EQUATING GENDER

EQUATING GENDER

Explorations in the Asia-Pacific

Edited by
Divya Upadhyaya Joshi
Chompoonuh K. Permpoonwiwat

RAWAT PUBLICATIONS
Jaipur • New Delhi • Bangalore • Guwahati • Kolkata

ISBN 978-81-316-0802-9

Published by
Prem Rawat for **Rawat Publications**
Satyam Apts, Sector 3, Jawahar Nagar, Jaipur 302 004 (India)
Phone: 0141 265 1748 / 7006 Fax: 0141 265 1748
E-mail: info@rawatbooks.com
Website: www.rawatbooks.com

New Delhi Office
4858/24, Ansari Road, Daryaganj, New Delhi 110 002
Phone: 011 2326 3290

Also at *Bangalore, Guwahati* and *Kolkata*

Typeset by Rawat Computers, Jaipur
Printed at Nice Printing Press, New Delhi

Contents

Contributors

Kalpana Agrahari, Associate Professor, Department of Political Science, Kumaun University, Nainital, Uttarakhand.

Chhavi Arya, Associate Professor, Home Science Department, Kumaun University, Nainital, Uttarakhand.

Poonam Bawa, Head, Department of Political Science and Former Director, UGC Sponsored Centre for Women's Studies, Jai Narain Vyas University, Jodhpur.

Rashi Bhargava, Research Scholar, Centre for the Study of Social Systems, School of Social Sciences, Jawaharlal Nehru University, New Delhi.

Ila Bisht, Research Scholar, Department of Sociology, Kumaun University, Nainital, Uttarakhand.

Petr Blizkovsky, Director, Economic and Regional Affairs, Secretariat General of the Council of the European Union, Brussels, Belgium.

Caroline Brassard, Assistant Dean (Academic Affairs) and Senior Lecturer Lee Kuan Yew School of Public Policy, National University of Singapore, Singapore.

Anup Shekhar Chakraborty, Head and Assistant Professor, Department of Political Science, St. Joseph's College, Darjeeling, West Bengal.

Ram Chandra, Senior Research Fellow (UGC), Department of Political Science, Jai Narain Vyas University, Jodhpur.

Ola Gamil Mahmoud El-Taliawi, Lee Kuan Yew School of Public Policy, National University of Singapore, Singapore.

Aruna Gyati, Assistant Professor, Department of Political Science, Dera Natung Government College Itanagar, Arunachal Pradesh.

Harumi Hosono, Professor, School of Information and Communication, Meiji University, Tokyo, Japan.

Jyoti Joshi, Associate Professor, Department of Sociology, Kumaun University, Nainital, Uttarakhand.

Suzaina Kadir, Assistant Dean (Student Affairs) and Senior Lecturer Lee Kuan Yew School of Public Policy, National University of Singapore, Singapore.

Padam Nepal, Associate Professor, Department of Political Science, St. Joseph's College, Darjeeling, West Bengal.

Lata Pande, Associate Professor, Home Science Department, Kumaun University, Nainital, Uttarakhand.

Chompoonuh Kosalakorn Permpoonwiwat, Associate Professor, School of Economics and Public Policy, Srinakharinwirot University, Thailand.

Triranjan Raj, Assistant Professor, Political Science, Ramlal Anand College, Delhi University, New Delhi.

Priyanka Neeraj Ruwali, Assistant Professor, Department of Sociology, Kumaun University, Nainital, Uttarakhand.

Reetesh Sah, Assistant Professor and Assistant Director, UGC-Academic Staff College, Kumaun University, Nainital, Uttarakhand.

Kittikorn Sankatiprapa, Graduate School, Srinakharinwirot University, Bangkok, Thailand.

Vandana Saxena, Associate Professor, CIE, Department of Education, University of Delhi, Delhi.

Bui Thi Minh Tam, School of Economics and Public Policy, Srinakharinwirot University, Thailand.

Hiromi Tanaka, School of Information and Communication, Meiji University, Tokyo, Japan.

Lalit P. Tirkey, Director, Department of Self-Financing Professional Courses, St Joseph's College, Darjeeling, West Bengal.

Ikushi Yamaguchi, Professor, School of Information and Communication, Meiji University, Tokyo, Japan.

Preface

The Asia-Pacific region shows great interregional and intraregional divergence in gender equity. There is a growing need to have interdisciplinary research spanning nations and regions in the Asia-Pacific with the aim of achieving a regional theoretical perspective and a more balanced picture of the root causes of gender inequity in the region. Keeping in mind the variance in the patterns of modernization and development among the societies in the region, it is pertinent to examine how to make research designs and how to undertake theoretical formulations about other societies, cultures and socio-political practices that affect women.

It is important for Asian-Pacific feminist theory that researchers and theorists make economic and socio-political assessments without merely endorsing ethnocentrism or socio-centrism, and while understanding the issue of gender equity in a larger perspective. The broad theme of the book is to include discussions on the changing paradigms in gender theory, policy and practices in the Asia-Pacific region.

There is an urgent need for academic discussion on the issues of practice and policy in achieving gender equity. Most countries of Asia and the Pacific do recognize equality between men and women as a matter of fundamental rights and citizenship. Yet, despite these formal and legal commitments, and the demonstrated benefits of gender equality to societies and economies, gender discrimination remains pervasive in the region. To ensure that all countries in the region make steady progress in narrowing the gender gaps and empowering women, rigorous exchanges of expertise and experience at various levels of policy research and feminist practice may essentially prove to be extremely valuable and beneficial.

In the first chapter of this compilation, Petr Blizkovsky keeps his focus on the relation between development aid and the situation of women for the purpose of analysing the gender situation in rural India. Examining the role of the global donors in the improvement of the conditions of women through the policy design of the development projects, the author also attempts to evaluate the actual potential of these international development projects in improving the women's situation. Situating the casual linkages between the 'feminization of poverty' and the 'feminization of agriculture', the chapter gives considerable importance to the rural poverty eradication programmes as a key rural gender concern. The author has tried to scrutinize six major international donors through an examination of 152 projects. Citing a good number of previous works and presenting enormous data, the chapter gives sufficient importance to monitoring the effectiveness of existing policies and projects from a gender perspective. The analysis demonstrates a relatively high positive effect of intervention projects on the gender situation. The author argues that international financial assistance could only be understood as complimentary to the systemic changes driven by the structural changes in the society, economy and trade.

In the second chapter of this compilation, Kadir et. al. discuss the role and limitations of public policy in ensuring gender equity. The theoretical dimensions of gender-related indicators have been systematically presented in the first part of the chapter. The main focus of the authors has been to delve into key debates and discourse relating to the public policy formulation and equalizing the role of women in politics and public sector in the Asia-Pacific region service in the last two decades. The central argument of this chapter is that in order to increase the participation of women in electoral politics, affirmative action might be the powerful and effective strategy. The authors argue that engendering politics would essentially make the women in political offices more effective advocates of the women's cause. The importance of party list system, sectoral representation, mobilization of women to vote for women, training investment in research and the impact of the business groups of women, besides female-dominated NGOs, have also been systematically emphasized. This leads to the central argument of the authors that increased political representation of women will necessarily lead to formulation of policies that would aid greater equality for women. The chapter vehemently argues that complimentary policies that may be supportive of a cultural shift for making growth inclusive can be enumerated as integration of gender equity as a part of the curriculum content; promotion of partnership between policy makers and religious leaders and increase in the representation of women in media positions. Interestingly, the authors have also identified areas of future research on various dimensions of gender equity and have given useful pointers to further research questions.

The chapter by Triranjan Raj presents a theoretical framework for understanding the discourse on differentiated rights by discussing the relationship between the concepts of feminism and multiculturalism. In order to examine the issue of culture-based discrimination, he first examines its specific articulation within contemporary theories of multiculturalism. He has also attempted to provide an overview of the reasons for most feminists emphasizing the principle of difference. He argues that the idea of women embodying a distinctive physiological perspective has immensely helped in providing justification for group representation and differentiated rights. In the same manner, while the defence for affirmative action policies is supported by the idea of compensating and reversing the effects of social discrimination, the radical feminists have sought group representation for women on account of their ideological and cultural difference. It has been contended that globalization has compelled different cultures and societies to be greatly linked and tightly interconnected, thereby making the societies increasingly multicultural. The equality of rights and dignity of every individual has to be recognized and ensured by the group, and collective efforts for protecting and promoting the differences and uniqueness of the individuals, groups and collectives. He concludes that in multicultural societies the women within a particular culture should be given freedom of choice in endorsing the values that are compatible with feminism as well as multiculturalism.

Anup Shekhar Chakraborty discusses the delicate issue of methodological and pedagogical contestations and complications in gender studies with special reference to queering gender in India. The main attempt of the chapter is to unravel and accentuate the less traversed terrain of queer methodologies and queering so as to accentuate the converging, diverging and overlapping folds between and among sexual or bodily located identities. He also tries to examine the institutionally recognized understanding of gender and to evaluate the polities of exclusion and inclusion within the same. The strategies challenging the negative conceptions and invisibility of the accomplishments of this group at an intellectual level have been highlighted by feminist sociologists, writers and activists. The author examines the bulk of literature available globally on queer methodologies and identifies their strengths. He describes how this academic contribution explores the diverse possibilities and impossibilities of queer and accentuates the limitations and potentials of queer engagements with social science research techniques and methodologies. According to him, queering social science research requires detoxification, alteration, mutation and hybridization of the available of options however limited they are at present.

Aruna Gyati and Kalpana Agrahari have attempted to explore the gaps and the possibilities of engendering governance, besides analysing the gender gap and examining various steps taken so far to engender governance. The authors have focused on three important domains of governance – state, market and civil society for the purpose of understanding and analysis. They posit that women are relatively excluded from positions of decision making in state institutions, market and civil society. It has been argued that because of the absence of specific goals of promoting gender equity in the objectives and functioning of the NGOs, any substantial correspondence between internal democracy within the organizations and institutions such advantage is not expected. Therefore, for the purpose of providing relatively better and more congenial environment within institutions for the interests of women, the nongovernmental organizations are not better than the state bureaucracies. Thus, the authors argue that promotion of NGOs, or even exclusive organizations of women, cannot be construed as an automatic panacea for gender equity. The chapter discusses the exclusion and marginalization of women in state institutions of governance, market and the private sector and the corporate businesses. Arguments for more research and exploration in this area have been forwarded in a forceful manner.

In the sixth chapter of this book, the research on the relationship between trade liberalization and economic integration has often come out with interesting findings. It has been demonstrated that gender inequalities in access to and control of domestic and social resources and decision making had different impact on men and women. The concept of masculinization of typical female employment fields has also been an area of concern for scholars studying the impact of globalization on gender situations. In this backdrop, the chapter by Bui Thi Minh Tam and Permpoonwiwat examines the change in the gender wage inequality between men and women in Thailand from a macroeconomic perspective and attempts to investigate the effects of trade liberalization on decreasing the wage gap. Having discussed the theoretical framework of the relationship between trade liberalization and gender wage inequality, the chapter provides some quantitative insight into the practical realities of the universe of study besides reviewing some significant works on gender wage inequality. The authors have concluded that because of limited access to resources, education and time, women were constrained from moving into more skilled, high-paying jobs created by liberalization.

Hiromi Tanaka raises the serious issue of the underrepresentation of women in the political set-up of Japan. Deviating from the traditional path of understanding the factors constraining the participation of women in politics, the author attempts to analyse the factors that have helped in promoting increased participation of women in politics. Arguing statistically, the author finds the underrepresentation of the half of the population in politics disturbing. Even research in this area of academic concern is unsatisfactory. For the purpose of constructing the main argument of the present research, the author has attempted to analyse the political biographies of two female politicians. Tanaka acknowledges the importance of politicization, particularly the development of political consciousness through non-legislative activities and processes such as preparation for the decision of women to run for political offices. The author argues that gender equality at home is not a prerequisite for the involvement of women in public life. It has been concluded that gender imbalance in the parliament still remains a key issue in gender equality policies. The major argument of this chapter is that an egalitarian marital relationship is not a precondition for the political participation of married women.

Harumi Hosono discusses the situation of the women in Japan with regard to the expression of their feelings and situations in written language instead of spoken language. The author begins with the argument that Japan established its own unique way of cultural expression by processing outside influences and maturing them internally, with little external dissemination. Japan does not have any history of being militarily invaded, besides having had very limited contact with the rest of the world. It has been argued that poverty is not directly linked to literacy in today's Japan; rather it is closely connected to the existing disparities in access to higher education and employment opportunities. In Japanese society, both among men and women, silence is considered a virtue. Postmodern influences of Western individualism have also not been able to make any dent in this social value of modesty, respect and obedience being expressed by way of not expressing one's intentions in words. In case of women, this silence has become a typical characteristic, although women in Japan do recognize its significance. The author argues that it is imperative that substantial efforts are put in the direction of finding different ways of enabling women to express themselves effectively for meaningful improvements in their lives.

Kittikorn Sankatiprapa's article deals with the Thai 'Kathoey' or Thai male to female transgender. This article highlights the myths surrounding the Thai Kathoey, their everyday struggle, their identity of the 'other' and their hidden voices in the mainstream. It delves into their private lives and inner world, putting forward their demands as a sexual minority group. Additionally, the article focuses on the marginalization of the Kathoey and its impact on human capital. Sankatiprapa brings to light the kinds of problems faced by a Kathoey in employment and also their exclusion from the job market.

Ikushi Yamaguchi attempts to explore the differences between the organizational attitudes and behaviour of male and female care workers in Japanese care facilities. The study is dependent on both qualitative and quantitative research, and examines the relationship between gender and behaviour of Japanese care workers. Perceptions about organizational justice, organizational commitment, job satisfaction and hierarchy have been measured in order to find out the similarities and dissimilarities between male and female workers. The concluding remarks confirm that in the quantitative data, the variations in interpersonal and informational justice and perceived organizational justice are not explained by demographic variables including sex. Gender is not related to organizational commitment or job satisfaction, but to ability of expression, and to the three dimensions of burnout. The study suggests that female workers are relatively in more disadvantageous situations than their male counterparts in Japanese care facilities.

Poonam Bawa and Ram Chandra have given an overview of the issues and the contemporary scenario of violence against women in India. The conceptual boundaries of the issue have been drawn, and a historical description of the problem has been provided in order to highlight the various dimensions of the problem in India. The authors have also described the legal provisions regarding women protection and rights. The diverse issues of female foeticide, female infanticide, education for girls, girls' health and education, domestic violence, crime against women, acid throwing incidents, sexual harassment, dowry deaths, child marriage, human trafficking, eve teasing, skewed sex-ratio, sanitation issues, rape cases and other such incidents have been discussed with sufficient data. The role of civil society in protecting the dignity and the rights of women has also been highlighted. A discussion on the contemporary legal developments in the cases relating to rape has also been provided.

Padam Nepal and Lalit Tirkey address the issue of gender in perspective of governance and livelihood security, with a special empirical reference to North Bengal tea region in the state of West Bengal, India. The study claims to be analytical, exploratory and descriptive with the use of a mixed or hybrid methodology, sensitizing the merits of both qualitative and quantitative approaches. The authors have got substantial empirical evidence from their primary data collected through field surveys, in-depth interviews, nonparticipant observation and informal discussions. The authors provide a detailed description of the study area and contextualize the existing governance patterns and accentuated livelihood insecurities. They find that the womenfolk in the North Bengal tea region have practically no access to the available commons in the garden premises, and their woes are compounded by the lack of education and capacity building, and consequent ignorance in the enclave economy of the tea gardens. The closure of tea plantations have made the female tea workers vulnerable to shocks and stresses such as malnutrition, hunger and diseases. The authors highlight the role of education in the empowerment of women in this context. They conclude by indicating a series of struggles emanating from micro-level politics in marginalized communities.

Rashi Bhargava has presented a travelogue that started from Lucknow in Uttar Pradesh routed through New Delhi and ended in Kohima in the state of Nagaland. The nature of this travelogue is investigative, and the author has confronted the historical reservations about the nature of conflicts which the state had with the national mainstream. Written in an interesting style and with an approach of social science research, the study makes informative reading.

Reetesh Sah attempts to study the impact of natural resource depletion in the Central Himalayan region of India with a perspective of water management systems and women. Beginning by way of giving a full length description of geographical dimension of the study area, he provides a summary of the conventional water management systems besides indicating the changing water scenario with regard to women. The author argues that judicious policies need to be formulated to address the needs of women with regard to protection of fresh water resources because they are the largest sufferers of natural water resource depletion. The systems of water resource management require approach that are capable of including modern knowledge and technology in the policy frameworks based on traditional knowledge systems and actual local requirements. The inclusion of people in the processes of planning and implementation as partners is essential for redeeming their interest in environment protection. The author provides a good number of suggestions for the improvement in the situation and pleads for empowerment of the women by providing food security, better health and education.

Chhavi Arya and Lata Pande's chapter is based on their extensive field study on the nutritional status of girls in government schools in Ludhiana in the state of Punjab. The study evaluates the socio-economic profile of the female children vis-à-vis their nutritional status. With the help of a good number of tables, charts and graphs, the authors have presented interesting and rescaling statistics about the health issues of female children. Economic condition, purchasing power, living conditions and daily intake of food such as pulses, cereals, green vegetables, fruits, milk and milk products, fats and oils and sugar are examined with regard to energy, calcium, iron and other nutritional parameters. The reasons of malnutrition along with its visible impact on the health of these children have been assessed. The authors plead for comprehensive strategies focusing on nutrition counselling and nutrition intervention.

Ila Bisht and Jyoti Joshi have touched upon the issue of health programmes and empowerment of rural women. The chapter is based on empirical evidences on gender equity and health issues emanating from a case study of women's awareness on health issues in Daholi village of district Almora in Uttarakhand. The study is aimed to understand the gender equity and health indicators by evaluating awareness level of rural women about health and suggesting measures for more and fundamental empowerment of rural women. The authors have come out with interesting and thought-provoking findings based on their empirical study. They have also made fruitful and imaginative suggestions for the improvement of the situation at ground level. It has been argued that the awareness among rural women regarding government health schemes and programmes has to be increased by concerted efforts of different levels.

Priyanka Neeraj Ruwali touches upon a relatively new dimension of social science research. Public health administration is an area wherein research studies have started very late. She has attempted to examine the status of women health in the perspective of contemporary health policies in India. She begins with the forceful argument that the endeavours to achieve gender equity essentially imply elimination of unnecessary, avoidable and unjust health inequalities existing as an outcome of imbalanced social construction of gender. The issue of gender is often neglected during planning and implementation of health promotion policies and strategies of disease prevention. Analysis of the enormous data presented by the author indicates that there exists a marked difference between the patterns of health and illness among men and women. The author argues that given the social realities in India, educating women regarding reproductive health issues is equally important as the need for educating their male counter parts. She has come out with a good number of suggestive measures to address the issue of gender inequities in health.

Vandana Saxena has made an empirical study of the gender gap in the study of physical sciences. She has argued that the available global data about the share of women researchers in science endorses the much contested position of women in science and at the same time reinforces the significance of continuous thinking and persistent focused action in this direction. It has been contended that unequal access and advancement and the disproportionate number of women from urban area and high social class background are some of the main sources and forms of gender inequality within Indian scientific institutions. The role of cultural and socio-economic obstacles has also been highlighted. The author has vehemently questioned the notion of science being masculine. By way of analysing the secondary data, the author has concluded that socio-cultural practices lead to discrimination on the basis of gender in the classrooms. The author asks for the practitioners of science to acknowledge the marginalizing nature of science studies in India and pleads for redesigning an inclusive epistemological basis of science.

This book includes articles representing both qualitative and quantitative research on gender in the Asia-Pacific. A wide canvas of issues are presented and it is hoped that this exercise of getting together researchers from different countries of the region on a common platform will serve as a starting block for further collaboration. The tradition of ethnographic research on sensitive issues of marginalization and the traditionally taboo 'personal' world needs to be revived. A balanced synchronization of empirical research and normative 'deep' enquiry are vital to relevant research in the region. The editors hope that this volume will be a first step in this direction by their collaborative group.

Acknowledgements

There are many people who have made this book possible and whose help we would like to acknowledge here. We are grateful to all the people who were involved in the conference that led to this book. The conference was made possible due to the funding from the National Commission for Women, Government of India. We thank Ms. Shamina Shafiq, former Member, the National Commission for Women, Government of India whose enthusiasm for this project remained crucial since its inception.

Colleagues have devoted time with generosity, and given thoughtful comments on the drafts. We thank these special people, family and friends for their emotional support in this venture. We thank the National Commission for Women, Government of India, for their support in this endeavour.

It would be amiss not to thank our respective University Administration, both at Kumaun University, India and Srinakharinwirot University, Thailand for facilitating the Memorandum of Understanding under which our collaboration has been initiated. We thank our collaborator in Meiji University, Japan, Associate Professor, Hiromi Tanaka for her enthusiastic support.

We especially thank our daughters, Ananya and Amy, for being so considerate and caring, sacrificing their time with us so that we could pursue our academic work.

Divya Upadhyaya Joshi
Chompoonuh K. Permpoonwiwat

Part I

Theorizing Gender Equity

CHAPTER 1

Is Development Aid Improving the Gender Situation in Asia?

Petr Blizkovsky

The objective of this chapter is to analyse the gender situation in rural India. The focus is on the relation between the development aid and women situation. The research question is whether the international donors aim at improving women's condition by the means of policy design of the development projects. The chapter also evaluates if such a possible focus actually impacts gender equity.

In Asia and the Pacific region, poverty is largely a rural problem, and the gap between rural and urban poverty is widening over time in spite of impressive progress, especially in economic growth and poverty reduction, in the last three decades. Two-thirds of the world's poor live in this region, and a large number of the marginalized poor are women. Most of them live in rural areas. In many rural areas of Asia, more women than men are among the 'working poor' than among the poor as a whole. The reinforcing causal link between the 'feminization of poverty' and the 'feminization of agriculture' is a key rural gender equality concern in the region with considerable importance to rural poverty eradication programmes. In India, 71 per cent of the population live in rural areas. According to FAO general information (FAO website), women accounted for 49 per cent of the rural population in 2001, accounting for 32 per cent of the agricultural labour force. Aside from the legal constraints hampering women's access to land, socio-cultural factors, such as the patriarchal practice of female seclusion, prevent women from claiming their rights to land.

The gender problems in rural India are a function of several factors of economic, social and cultural nature. Rural areas in India expose women to a complex situation. In the last few decades, India has remained more of a male-dominated society. Girls' education in villages, health issues and poverty existing in rural India are the most powerful reform acts started by Indian government. The work of rural Indian women is left unrecognized and has less autonomy (Ramachandran 2006). According to the Indian census, half of the women work as agricultural workers. Factors such as 25 per cent of domestic violence against women, 50 per cent of women's access to land, 50 per cent of women's access to bank loans and 50 per cent of women's access to property other than land are reducing women's quality of life in India (OECD 2013; Udry et al. 2005). In rural India, agriculture and industrial sectors employ as much as 89.5 per cent of the total female labour. The role of women engagement in taking responsibility in the local decision making has improved. By 2011, India had achieved acknowledge for the level of gender parity in political participation and empowerment.

In 2005, the unorganized sector accounted for 99 per cent of Indian manufacturing establishments, 80 per cent of Indian manufacturing employment (National Sample Survey Organisation 2013). There was heightened women's entrepreneurship in the organized sector. Manufacturing employment grew 17 per cent from 1994 to 2005; employment in new women-owned establishments in the unorganized sector grew 138 per cent and associated employment of 40 per cent after political reservations were implemented, but not to increased employment generally of women in manufacturing. Female participation has dropped over the past decade in contrast to other emerging markets. Less than a third of working age women in India leave their jobs (*Forbes* 2015).

Although activities were implemented in favoured industries where women have historically owned more establishments nationally (Ghani et al. 2011), however the reported crimes against women increased (Lakshmi et al. 2012). As the study of Srivastava and Srivastava (2009) in rural India made clear that higher work participation does not lead to better employment outcomes unless accompanied by higher education and better access to assets. Monitoring the effectiveness of existing policies and projects from a gender perspective must take into account distinct gender contexts (Sancar and Bieri 2009).

The workforce participation rate at national level is 25.51 compared to 53.26 for males 41.1 per cent are agricultural labour, 24.0 per cent are cultivators, 5.7 per cent are household industry workers and 29.2 per cent are engaged in other work (NSSO 2013).

Women occupy only 30 per cent of total posts as senior corporate managers or leaders. This is higher than global average of 24 per cent.

METHODOLOGY

The methodology is based on the empirical qualitative analysis. Six international donors that donate to rural areas of India are scrutinized: the World Bank, Food and Agricultural Organization of the United Nations (FAO), the International Fund for Agricultural Development (IFAD) – a specialized agency of the United Nations, the European Union (EU), the Asian Development Bank (ADB) and the United Nation Women (UNW).

The individual project of these six donors was analysed at the project level. The period under scrutiny covers 1995–2013. The sources of data were public websites of the international donors. The gender conditionality test was run at the project level. Where available, the impact on the factual improvement on the women situation was checked.

RESULTS

In total, 152 projects of six international donors were analysed with regard to their conditionality to improve the gender situation of women.

Table 1 *Overview of international projects in India*

Donor	*Number of Projects*	*Period*	*Budget*	*Number of Projects with Gender Conditionality*
World Bank	13	1997–2012	1.950 million USD	6
FAO	30	2004–2013	61.400 million USD	0
International Fund for Agricultural Development	11	2000–2012	376 million USD(*)	3
European Union	16	2008–2012	15 million Euro	9
Asian Development Bank	67	2004–2012	NA	1
UN Women	15	2004–2011	NA	12

Table 1 shows the results of the gender focus of the projects under scrutiny. The empirical analysis results show that 20 per cent of the project (31 projects) contained gender conditionality. The gender focus was highest in the case of the projects of the UN Women where 80 per cent of the project contained women-related conditionality. In case of the European Union, there were 56 per cent of the projects containing gender-related conditionality, followed by the World Bank that had 46 per cent of its projects that were gender related. In the case of the International Fund for Agricultural Development (IFAD), this was 27 per cent of the projects. Projects of the Asian Development Bank and of the FAO were focused to issues other than gender ones (FAO 2010).

Table 2 *List of projects and their link to gender conditionality*

Donor	*Title of Project*	*PERIOD (Approval Date)*	*Sector/Themes*	*Budget (*)*	*Gender Conditionality*
WB	Bihar Rural Livelihood	2012	Civic engagement, gender (25%)	$ 140 million	Y
WB	North East Rural Livelihoods	2011	Rural markets	$144.4 million	N
WB	Kerala Rural Water Supply and Sanitation	2011	Rural development	NA	N
WB	PMGSY Rural Roads	2010	Rural development	NA	N
WB	Economic Empowerment Project for Women	2010	Gender (25%), other	$ 182 million	Y
WB	Maharashtra Agricultural Competitiveness	2010–2016	Rural markets	$ 100 million	N
WB	Andhra Pradesh Rural Water Supply	2009	Rural services and infrastructure	$ 180 million	N
WB	Orissa Rural Livelihoods	2008	Rural markets, gender (10%)	$ 90.50 million	Y
WB	Emergency Tsunami Reconstruction	2005	Natural disaster management infrastructure	$ 682.8 million	N
WB	Rural Women's Development and Empowerment	1997	Gender (20%)	$ 53.50 million	Y
WB	Assam Rural Infrastructure and Agriculture Services	1995	Rural services, infrastructure, gender (17%)	$146.6 million	Y
WB	Rural Telecommunication Development	NA	Rural services, infrastructure	$ 60 million	N
WB	Woman and Child Development	1998	Nutrition, children gender (22%)	$ 350 million	Y
FAO	Andhra Pradesh Farmer-Managed Groundwater Systems	2004–2009	Farm management	$ 6,784.539 million	N

Cont'd...

...Cont'd

FAO	Support to Nationally Executed Land and Water Programme	2004–2013	Rural services	$ 4,695.903 million	N
FAO	Andhra Pradesh Water Management	2004–2010	Rural services	$ 4,646.7565 million	N
FAO	Livelihood Improvements in Dryland Farming on the Deccan Plateau	2004–2008	Rural management	$ 3,161.023 million	N
FAO	Apples Production Improvement	2004–2005	Agriculture	$ 365.277 million	N
FAO	Development of Technical Capacity Base for the Promotion of Organic Agriculture	2005–2007	Agriculture	$ 212.140 million	N
FAO	Support to Fisheries Sector of the Post-Tsunami Recovery Framework	2006–2008	Fisheries management	$ 146.849 million	N
FAO	Developing a National Food Insecurity and Vulnerability Information	2006–2007	Nutrition	$ 103.000 million	N
FAO	Capacity Building in Support of Cleaner Fishing Harbours	2007–2009	Fisheries management	$ 318.000 million	N
FAO	Technical Assistance to Strengthen the Control of Highly Pathogenic Avian Influenza	2008–2011	Farm services	$ 1,220.000 million	N
FAO	TCP Facility	2008–2009	NA	$ 216.601 million	N
FAO	Fisheries Management and Sustainable Livelihoods in Tamil Nadu and Puducherry	2010–2011	Fisheries management	$ 2,125.000 million	N

Cont'd...

...Cont'd

FAO	Reversing Environmental Degradation and Rural Poverty through Adaptation to Climate Change in Drought Stricken Areas in South India	2010–2013	Rural services	$ 909.090 million	N
FAO	Improving the Productivity and Quality of Litchi in Bihar	2010–2011	Agriculture	$ 396.000 million	N
FAO	Strategy for an Animal Identification and Traceability System	2011–2013	Livestock management	$ 182.000 million	N
FAO	Workshop on Policy Options and Investment Priorities for Accelerating Agricultural Growth	2011–2013	Agriculture	$ 273.000 million	N
FAO	Improving the Productivity and Quality of Litchi in Bihar	2012–2013	Agriculture	$ 48.000 million	N
FAO	Complimentary Assistance to the FAO-IFAD Collaborative Programme on Pro-Poor Policy Formulation, Dialogue and Implementation at the Country Level	2008–2011	Development	$ 354.517 million	N
FAO	Improving Postharvest Practices and Sustainable Market Development for Long-line Fisheries for Tuna and Other Large Pelagic Fish Species	2010–2013	Fisheries	$ 429.000 million	N
FAO	Re-inventing Irrigation and Agricultural Water Governance in the Asia Pacific	2010–2013	Agriculture	$ 487.000 million	N

Cont'd...

...Cont'd

FAO	Conservation and Management of Pollinators for Sustainable Agriculture through an Ecosystem Approach	2009–2013	Agriculture	$ 7,810.682 million	N
FAO	Sustainable Management of the Bay of Bengal Large Marine Ecosystem	2009–2014	Marine	$ 12,082.107 million	N
FAO	Biennial Sessions of Asia and Pacific Plant Protection Commission	2010–2021	Agriculture	$ 339.000 million	N
FAO	Improvement of Regional Capacities for the Prevention, Control and Eradication of Highly Pathogenic and Emerging Diseases	2009–2013	Health	$ 10,939.608 million	N
FAO	Reversing Environmental Degradation and Rural Poverty through Adaptation to Climate Change in Drought Stricken Areas in South India	2010–2013	Rural development	$ 909.091 million	N
FAO	Incorporating International Best Practices in the Preparation of Agricultural Outlook and Situation	2012–2014	Agriculture	$ 458.298 million	N
FAO	Policy and Technical Support for National Contingency Planning in Countries at Direct Risk of New Virulent Races of Wheat Rusts	2010–2013	Health	$ 185.000 million	N
FAO	Medium-term Cooperation Programme with Farmers' Organizations in Asia -Pacific Region	2009–2012	Farm management	$ 1,083.000 million	N

Cont'd...

...Cont'd

FAO	Enhancing Understanding and Implementation of the International Treaty on Plant Genetic Resources for Food and Agriculture in Asia	2012–2015	Nutrition	$ 435.000 million	N
FAO	India's Contribution to the Bay of Bengal Large Marine Ecosystem	2011–2013	Marine	$ 84.932 million	N
IFAD	Jharkhand Tribal Empowerment and Livelihoods	September 12	Agriculture development	$ 51 million	N
IFAD	Integrated Livelihood Support Project	December 11	Agriculture development	$ 8.9 million	N
IFAD	Convergence of Agricultural Interventions in Maharashtra's Distressed Districts Programme	April 09	Agriculture development	$ 40.1 million	N
IFAD	Mitigating Poverty in Western Rajasthan Project	April 08	Rural development	$ 30.4 million	N
IFAD	Women's Empowerment and Livelihoods Programme in the Mid-Gangetic Plains	December 06	Credit and financial services	$ 30.2 million	Y
IFAD	Tejaswini Rural Women's Empowerment	December 05	Credit and financial services	$ 39.4 million	Y
IFAD	Post-Tsunami Sustainable Livelihoods Programme for the Coastal Communities of Tamil Nadu	April 05	Credit and financial services	$ 15 million	N
IFAD	Orissa Tribal Empowerment and Livelihoods Programme	April 02	Agriculture development	$ 20 million	N

Cont'd...

...Cont'd

IFAD	Livelihoods Improvement Project in the Himalayas	December 03	Credit and financial services	$ 22.9 million	N
IFAD	Livelihood Security Project for Earthquake-Affected Rural Households in Gujarat	September 01	Agriculture development	$ 15 million	N
IFAD	National Microfinance Support Programme	May 00	Credit and financial services	$ 22 million	N
EU	Support to Stop Trafficking Women and Girls through Community Action at the Panchayat Level	2011–2014	Human rights	240.000 million € (80% of total)	Y
EU	Empowering Women: Access and Ownership over Land and Land based Activities through Education, Legal Literacy and Advocacy in Rural India	2010–2012	Women's equality organizations and institutions	475.200 million € (88% of total)	Y
EU	Synthesising Rural Employment Needs and Poverty Reduction in Backward Regions	2010– 2014	Vocational training	1,000.000 million € (87% of total)	N
EU	Revitalising Sustainable Rural Livelihoods among Small and Marginal Dryland Farmers and Landless Poor of Anantapur District	2008–2013	NA	NA	N
EU	Support to Livestock Services	NA	NA	3,988.121 million € (69% of total)	N
EU	Promoting Older People-led Community Action to Reduce Poverty among Vulnerable Groups in Rural Rajasthan	2008–2013	Rural development	749.138 million € (75% of total)	N

Cont'd...

...Cont'd

EU	Revitalising Sustainable Rural Livelihoods (Small, Marginal Dryland Farmers, Landless Poor of Anantapur District)	2008–2012	Rural development	749.000 million € (69% of total)	N
EU	Socio-economic Empowerment for Marginalized Farmer and Landless Families through Integrated Watershed Development, Dindigul	2008–2012	Rural development	491.292 million € (75% of total)	N
EU	Community Empowerment and Strengthening of Advocacy Groups for Disadvantaged People in Deoghar District, Jharkhand	2008–2012	Rural development	242.250 million € (75% of total)	N
EU	Project Swavlamban – Empowering Poor Informal Sector Women through Market Relevant Capacity Building	2010–2014	Vocational training	995.896 million € (87% of total)	Y
EU	Reduction of Mother to Child Transmission of HIV in India: Improving access to Positive Women to Public Health Services	2009–2012	Infectious disease control	750.000 million € (75% of total)	Y
EU	Vocational Education and Training for Vulnerable Groups of Women in 4 States	2010–2012	Vocational training	507.485 million € (72.39% of total)	Y
EU	Revitalising Sustainable Rural Livelihoods among Small and Marginal Dryland Farmers and Landless Poor of Anantapur District, India	2008–2012	Rural development	749.000 million € (68.97% of total)	Y

Cont'd...

...Cont'd

EU	Promoting Community Action Led by Older People in Rural Rajasthan, India	2008–2012	Health, services, infrastructures	749.000 (75 % of total)	Y
EU	Helping Rural and Tribal Youth in India, HIV Prevention and Care	2003–2006	Health	3 million € (90% of total)	Y
EU	Preventing HIV/AIDS among Women of Childbearing Age in North-East India	2002–2006	Health	1,02 million € (90% of total)	Y
ADB	Off Grid Pay-As-You-Go Solar Power	January 13	Energy	NA	N
ADB	Poverty Reduction – Capacity Building and Institutional Strengthening for the Assam Urban Infrastructure Investment Program	December 12	NA	NA	N
ADB	Chhattisgarh State Road Sector Project	December 12	Infrastructure	NA	N
ADB	Livelihood Improvement for River Erosion Victims in Assam	October 12	Infrastructure	NA	N
ADB	Rural Connectivity Investment	August 12	Communication	NA	
ADB	Poverty Reduction – Updating Load Forecast and Power System Master Plan for Assam	August 12	Communication	NA	N
ADB	Advanced Project Preparedness for Poverty Reduction – SASEC Sub-regional Road Connectivity Project	July 12	Communication	NA	N
ADB	Rural Connectivity Investment Program	July 12	Communication	NA	N
ADB	Poverty Reduction – Capacity Building for North Eastern State Roads Sector	March 12	Infrastructure	NA	N

Cont'd...

...Cont'd

ADB	Poverty Reduction – Gender Inclusive Capacity Development for Electricity Distribution Loss Reduction in Rural Madhya Pradesh	March 12	Rural services	NA	N
ADB	Poverty Reduction – Rajasthan Urban Development Program	December 11	Urban development	NA	N
ADB	Poverty Reduction – Preparing State Road Projects	December 11	Infrastructure	NA	N
ADB	Poverty Reduction – Preparing the Rajasthan Renewable Energy Transmission Program	December 11	Energy	NA	N
ADB	Skills Development for Inclusive Growth	December 11		NA	N
ADB	Poverty Reduction – Designing and Capacity Building for Strengthening State Finances and Service Delivery in West Bengal	December 11	Finances	NA	N
ADB	Madhya Pradesh Energy Efficiency Improvement Investment Program	December 11	Energy	NA	N
ADB	Poverty Reduction – West Bengal North South Road Corridor Project (formerly Haldia Port Connectivity)	December 11	Infrastructure	NA	N
ADB	Karnataka Integrated and Sustainable Water Resources Management Investment Program	December 11	Services	NA	N
ADB	Support to Jawaharlal Nehru National Solar Mission	November 11	Energy	NA	N

Cont'd...

...Cont'd

ADB	Poverty Reduction – Supporting Clean Village Environments for MDGs	November 11	Environment	NA	N
ADB	Poverty Reduction – Capacity Building for Bihar Urban Infrastructure Development Project	October 11	Infrastructure	NA	N
ADB	Poverty Reduction – Capacity Building and Institutional Strengthening for the Assam Urban Infrastructure Investment Program	September 11	Infrastructure	NA	N
ADB	Developing the Power System Master Plan for Bihar	August 11	NA	NA	N
ADB	Madhya Pradesh Energy Efficiency Improvement Investment Program	July 11	Energy	NA	N
ADB	Poverty Reduction – Gujarat Solar Vocational Training and Livelihoods Project	May 11	Energy	NA	N
ADB	Poverty Reduction – Rajasthan Solar Park Capacity Development Project	May 11	Energy	NA	N
ADB	Poverty Reduction – Capacity Development for Jharkhand State Roads Sector	December 10	Infrastructure	NA	N
ADB	Poverty Reduction – Institutional Development for a Value Chain Approach to Agribusiness in Bihar and Maharashtra	December 10	Finances, agriculture	NA	N

Cont'd...

...Cont'd

ADB	Poverty Reduction – Capacity Development for Community-based Flood Risk Management in Assam	December 10	NA	NA	N
ADB	Capacity Development for Project Management of Infrastructure Development for Rural Livelihood Enhancement	November 10	Infrastructure	NA	N
ADB	Poverty Reduction – Meghalaya Public Resource Management Development Program	November 10	NA	NA	N
ADB	MFF – Assam Integrated Flood and Riverbank Erosion Risk Management Investment Program	October 10	Infrastructure	NA	N
ADB	MFF – Sustainable Coastal Protection and Management Investment Program	October 10	Infrastructure	NA	N
ADB	Agribusiness Infrastructure Development Investment Program	September 10	Finances	NA	N
ADB	Improving Small Farmers' Access to Market in Bihar and Maharashtra	July 10	Farm management	NA	N
ADB	Preparing an Investment Plan for Himachal Pradesh Urban Development	July 10	Urban development	NA	N
ADB	MFF – Rural Roads Investment Program	July 10	Infrastructure	NA	N
ADB	Poverty Reduction – Water Users Association Empowerment for Improved Irrigation Management in Chhattisgarh	February 10	Services	NA	N

Cont'd...

...Cont'd

ADB	Addressing Social and Health Issues Associated with Road Improvement in Selected North Eastern States (Assam, Meghalaya, Mizoram, Manipur and Nagaland)	December 09	Health	NA	N
ADB	Integrated Water Resources Management and Sustainable Water Service Delivery in Karnataka	December 09	Services	NA	N
ADB	Poverty Reduction – Capacity Development for Sustainable Coastal Protection and Management	December 09	Infrastructure	NA	N
ADB	Jharkhand State Roads Project	December 09	Infrastructure	NA	N
ADB	MFF – Assam Power Sector Enhancement Investment Program	November 09	NA	NA	N
ADB	Poverty Reduction – Capacity Development of Bihar Power Sector Entities	November 09	NA	NA	N
ADB	Poverty Reduction – Support for the Jawaharlal Nehru National Urban Renewal Mission	September 09	Urban development	NA	N
ADB	Poverty Reduction – Madhya Pradesh	September 2009	NA	NA	N
ADB	Supporting an Initiative for Mainstreaming Public-Private Partnerships for Providing Urban Amenities in Rural Areas	September 09	Rural development	NA	N

Cont'd...

...Cont'd

ADB	Chhattisgarh Irrigation Development Project	August 09	Agriculture	NA	N
ADB	MFF – Rural Roads Sector II Investment Program	August 09	Infrastructure	NA	N
ADB	Capacity Building & Livelihood Enhancement of Poor Water Users	June 09	Services	NA	N
ADB	Study on Cross-Sectoral Implications of Biofuel Production and Use	March 09	Energy	NA	N
ADB	Rajasthan Urban Sector Development Investment Program	January 09	Urban development	NA	N
ADB	Agribusiness Infrastructure Development Investment Program	December 08	Finances	NA	N
ADB	Rural Electrification Corporation of India	November 08	Energy	NA	N
ADB	Khadi Reform and Development Program	October 08	NA	NA	N
ADB	Preparing the Integrated Flood and Riverbank Erosion Risk Management Project – Assam Processing and Institutional Strengthening	September 08	NA	NA	N
ADB	MFF – Rural Roads Sector II Investment Program	September 08	Infrastructure	NA	N
ADB	IND: GTL Infrastructure Limited Phase-II Telecommunication Infrastructure Project	May 08	Communication	NA	N

Cont'd...

...Cont'd

ADB	Mainstreaming Public-Private Partnerships at Central Line Ministries of the Government of India	November 07	NA	NA	N
ADB	Deploying Innovative Information and Communications Technology for Supporting e-Governance in Assam	November 07	Communication	NA	N
ADB	MFF – Madhya Pradesh Power Sector Investment Program	April 07	NA	NA	N
ADB	MFF – Uttarakhand State-Road Investment Program	December 06	Infrastructure	NA	N
ADB	Rural Cooperative Credit Restructuring and Development Program	December 06	Rural development	NA	N
ADB	Kerala Sustainable Urban Development (formerly Urban Infrastructure Development and Environment II)	December 05	Urban development	NA	N
ADB	MFF – Rural Roads Sector II Investment Program	December 05	Rural infrastructure	NA	N
ADB	Multi-sector Project for Infrastructure Rehabilitation in Jammu and Kashmir	December 04	Infrastructure	NA	N
ADB	Assam Power Sector Development Program	December 03	NA	NA	N
UN Women	Strengthening Women's Legal Rights in Aceh, Indonesia	2009	Women, gender	NA	Y

Cont'd...

...Cont'd

UN Women	Supporting Gender Equality and Women's Human Rights in Nation-building of Timor-Leste	2010	Women, gender	NA	Y
UN Women	Mid-Term Evaluation of the Integrated Programme for Women in Politics and Decision-Making in Timor-Leste	2011	Women	NA	Y
UN Women	Deepening Democracy, Women's Participation in Peace and Politics in South Asia	2009	Women	NA	Y
UN Women	Project on Promoting Women in Democratic Decision Making in Cambodia	2009	Women	NA	Y
UN Women	Regional Programme on Expansion of Employment Opportunities for Women (EEOW), Cambodia Chapter	2005	Women	NA	Y
UN Women	Asian Regional Programme on Expansion on Employment Opportunities for Women Vietnam Chapter	2004	Women	NA	Y
UN Women	Decent Employment for Women in India Project	2005	Women	NA	Y
UN Women	Equality and Decent Work Promotion for Asian Women through Prevention of Human Trafficking, Protection of Domestic Workers and Gender Capacity Building	2010	Women	NA	Y

Cont'd...

...Cont'd

UN Women**	India: Promoting Urban Social Development through Self-help Groups in Karnataka	2007	Urban development	NA	Y
UN Women	Empowering Women through Self-help Groups, India Country Programme Evaluation	2009	Women	NA	Y
UN Women	Evaluation of Gender within the Livelihoods Programme on Nias Island, Indonesia	2007	Gender	NA	Y
UN Women	Nepal: Gender Equality &Social Inclusion Promoting Rights of Marginalised for Sustained Peace and Inclusive Development	2011	Gender	NA	Y
UN Women	Country evaluation of the age and gender mainstreaming pilot project India	2005	Gender	NA	Y
UN Women	Entrepreneurship development programme for women in food processing in central Vietnam	2007	Women	NA	Y

* The budget refers to the budgetary implication of the Institution/donor.

** This project is co-financed by the ADB and UN Women, therefore it is mentioned twice.

Table 3 *Effects on conditionality on the projects that aim to improve gender situation in rural India and in Asia*

Donor	Project	*Conditionalities*	*Positive Effects*
WB	Bihar Rural Livelihoods Project	Measures to facilitate favourable climate and efficient delivery of public services. Effectiveness through scaling up federating and build livelihood organizations and vertically federate the village organizations	**YES** (Mobilized 515, 000 poor women, into 46,000 self-help groups and 3,500 village organization. Saved $5.5 million, positively impacted savings of households, reduced cost indebtedness, and increased food security, women empowerment significantly.)
WB	Economic Empowerment Project for Women	Partnerships initiated with organizations to set up centres in the states concerned. Business plans, support from management, local economic activities to farmers through training, tele-agriculture, demonstration plots, tools libraries, spot and future price information distributed by mobile (technology tools), linkages to markets through agricultural trading cooperative	**YES** (7 Community Resource Centres to be scaled up to Business Resource Centres were identified through a participatory process.)
WB	Orissa Rural Livelihoods Project	Interventions through partnership with Technical Support Agencies. The project has developed a strategy for forming producer groups to support producers across the production cycle. Signed a Memorandum of Understanding with Odisha Rural Development and Marketing Society to provide skills training placement services.	**MODERATELY** (Some progress, many of planned activities behind schedule, pending. Delays in the implementation of planned activities impacted the planned expenditures over years. 100 producer groups formed mostly in the farm sector. 75% of the households reduced dependency from high cost from private money lending.)

Cont'd...

...Cont'd

WB	Assam Rural Infrastructure and Agricultural Services Project	Offering better opportunities for poorer farmers and women to contribute to agricultural growth and income generation; induced key policy reform initiatives, better use of ground water, crop diversification and better rural connectivity.	**YES** (Improve equity and alleviate poverty. Increase productivity of agriculture, livestock and fisheries by > 34%.)
WB	Woman and Child Development Project	Programme Support; Management and Institutional Development, Information, Education and Communication (home visits, nutrition and health education session, social mobilization through door-to-door contacts, rallies, gold art, mobile video van, exhibitions, special campaign days). Nutrition Surveys and National Training. Help from the new Bank supervision team: institutional changes on service quality improvement; decentralization; targeting and enhancing community participation. The central government provides financial assistance. Preventive strategies in malnutrition reduction, providing training in life skills. Infrastructure development: hand pumps for safe drinking water and provision of equipment. Free Expression for Quality Improvement (FREQI): powerful tool involving every functionary to have positive impacts.	**MODERATELY** (Bank performance moderately satisfactory. The direct beneficiaries were increased by 5.3 million children and 1.3 million pregnant and lactating women. Implementation delayed [had not made much progress, falling into a crisis]. Implementation progress was rated 'satisfactory' and development objectives 'moderately satisfactory'.)

Cont'd...

...Cont'd

IFAD	Women's Empowerment and Livelihoods Programme in the Mid-Gangetic Plains	Support structure to evolve into sustainable People's Organizations. Community Institutions Development sub-component provides support services in strengthening existing community organizations and promoting new organizations with training and capacity building using the services of national NGOs. Involving women in enterprises and activities supported by extensive training and orientation.	**NO** (Large number of women could not be linked with bank credit and affected the livelihood promotion activities, delays in recruitment, high turnover, bureaucratic procedures and insufficient decentralization. Increases in women's incomes are small, negative high levels of women's participation.)
IFAD	Tejaswini Rural Women's Empowerment Programme Documents	Sexual harassment policies and redressal mechanisms as per Supreme Court directive developed. Gender strategy prepared by an external consultant that gives a good analysis of position of women and gender concerns in Maharashtra. The National Alliance for Women Organizations developed a manual for conducting mock parliament. Women's access to basic infrastructure and facilities addressed through convergence with government programmes, improved considerably in terms of achieving physical and financial targets.	**MODERATELY** (Satisfactory: training on governance issues to 3,030 women who have contested elections in the previous year. 27% and 59% of the respondents are very satisfied with the empowerment-related activities. 2% unsatisfied Moderately satisfactory on physical and financial assets, as mobilized saving INR 1.794 million. Moderately satisfactory in food security. Moderately satisfactory in increase in incomes. Moderately satisfactory in policy Impact.)
EU	To Support the Government of India's Efforts to Stop Trafficking Women and Girls through Community Action at the Panchayat Level	Creating institutionalized prevention mechanisms to stop trafficking at the source districts get supported and enhanced through community action	**YES** (Community actions enhanced.)

Cont'd...

...Cont'd

EU	Empowering Women: Access and Ownership over Land and Land-based Activities through Education, Legal Literacy and Advocacy in Rural India	Literacy including functional and legal literacy among dalit and tribal women; Access to and control over property, income and natural resources	**YES** (100 villages from the states of Jharkhand, Orissa, Rajasthan, Madhya Pradesh. Target Groups: 3,300 tribal, dalit and socially disadvantaged women.)
EU	Project Swavlamban—Empowering Poor Informal Sector Women through Market Relevant Capacity Building	Will build skills among self-employed women, in textile, garment and other economic fields such as agro-processing and renewable energy	**YES** (Gujarat and Rajasthan states covering 25,000 women.)
EU	Reduction of Mother to Child Transmission of HIV in India: Improving access to Public Health Services	Reversing the HIV epidemic in India. Through access to, equality, services and information	**YES** (Vulnerable populations in two high prevalence and one highly vulnerable state).
EU	Vocational Education and Training for Vulnerable Groups of Women in 4 States	Building on existing rural business hubs for skills development in the supply chain (vegetables, honey, non-timber forest products and bamboo) for women. Training in quality segregation, value addition and packaging; enterprise management. Get support for infrastructure, capital and insurance	**YES** (Covering 5,200 women in 4 states: Jharkhand, Bihar, Uttarakhand and Rajasthan.)

Cont'd...

...Cont'd

EU	Revitalising Sustainable Rural Livelihoods among Small and Marginal Dryland Farmers and Landless Poor	Promote a sustainable use of natural resources in a drought-prone area in India. The involvement and strengthening of women's cooperatives aims to contribute to gender equality.	**YES** (Anantapur district and Andhra Pradesh)
EU	Promoting Community Action Led by Older People in Rural Rajasthan, India	The construction of a Rain Water Harvesting Structure (Taanka). Using saved money and spending on buying livestock.	**YES** (Improving economic situation of women)
EU	Helping Rural and Tribal Youth in India, HIV Prevention and Care	Through access to information and services on HIV and reproductive health for young people (especially girls). To promote a supportive environment to meet the reproductive, sexual and HIV-related health-needs of rural and tribal youth.	**YES** (400 young women/men's support groups formed health services for STI testing and treatment support.)
EU	Preventing HIV/AIDS among Women of Childbearing Age in North East India	Establishment of previously non-existent maternal and child health services. Providing information and raise awareness among women in the reproductive age group of HIV. Providing integrated health services opening of health centres and mobile clinics.	**YES** (Improving social and health situation of women.)
UN Women	Strengthening Women's Legal Rights in Aceh, Indonesia	Higher levels of awareness of gender issues, legislators and policy makers, government staff in the province and districts, judges and prosecutors, law enforcement staff. Using law in more districts and pursue a preventive approach, law enforcement training centres and women's studies programmes and work towards creating a provincial masterplan for the development of women's rights.	**YES** (Very relevant to the context and effective in contributing to improving women's realization of their rights in Aceh. Some partners needed more capacity to use results-based management tools and training is planned.)

Cont'd...

...Cont'd

UN Women	Supporting Gender Equality and Women's Human Rights in Nation-building of Timor-Leste	Through quality social welfare and social protection services. Outcome 1: change in laws and plans through establishment of legal frameworks and mechanisms to uphold their rights; national action plans to prevent-combat domestic violence and human trafficking; upgrade the knowledge and skills of government officials, NGOs and CBOs involved in implementing action plans, Information, education and communication strategies. Outcome 2: seeks to improve social services and schemes through improved outreach mechanisms and services and the establishment of a social protection scheme Outcome 3: tools on gender sensitive planning and gender responsive budgeting; civil society trained on gender sensitive planning and gender responsive budgeting.	**YES** (Stronger democratic institutions and mechanisms for social cohesion are consolidated and vulnerable populations benefit) Outcome 1: improved protection of women and girls. Outcome 2: reduced vulnerability of women and girls. Outcome 3: increase the knowledge and skills of senior government officials.)
UN Women	Mid-Term Evaluation of the Integrated Programme for Women in Politics and Decision-Making (IPWPDM) in Timor-Leste	Enable greater and more meaningful participation by women in the national parliament and councils. Interventions are building the capacities of women-candidates so they can participate in the electoral processes. Absence of local sustainable institutions and the manner of project execution. Deficiencies in the formulation of the programme results frameworks and its links. Inadequacy of the funds raised compared to the projected total programme budget.	**NO** (Only minimal changes in the number of women elected as chiefs and council members over the last two electoral cycles. NGOs which supported the women did not have the technical competence required for the tasks. There was no uniform method for the allocation of resources. Inefficiencies being incurred in the centralized management system of UNIFEM/UN Women. Inefficiencies in the programme implementation).

Cont'd...

...Cont'd

UN Women	Deepening Democracy, Women's Participation in Peace and Politics in South Asia	Inclusion of gender concerns and women's rights in the New Constitution of Nepal. UNIFEM Nepal's ability to jointly mobilize Nepali women activists. Through a good communication between and among related stakeholders. Timely mobilize the activists on appropriate issues.	**YES** (Contribution significantly to influence the decision makers in the Nepali politics to increase participation of women in political and peace processes. Some of the planned activities were completed with a very tight budget.)
UN Women	Project on Promoting Women in Democratic Decision Making in Cambodia	Through promoting women in decision making in the 2007 and 2008 elections. Through the collaboration among the CPWP member organizations and NGOs. Mobilizing financial resources to support their own campaigns and women's greater participation in development. Organizing a women's group at the village level to facilitate the work of commune-level women leaders.	**YES** (The project has effectively contributed to greater visibility of women in elected offices at the commune, provincial and national levels.)
UN Women	Regional Programme on Expansion of Employment Opportunities for Women (EEOW), Cambodia Chapter	Providing various training workshops, gender equality promotion in enterprise development and workers' rights. Implementing partners and other organizations working in the related fields. Providing direct assistance to beneficiaries in the areas of gender awareness raising, technical training on agriculture, handicrafts, animal raising and microfinance. Integrating gender issues in the Local authorities' programmes and men sharing reproductive work. Combination of institutional capacity building, direct assistance to women and networking.	**YES** (Progress in improving the socio-economic status of women in the target areas. Beneficiaries raised awareness on gender issues and gained new skills and knowledge together with credit to earn additional income. Women gained self-confidence with new skills; they are more involved in community activities and decision making.)

Cont'd...

...Cont'd

UN Women	Decent Employment for Women in India Project (DEW)	Through public vocational training institutes in India: formal-training. The government would launch, expand and institutionalize non-formal training in its training institutions, providing vocational and soft skills to poor women, technical staff, monitoring of activities, cross sharing of experiences between implementing partners, traditional and non-traditional vocational skills.	**YES** (Workable to provide employable training for poor women in the informal sector. 70% of the women trained have found employment.)
UN Women	Equality and Decent Work Promotion for Asian Women through Prevention of Human Trafficking, Protection of Domestic Workers and Gender Capacity Building	Institutional interventions facilitated, networks built, local legislation strengthened, skills imparted, locally adapted materials distributed. New funding modality, investment in adaptation and translation of materials, training and application of gender mainstreaming tools.	**YES** (Constructive balance between responsiveness to the constituents and bridge-building most involved in anti-trafficking and domestic worker protection issues. For the Asia Pacific, there is a clear disadvantage to earmarked funds.)
UN Women	India: Promoting Urban Social Development through Self-help Groups in Karnataka	NGOs with women empowerment have continued to support the groups and are keen on sustaining the groups	**UNCERTAIN** (For the NGOs, the operational cost of maintaining the SHGs is high. Groups have contributed to the NGOs' survival.)

Cont'd...

...Cont'd

UN Women	Nepal: Gender Equality and Social Inclusion Promoting the Rights of Women and the Excluded for Sustained Peace and Inclusive Development	Supported participatory and inclusive constitutional processes to further peace. International standards on human rights have been ratified or signed. Consent of formal political institutions once in place. Hardening of boundaries between groups, and a heavy focus on rights as entitlements. Enforcement mechanisms to the success of legislation in reducing inequalities and in promoting more inclusive development.	**YES** (In spite of the uncertain political situation and the absence of local government bodies the mission observes that substantial progress has been made.)
UN Women	Country Evaluation of the Age and Gender Mainstreaming Pilot Project India	Mainstreaming of age and gender by representatives essential to success. The participatory tool should be applied thoroughly and in a structured manner in order to guarantee the continuity of the benefits identified by the pilot scheme.	**YES** (Methodology project had enthusiastic acceptance by UNHCR.)
UN Women	Entrepreneurship Development Programme for Women in Food Processing in Central Vietnam	Ownership and interest by key partners in project activities. Continuity in the approach (use of expertise, materials from previous projects). Consideration for socio-cultural aspects through series of awareness building events. Intensity of cooperation between the project and counterparts at the provincial, district and commune levels.	**YES** (Awareness and cooperation gains.)

The overview of the projects under scrutiny is listed in Table 2. It demonstrates the main thematic focus of the projects that explains key policy aim of the international donors. While the UN Women, the European Union and the World Bank projects are often of micro-societal nature, they tend to address gender issues in more cases. On the other hand, projects of FAO and the International Fund for Agricultural Development (IFAD) are typically infrastructure-oriented and thus gender neutral (Budlender 2010).

Finally, Table 3 provides an overview of the types of gender conditionality included in the projects under scrutiny. This analysis demonstrates that the range of tools chosen to improve the gender situations varies from the organizational measures at regional or local level to economic and social instruments. Table 3 also indicates whether actually there are positive gender effects achieved. In majority of the cases, the evaluation is of the qualitative and not of the quantitative nature due to the publicly available information.

The results show that out of 28 evaluated projects with gender conditionality, 22 generated positive results. Three other projects offered moderate positive effects. The moderation came mainly from the delays in the implementation. In one case, the gender-impact results are uncertain. Finally, in the case of two projects, no positive effects could have been identified due to the implementation delays of the projects or project management issues.

CONCLUSION

The chapter analysed 152 projects of six international donors to rural India and some other Asian countries. The gender conditionally was contained in 31 projects, which is smaller of the total number. However, gender conditionality focus varied according to the donors' priority. UN Women had the highest gender focus (86% of the project contained women-related conditionality), followed by the European Union (56%), the World Bank (46%) and the International Fund for Agricultural Development (27%). Other two donors were focused to issues other than gender focus.

In terms of efficiency of the conditionality, the analysis shows a relatively high positive effect with 22 out of 28 projects having a positive impact on gender situation. The reservation should be kept concerning the quantitative effect of project on the real improvement of the women situation in rural India and Asia.

In conclusion, the international donors under the scrutiny focus on gender issues were not in the centre of the policy orientation. However, once a women-related conditionality was part of the project, it generally helped in improving women's situation. Nevertheless, the international aid should be seen only as a complement to the systemic change driven by structural changes in the society, economy and trade.

REFERENCES

Budlender, D. (Ed.) (2010). *Time Use Studies and Unpaid Care Work*. London: Routledge.

FAO (2010). *The State of Food and Agriculture 2010–11: Women in Agriculture*. Rome: FAO.

Forbes (2015). Why India Needs More Women Entrepreneurs. www.forbesindia.com on 8/12/2015.

Ghani, E., Kerr, W. and O'Connell, S. (2011). Spatial Determinants of Entrepreneurship in India. NBER Working Paper 17514.

Lakshmi, I., Mani, A., Mishra, P. and Topalova, P. (2012). The Power of Political Voice: Women's Political Reservation and Crime in India. *American Economic Journal: Applied Economics 4*(4), pp. 165–193.

National Sample Survey Organisation (2013). Report. India – Employment and Unemployment, July 2011 – June 2012, NSS 68th Round – Overview – Micro Data Archive. New Delhi: Ministry of Statistics and Programme Implementation.

OECD (2013). Gender, Institutions and Development. International Development Statistics, Development: Key Tables from OECD.

Ramachandran, N. (2006). Women and Food Security in South Asia: Current Issues and Emerging Concerns. Research Paper No. 2006/131, UNU/WIDER.

Sancar, A. and Bieri, S. (2009). Power and Poverty: Reducing Gender Inequality by Ways of Rural Employment? University of Berne (Switzerland) and the Swiss Development Agency (Switzerland).

Srivastava, N. and Srivastava, R. (2009). Women, Work, and Employment Outcomes in Rural India. University of Allahabad (India), Jawaharlal Nehru University (India).

Udry, C. et al. (2005). Gender Differentials in Farm Productivity: Implications for Household Efficiency and Agricultural Policy. *Food Policy 20*(5), pp. 407–423.

CHAPTER 2

The Role and Limitations of Public Policy in Ensuring Gender Equity

Suzaina Kadir, Caroline Brassard and Ola Gamil Mahmoud El-Taliawi

If we consider the relatively short time frame, from the start of the women's movement at the end of the nineteenth century till now, we should acknowledge the significant improvements towards gender equality worldwide. From a time when women were universally relegated to the private realm of the family, without any political or economic rights, now women are on the whole regarded as equal citizens along with the men. This was not an easy achievement and came about as a result of real fights over public policy at the national and international level, led by feminists and other advocates for gender equality.

This chapter delves into the role and limitations of public policy in ensuring gender equity. After a discussion on gender-related indicators, it focuses on three key debates about generating policies to equalize women's role in politics and the public sector in the Asia-Pacific region, since the late 1990s. The first debate centres on political representation of women as a means to generating policies to encourage greater equality for women. The second major debate concerns the obstacles against women's equality or ability to rise up the ranks. Here the focus is on removing institutional constraints such as acknowledging the double burden, and the need for pro-family policies. The third and last debate relates to the need for a culture shift, arguing that policies have major limitations. This cultural shift requires specific focus on education and strong political will. The chapter concludes on the implications for public policy research on gender equity for countries in Asia and the Pacific.

GENDER-RELATED INDICATORS AND PUBLIC POLICY

The Convention of the Elimination of Discrimination against Women (CEDAW), the Beijing Declaration, and the Millennium Development Goals have all situated the call for gender equality squarely at the centre of public policy debates and objectives. In the UNDP's human development perspective which started in 1990 and has continued every year until now, development has been looked at in terms of 'human development', which is defined as 'the process of broadening the people's choices' (Roces and Edwards 2000).

In order to determine the extent of human development, the Human Development Index (HDI) measures life expectancy at birth, adult literacy and gross domestic product per capita. To broaden human development, it prescribes the provision of minimum basic needs – food, shelter, health, education and livelihood, to people. The UNDP also devised the Gender-sensitive Development Index (GDI), which looks at the same indicators, but comparing male and female for states where gender disaggregated data already exist.

In 1995, the UNDP specifically looked at women's role in politics and decision making, devising the Gender Empowerment Measure (GEM). It specifically looks at the following points:

(1) Number of seats in the parliament held by women;

(2) Proportion of female legislators, senior officials and managers;

(3) Proportion of female professional and technical workers and

(4) Ratio of estimated female to male earned income.

The call now is to focus on the GDI as much as the HDI, as countries plan out their development agendas and objectives. The GEM makes the core argument that women's political participation and leadership are central to our measure of gender equality. The UNDP replaced GDI with the Gender Inequality Index (or GII) in 2011 as a better reflection of gender inequalities in countries under review.

As much as there is variation in the HDIs across countries, there are similarly wide variations in the GDI and GEM. This reflects the persistent challenges in achieving gender equality, and more importantly, in areas where it matters most. It is worth noting that there is the evidence of contradictions in the HDI and GDI data available.

For example, UNDP statistics show that the HDI, GDI and GEM of many countries do not coincide. Singapore is one of those states with near ranks of HDI, GDI and GEM. In 1995, Singapore's HDI was ranked 35 from among 175 countries, GDI ranked 28 and GEM 35. In 2000, Singapore's HDI ranked 24, GDI also 24 and GEM 38; in 2004, HDI was 25, GDI was 28 and GEM was 20 (Chew 2001).

But Philippine data show an inherent contradiction. In 1995, the Philippine HDI ranked it as 100; GDI was 64, but GEM was a high 28. The response from women's groups in the Philippines indicated incredulity at these scores (Tapales 1992). In 2000, Philippine HDI was 77, its GDI was 64 and its GEM was 44. In 2004, the HDI was 83, GDI was 66 and GEM was 37. In contrast, some countries have high HDI but low GEMs. This problem is compounded by the fact that many countries do not have data to compute the GEM (see Table 1).

Table 1 *Ranking of development and gender indicators in selected Asian countries (1995, 2000, 2004, 2012)*

Country	*1995*			*2000*			*2004*			*2012*		
	HDI	*GDI*	*GEM*	*HDI*	*GDI*	*GEM*	*HDI*	*GDI*	*GEM*	*HDI*	*GDI**	*GEM*
Japan	3	8	27	9	9	41	9	12	38	10	—	54
Singapore	35	28	35	24	24	38	25	28	20	18	—	16
Korea, Rep.	31	37	90	31	30	63	28	29	68	12	—	64
Malaysia	59	38	49	61	57	47	59	52	44	64	—	65
Thailand	58	33	54	76	62	—	76	61	57	103	—	73
Philippines	100	64	28	77	64	44	83	66	37	114	—	45
Sri Lanka	97	58	79	84	68	66	96	73	74	92	—	85
China	111	71	—	99	79	—	94	71	—	101	—	57

Source: Human Development Reports (1990–2013), United Nations Development Programme (UNDP), available at http://hdr.undp.org/en/

* The United Nations replaced the Gender Development Index (GDI) with the Gender Inequality Index (GII) in 2011.

Despite the contradictions, these GEM scores are an important starting point in highlighting the persistent challenges for gender equality. If we take the Philippines as an example, women's quantitative participation in areas of politics and decision making has not been increased despite what the GEM scores may suggest. Bills providing for direct woman empowerment through greater participation in politics have not been passed by the Philippine Congress. The relative high score of the Philippines in the GEM comes from the more covert areas of women's participation in technical and managerial positions. In fact, it would have been higher had the ratio of male/female income not been very unequal: for every one peso the man earns, the woman earns only 0.59 centavos (Aguilar 1990).

Careful research has pointed to similar challenges in Singapore, where the GEM scores are relatively impressive. Like in the Philippines, unequal pay between men and women persists, yet Singapore rejects quotas as an option on the principle of meritocracy. Institutional constraints continue to make women's empowerment in political decision making difficult (Chew 2001).

Other countries, in Asia as in the West, have provided for affirmative action for women in politics as the best and most practical strategy to improve GEM scores. In addition, quotas make women less reluctant to seek political office, as in the case in many Asian countries. For example, both India and Pakistan have passed a law that reserves 33 per cent of seats for women in local councils.

In order to get women to run for office, some electoral reforms such as party list systems to encourage women to form political parties have proven to be a useful approach. Sectoral representation in local councils is a strategy that needs to be more rigorously implemented, and not just written in law (Roces 1994). For now, affirmative action may be the more practical strategy, but ultimately, women should be mobilized to vote for women. This requires women to be more aware of their latent power, and public policies have only limited impact on this aspect.

Engendering politics also connotes making the women in office effective advocates of the women's cause. Here is where business groups of women and NGOs need to make greater impact. They can provide funds for training or train women themselves. They can invest in research that will help governments consider options that will best address the persistent challenges against women's empowerment. This can all feed into the many areas needed: training of women candidates for office, orientation programmes to provide women in office the gender perspective and training women public officials in much needed management skills (Tapales 1992). In the end, it is crucial to get women into positions of power, to enable them to make decisions that will lead to significant improvements in gender equity, as discussed next.

POLITICAL REPRESENTATION OF WOMEN

In this section, we argue that political representation of women is a means to generating policies towards greater equality for women. Encouraging greater equality for women has been the quest of women's rights movements, international development agencies and governments for many decades. From an economic perspective, it has been argued that rapid economic transformation cannot occur with almost half the population – its women – deprived of jobs, health and education (Tinker 2009).

With this in mind, the calls for equal political participation of women started to emerge. It was seen not only as a human right, where the concept of 'citizenship' itself is directly linked with the ability to vote and run for political office, but also as a developmental necessity (UN Division for Advancement of Women 2005). The call for women's equal political participation was also based on the notion of democracy, where the ability of citizens to participate equally in their self-government was at the heart of democratic values (UN Division for Advancement of Women 2005).

Thus, increasing the political participation of women as both voters and elected officials in the different tiers of government became a goal for both policy makers and women's rights movements, in order to ensure better equality for women. As a result, affirmative action policies aiming at an increased number of elected women began to be implemented by countries all over the world, in the form of gender quota provisions. These were either legal quota imposed through constitutional amendments or changes to electoral laws; or party quotas, where major parties included quota provisions in their internal statutes (Wängnerud 2009). Many Asian countries introduced quota provisions at the local, provincial and/or national levels, and this policy was behind the increase in the number of women legislators since the late 1990s (see also Figure 1) (Ayaz and Fleschenberg 2009).

However, as researchers' understanding of the interplay between gender and politics evolved, there was no longer a perception that women's political participation was an *end* in itself, but rather a *means* to achieve better equality for women. This effectively shifted the literature away from *descriptive* representation centred on the number of female parliamentarians, towards *substantive* representation, concerned with the effects of the presence of women in the parliament. According to the 'Politics of Presence' theory by Phillips (1995),

Figure 1 *Proportion of seats held by women in national parliaments in 2012 (%)*

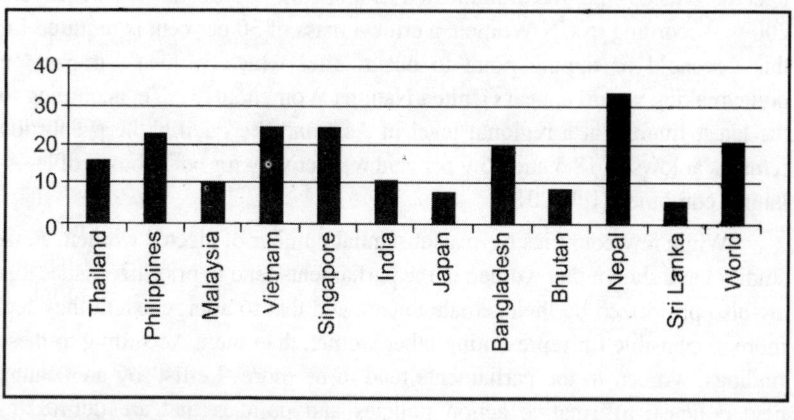

Source: World Bank (2013).

'equal rights to a vote are not strong enough to guarantee that women's issues are addressed there must also be equality among those elected to office'.

Hence, the idea of representation, as opposed to mere participation, started to appear. It was based on the argument that women's daily life experiences differed considerably from men, because of 'child-rearing, education, divisions of paid and unpaid labour, and exposure to violence and sexual harassment' (Wängnerud 2009). Female politicians, who share these same experiences, would be more able to advance women's interests and needs on the agenda.

Proponents of this view advocate that policies seeking gender equity would become more prominent as women's power grows, and that women's interests would remain inadequately addressed in a political sphere that is dominated by men (Wängnerud 2009; Tinker 2009). Additionally, women's presence in legislatures would change the 'substance' of policymaking by acting on behalf of women; by influencing legislative activities and providing oversight of policies; holding ministers accountable and raising the awareness of men in the parliament (Costa et al. 2012). In terms of government legitimacy, it was also suggested that women's increased political representation would improve legitimacy, as governments seek to address issues relevant to all members of society (Ayaz and Fleschenberg 2009).

Some argue that women need to not only be present in legislative assemblies, but also move from being small minorities to larger groups to be able to make a difference. Otherwise, women would tend to adapt to the surrounding environment and act more like their male counterparts. In other words, a 'critical mass' of female legislators is required and only then they are empowered to push for women-friendly policies (Tinker 2009: 1). According to this argument, there needs to be a significant number of women for them to operate outside the male-dominated framework (Ayaz and Fleschenberg 2009). According to UN Women, a critical mass of 30 per cent is required for this threshold or tipping point to occur, after which women's impact on policymaking would appear (United Nations Women 2013). Yet according to the latest figures, at a regional level in Asia and the Pacific, the proportion remains at lows of 18.5 and 15.9 per cent respectively for both houses of legislatures combined (IPU 2013).

While few countries have a substantial number of elected women, some studies have shown that women in the parliaments tend to prioritize issues that are also prioritized by their female voters, and that to a large extent they feel more responsible for representing other women than men. According to these findings, women in the parliaments tend to be more 'Leftist' by advocating new policies, affirmative action policies and policies that are defined as women's issues (Wängnerud 2009).

Although the impacts of women in the parliament are not yet conclusive, it is fair to say that increasing women's political participation and representation is an important means to generate policies that would encourage gender equity. However, further research in this area is sorely needed, as discussed in the last section of this chapter. It is also essential in enabling women to craft policies to help remove the barriers that hinder other women's political representation, including cultural attitudes that discourage women from participating in public forums (Tinker 2009).

However, quotas alone cannot do the trick. Laws that stipulate gender quotas should be more binding. Often, noncompliance only results in fines, where large parties opt for paying the fines rather than sacrificing the chance of a 'winning' candidate (Tinker 2009). Other hindrances that women can empathize with and aim to address include working conditions that are incompatible with family responsibilities.

Such barriers faced by women prior to and after election play a significant role in diminishing their opportunities for participation, chance of winning and eventual impact. Understanding these hindrances and developing policy options to address them requires in-depth research on a local and regional level. However, the research agenda of international organizations such as the United Nations has tended to focus more on a national-level perspective, which provides limited understanding of local contexts.

WOMEN RISING UP THE LADDER

Ensuring that women can attain high levels of leadership as equally as men is an important aspect of gender equity; not just in politics, but in the professional sphere as well. Their equal representation in managerial ranks, in both business and public administration, and the availability of equal opportunities for them to rise up the career ladder is a reflection of the state of gender equity in the society at large. Therefore, a society where women are obstructed from reaching higher managerial levels based on their gender signals an imbalance in its gender equity scales (Chou et al. 2005). This section discusses some of the major institutional (and to a certain extent cultural) obstacles that impede women from moving up the organizational ranks.

The inability of women to rise up the organizational ladder, because of exclusivist practices, negatively influences the motivation of those at the lower ranks, as they lose the desire for what they perceive as 'useless' competition. Hence, their productivity levels and sense of organizational commitment becomes affected (Dreher 2003). A society that hinders women's ability to rise up the ladder also loses out on the added value women can impart in their organizations.

Indeed, recent studies have shown that diversity in the different tiers of organizations, from the bottom to the utmost top, is 'organizationally healthy'. By tapping into the overall available talent pool, regardless of gender, an organization increases its profit potential. In terms of innovation, studies on group behaviour have shown that diverse groups make more innovative initiatives, as compared to non-diverse groups (Lansing and Chandra 2012).

As for accountability, the issue of promoting women's advancement onto boardrooms first gained international attention after the recent global economic meltdown, where there was an increased need for corporate accountability. This was supported by research findings demonstrating that when women were present on corporate boards, more formal board evaluations were conducted (Lansing and Chandra 2012). The link between accountability and the participation of women in senior positions is an area that required more attention from a policy research perspective and will be discussed further later.

Overall, the rapid growth from many Asian economies over recent years, along with higher education levels and lower fertility rates, has all contributed to increasing women's labour force participation (Yukongdi and Benson 2005). But the scarcity of women at the top echelons of organizations is a global phenomenon (Chugh and Sahgal 2007). While women have made progress in reaching managerial positions at the low and middle management levels, the gender gap increases and becomes more apparent at the more senior levels (Chugh and Sahgal 2007). Evidence has shown that the higher the ranks, the more women experienced gender inequality in terms of rewards and benefits (Chou et al. 2005).

Figure 2 *Percentage of women in senior management in 2012*

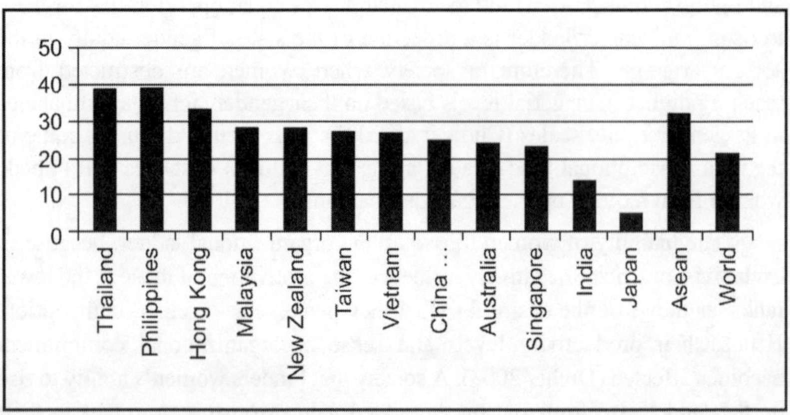

Source: Adapted from Grant Thornton (2012).

Figure 3 *Percentage of businesses headed by women CEOs in 2012*

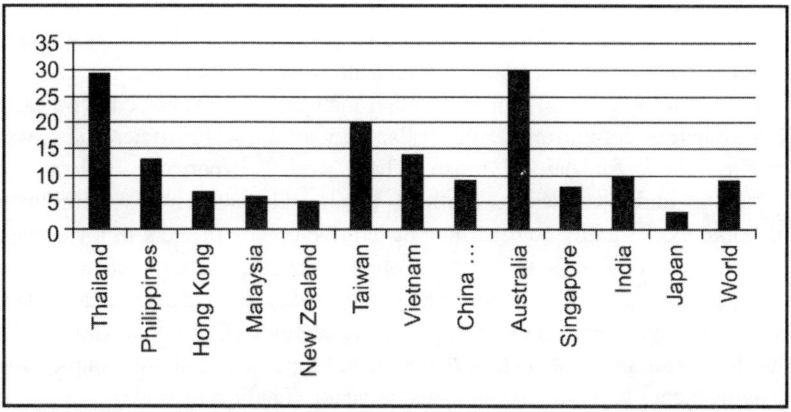

Source: Adapted from Grant Thornton (2012).

A recent survey by Grant Thornton (2012), based on 6,000 interviews with senior executives in listed and privately held businesses internationally, showed that the percentage of women in senior management positions in 2012 varied greatly in the Asia-Pacific region: between a low 14 per cent in India and a high 39 per cent in Thailand (see Figure 2).

Furthermore, with respect to women chief executive officers (CEOs) or chief financial officers (CFOs), the proportion dropped even further, where the percentage of businesses studied headed by a female CEO ranged between a low of 10 per cent in India and a high of 29 per cent in Thailand (see Figure 3). These figures strongly suggest the presence of significant gender barriers faced by women as they attempt to climb up their organizational ladders and advance their careers.

Some of the obstacles cited in the literature on the factors that impede women's career advancement include women's tendency to accumulate less human capital, in terms of education and work experience that makes them less likely to advance in comparison to men (Dreher 2003). Other obstacles arise from within the organization itself, where informal men's groupings, or what is also referred to as 'the old boys' network' exist. These tend to exclude women and give men more visibility during managerial position selections (Chugh and Sahgal 2007; Chou et al. 2005). Human resource management practices in some Asian countries have also been cited by researchers, including restrictive recruitment in certain industries, such as aviation and transport, where jobs are often labelled as 'male' jobs (Chou et al. 2005; Yukongdi and Benson 2005).

As discussed more deeply in the next section, cultural attitudes also feature prominently, where certain cultural and religious traditions contribute to the underrepresentation of women in managerial positions in Asia (Yukongdi and Benson 2005). In such cultures, women's roles are still seen through a traditional lens as restricted to the family. In the instance where women are part of the labour force, their work is often seen merely as a supplement to the family income, rather than as a career choice (Chou et al. 2005). Family responsibilities have also been attributed to women's ability to rise up the organizational ranks, where women experience difficulty in assuming multiple roles, as mothers, wives and managers. Concerns over possible work–family conflict may have driven many of them to lower their career aspirations. Research has shown that married women who wished to assume both career and family tracks also tended to be stereotyped by their senior managers as uncommitted to the organization (Chou et al. 2005). This has led researchers to conclude that women face a 'labyrinth' of complex and heterogeneous barriers on their paths to the top (Eagly et al. 2007).

Public policies aimed at empowering women's career advancement need to target the removal of the institutional and cultural obstacles that exist and impede women from moving up the organizational ranks. While some countries in the Asia-Pacific region, such as China, Hong Kong and others, have introduced antidiscrimination and equal opportunity legislation, policies need to acknowledge women's 'double burden' (Yukongdi and Benson 2005). Adopting pro-family or family-friendly employment policies, such as flexible working conditions, that allow women to balance family and work responsibilities would be a major step towards gender equity, since a major portion of the 'labyrinth' women face is derived from their inability in most cases to commit to both (Eagly et al. 2007).

CULTURAL SHIFT AND PUBLIC POLICY

Culture as a withholding force of gender equity, whether in the political or the professional domain, has featured in both debates discussed earlier. It has been argued that culture, beliefs and values are part of the main impediments to women's progress as political representatives and managers, especially in cultures where there is a strong preference for son (Yukongdi and Benson 2005). While this is a global phenomenon, the Asia-Pacific region has a specific stake in addressing it as undergoing a rapid change. In order for that growth to become sustained, it needs to be socially inclusive. In this section, we argue that three types of complementary policies may support cultural shift: integrating gender equity as part of the curriculum content, promoting partnerships between policy makers and religious leaders and increasing the representation of women in media positions.

Even though public policies such as quotas and pro-family policies and others are important for empowering women and removing institutional, they alone cannot create the sustained impact required to achieve gender equity (MenEngage 2013). What is equally important is a simultaneous cultural shift to take place, in order for such policies to create the change needed (United Nations Population Fund [UNFPA 2013a]). This is especially important since it has been argued that 'societies based in religious values are most likely to retard acceptance of gender equality' (Inglehart and Norris 2003). Therefore, policies need to be crafted in such a way that they address the institutional and cultural barriers that impede women's progress.

First, education policy is one of the main policy areas advocated by international organizations as a tool for cultural change. However, policies should focus not only on increasing female enrolment and completion rates (quantitative approach) but also on curriculum content (qualitative approach). This would have an impact not only on girls' education but also on boys' education.

The importance of the role of men and boys in achieving gender equity has long been highlighted by the United Nations as a cornerstone for advancing gender equity. This is especially important in the Asia-Pacific context, where evidence from Taiwan showed that husbands' negative attitudes towards women's working arrangements or political involvement often played a more significant role in discouraging them from participating than having child-rearing responsibilities (Chou et al. 2005).

Second, promoting a more moderate understanding of religion is another policy area, which can help create a cultural shift. Religious and tribal leaders (mostly male figures) are often the gatekeepers to what a society can accept or reject. Partnering with religious figures and leaders, who believe in women's equality and human rights, can create a societal dialogue and advance gender equality based on moderate religious grounds.

It is, therefore, imperative to partner with religious figures to advance women's equal right to political representation and career advancement. Including them in the process can help change perceptions of gender roles among both women and men. The United Nations Population Fund has taken this approach in some countries, such as Uganda, to help end harmful traditional practices such as female genital mutilation (UNFPA 2013b).

The third important sphere where policy can play a role in advancing gender equity is through media policies and women representation in senior media positions. Women are both underrepresented in media positions and are continuously portrayed in stereotypical roles. Ayaz and Fleschenberg (2009) argue that 'media should not present women politicians as models, but as role models; covering their success stories and not only their outfits and failures'. Further, according to a report issued by Women Watch, women are often depicted as 'sexualized images' for commercial interests (United Nations

Women 2002). The combination of these poor practices negatively influences cultural perceptions of women and attitudes towards them.

Therefore, accreditation and standard setting for the media, as well as self-regulatory mechanisms, and codes of conduct and ethics, are policy tools that have been promoted to create awareness about gender equity issues in the media, with the aim of reducing this trend. Moreover, the representation of women in media positions can ensure that women's perspectives are also taken into account.

Designing such policies require strong political will in order to achieve a cultural shift. In order to design such policies in a consistent and implementable manner, policy makers need to partner with and gain the support of agents of change and local power structures. This will enable policy makers to better understand the roots of the cultural and traditional biases against women and to harness their support later on when implementing or advocating policies (UNFPA 2013c). This is a challenging task and requires the coordination, resources and patience of a dedicated government. It is also essential because crafting policies aimed at cultural change requires the development of strong evaluation mechanisms to track changes over time.

IMPLICATIONS FOR POLICY RESEARCH AND CONCLUSIONS

Finally, we reflect on the design of public policy research about gender equity in order to help shape the three debates discussed in this chapter and influence policy making. This section draws key implications in four cross-cutting areas: from generating new types of data, to understanding multiple relationships, using systematic qualitative analysis and disseminating research findings. The methodologies used in the recent academic literature and by think tanks tend to rely on the quantifiable aspects of gender equity such as targets, quotas and remuneration. However, as discussed throughout this chapter, barriers to gender equity are often deeply rooted in cultures and values, and are less tangible.

Hence, the first step into improving the relevance and impact of policy research is to re-look at the issues of problem definition and measurement, also known as construct validity. In the first debate in particular, in relation to the political representation of women, an area worth investigating is to test the importance of formal and informal networks, and the comparison between men's and women's networks. This may be done via several complementary methods, such as in-depth case studies of women in the parliament, as well as perception surveys.

Perception surveys may be used as advocacy tools to highlight prevailing stereotypes and historical legacies (see Bessel 2004) and provide evidence on the perceived barriers of entry for women into parliament and other public roles. Case studies may also be used to increase the visibility or profile of women leaders, by highlighting their perspectives and views on the challenges as well as enabling factors to their success. Unfortunately, single case studies are still underused, due to their perceived lack of generalizability (Flyvbjerg 2006).

Strategies to enable women to be an integral part of political life need to go beyond quotas (Rai et al. 2006). The concept of 'gender equality' includes equality of opportunity to engage in political debates. Research that demonstrates the impact of women in the parliament is another glaring area of research.

But, instead of looking for causality, collaborative research with individual communities can be developed to establish their contribution to increased awareness about equity issues and also the increased importance of accountability. Moving beyond anecdotal evidence and into creating reliable source requires developing qualitative data analysis skills. In-depth interviews with policy makers and political leaders may also uncover the important contribution of women in the soft power of localities, regions and ultimately of nations. An important context in which such research is needed is in conflict-affected areas (see also True et al. 2012).

Second, understanding local and historical contexts with respect to the ability of women to rise up the ladder requires more systematic qualitative data analysis. Given the emergence of indicators such as the GEM discussed previously, the trend towards using international quantitative data on gender equity can be deceiving. It often masks or diffuses the less tangible and more contextual aspects that compound challenges of achieving gender equity.

We argue that the lack of evidence which can reflect the richness and complexity of communities poses severe limitations to the advancement of policies towards gender equity. Moreover, recent developments in the possibilities offered by qualitative data analysis software have not been taken advantage of by researchers on gender equity. This comment also applies to the third debate on the need for a cultural shift.

The wealth of information contained in social media and blogs remains untapped from a research point of view. This is partly due to the lack of training but also due to limitations of such software in terms of enabling analysis of data other than in the English language. Indeed, local research on gender equity, which targets a local audience, is rarely translated from the local language into English. Consequently, this rich body of the literature does not sufficiently surface in the international academic literature.

Broadening the agenda and strengthening public policy research on gender equity require researchers to understand what explains government's choices of policy tools and instruments, given all the options considered. The relative importance given to values, resources and criteria such as acceptability and feasibility would require researchers to conduct systematic qualitative data collection from policy makers and decision makers influencing the policy process. Other areas of investigation concern partnerships between policy makers and religious leaders and increasing the representation of women in media positions.

Moreover, it has long been established that public opinion surveys can also play an important role in influencing policies (Benjamin and Shapiro 1983). However, the relationship with public opinion is less clear when it comes to gender equity issues and requires further research. Establishing causal linkages within the decision-making process is only part of the story that needs uncovering.

More systematic research is required on areas such as the unexpected impacts of various policies on gender equity. The limitations of public policy given the importance of informal employment also require the attention of researchers. Innovative approaches teaming researchers with community-based monitoring mechanisms can greatly enrich this process and give immediacy to these policy issues in terms of advocacy and improved communication.

Finally, perhaps the most complex area is to increase our understanding of the difference between policy narratives and *policy* norms and how this relates to *societal* norms and values. These could be approached through in-depth interviews and surveys, and complemented by narrative analysis, textual analysis or discourse analysis. Much can be learned from analysing the private sector, and how effective partnerships can be leveraged in order to address gender equity issues (see, for example, Bexell 2013).

This chapter looked at the role and limitations of public policy in ensuring gender equity, focussing on three key debates about generating policies to equalize women's role in politics and the public sector in the Asia-Pacific region. We advocate for the need to produce an analyse evidence that track changes over time, record gains made in terms of gender equity and use multiple channels of communication to share these research findings. This will bring gender equity an integral part of overall political conscience and ultimately foster greater political will to tackle the enduring and deeply rooted problems.

REFERENCES

Aguilar, C.T. (1990). Women in Politics in the Philippines. *Philippine Political Science Journal 29*(30), pp. 39–74.

Ayaz, A. and Fleschenberg, A. (2009). *The Gender Face of Asian Politics*. London: Oxford University Press.

Benjamin, P. and Shapiro, R.Y. (1983). Effects of Public Opinion on Policy. *The American Political Science Review 77*(1), pp. 175–190.

Bessel, S. (2004). Women in Parliament in Indonesia: Denied a Share of Power. Policy and Governance Discussion Paper 04–07, Asia Pacific School of Economics and Government, Australian National University. Available at http://www.crawford.anu.edu.au/degrees/pogo/discussion_papers/pdp04-7.pdf (accessed on 24 September 2013).

Bexell, M. (2013). UN-Business Partnerships for Women's Empowerment. *International Feminist Journal of Politics 14*(3), pp. 389–407.

Chew, P.G. (2001). Political Women in Singapore: A Socio-Linguistic Analysis. *Women Studies International Forum 24*(6), pp. 727–736.

Chou, W.C., Fosh, G.P. and Foster, D. (2005). Female Managers in Taiwan: Opportunities and Barriers in Changing Times. *Asia Pacific Business Review 11*(2), pp. 251–266.

Chugh, S. and Sahgal, P. (2007). Why Do Few Women Advance to Leadership Positions? *Global Business Review 8*(2), pp. 351–365.

Costa, M., Sawer, M. and Sharp, R. (2012). Women Acting for Women: Gender-Responsive Budgeting in Timor-Leste. *International Feminist Journal of Politics*, pp. 1–20.

Dreher, G.F. (2003). Breaking the Glass Ceiling: The Effects of Sex Ratios and Work-Life Programs on Female Leadership at the Top. *Human Relations 56*(5), pp. 541–562.

Eagly, L.L., Carli, A.H. and Carli, L.L. (2007). *Through the Labyrinth: The Truth about How Women Become Leaders.* Boston, MA: Harvard Business Press.

Flyvbjerg, B. (2006). Five Misunderstandings about Case-Study Research. *Qualitative Inquiry 12*(2), pp. 219–245.

Grant Thornton (2012). Corporate Governance Review 2012: The Chemistry of Governance – A Catalyst for Change, www.grantthornton.com

Inglehart, R. and Norris, P. (2003). *Rising Tide: Gender Equality and Cultural Change around the World.* Cambridge: Cambridge University Press.

Inter-Parliamentary Union (IPU) (2013). Statistics on Women in National Parliaments as of 1 November 2013. Available at http://www.ipu.org/wmn-e/world.htm (accessed on 21 November 2013).

Lansing, P. and Chandra, S. (2012). Quota Systems as a Means to Promote Women into Corporate Boardrooms. *Employee Relations Law Journal 38*(3), pp. 3–14. Retrieved from http://search.proquest.com/docview/113879501

MenEngage (2013). Africa Policy Report Series: Prioritizing the Engagement of Men Within Policy for Gender Equality. Available at http://www.menengage. org/index.php?option=com_docman&task=cat_view&gid=51&limit=5&limitstart=0&order=hits&dir=desc&I=itemid=86 (accessed on 1 November 2013).

Phillips, A. (1995). *The Politics of Presence*. Oxford: Oxford University Press.

Rai, S.M., Bari, F., Mahtab, N. and Mohanty, B. (2006). South Asia: Gender Quotas and the Politics of Empowerment – A Comparative Study. Chapter 9, in D. Dahlerup (Ed.), *Women, Quotas and Politics*. New York: Routledge.

Roces, M. (1994). Can Women Hold Power Outside the Symbols of Power? *Asian Studies Review 17*(3), pp. 14–22.

Roces, M. and Edwards, L. (Eds) (2000). *Women in Asia: Tradition, Modernity and Globalization*. Sydney: Allen and Unwin.

Tapales, P.D. (Ed.) (1992). *Filipino Women and Public Policy*. Manila: Kalikasan Press.

Tinker, I. (2009). Assumptions and Realities: Electoral Quotas for Women. *Georgetown Journal of International Affairs 10*(1), pp. 7–16. Retrieved from http://search.proquest.com/docview/221189637.

True, J., Niner, S., Parashar, S. and George, N. (2012). Women's Political Participation Report in Asia and the Pacific. SSRC Conflict Prevention and Peace Forum, United Nations Department of Political Affairs. Available at http://artsonline.monash.edu.au/thebordercrossingobservatory/files/2013/02/undpawomen%e2%80%99s-political-participation-in-asia-and-the-pacific.pdf (accessed on 24 September 2013).

United Nations Division for Advancement of Women (2005). Equal Participation of Women and Men in Decision-Making Processes, with Particular Emphasis on Political Participation and Leadership. Available at http://www.un.org/ women watch/ daw/egm/eql-men/finalreport.pdf (accessed on 15 November 2013).

United Nations Population Fund (2013a). Promoting Gender Equality: Engaging Men and Boys. Available at http://www.unfpa.org/gender/men (accessed on 19 November 2013).

—- (2013b). Culturally Sensitive Approaches: Guiding Principles on Working from Within. Available at http://www.unfpa.org/culture/guiding.htm (accessed on 19 November 2013).

—- (2013c). ibid.

United Nations Women (2002). Participation and Access of Women to the Media, and the Impact of Media and its Use as an Instrument for the Advancement and Empowerment of Women. Division for Advancement of Women, Report of the Expert Group Meeting on Women and the Media. Available at http://www.un.org/womenwatch/daw/egm/media2002/reports/egm,finalreport.pdf (accessed on 19 November 2013).

— (2013). Facts and Figures: Leadership and Political Participation. Available at http://www.unwomen.org/en/what-we-do/leadership-and-political-participation/facts-and-figures (accessed on 19 November 2013).

Wängnerud, L. (2009). Women in Parliaments: Descriptive and Substantive Representation. *Annual Review of Political Science 12*, pp. 51–69.

World Bank (2013). Proportion of Seats Held by Women in National Parliaments. Available at http://data.worldbank.org/indicator/sg.gen.parl.zs/ countries/1w?display=default

Yukongdi, V. and Benson, J. (2005). Women in Asian Management: Cracking the Glass Ceiling? *Asia Pacific Business Review 11*(2), pp. 139–148.

CHAPTER 3

Discourse on Differentiated Rights

Feminism and Multiculturalism

Triranjan Raj

Multiculturalism is a form of identity politics in which the main emphasis is on the range of cultural diversity and identity-related differences. Although such diversity may be linked to age, social class, gender or sexuality, but multiculturalism is usually associated with cultural differentiations. Multiculturalism not only recognizes the fact of cultural diversity, but also holds that such differences should be respected and publicly affirmed. It accords positive value to group difference. They accept that marginalized and discriminated communities within the nation-state deserve special rights. At least, identified minorities must have access to their culture and the freedom to live by the norms of their distinct way of life. This could be done by granting recognition to their cultural practices and norms and exemptions from the prevailing laws. Thus, multiculturalism is a philosophy of minority rights.

The significance of multiculturalism lies in the fact that it raises the issue of culture-based discrimination in society. While previous liberal theories emphasized that individuals were culture-blind, multiculturalism tried to show that indifference to cultural difference can be a cause of injustice in society and can shelter prejudice in a liberal democracy. In a liberal democracy, culture blindness often entails an unquestioned acceptance of the norms that express the culture of the majority. This does not mean that other groups and communities are excluded from the public domain. They may be included but they are expected to conform to the practices of the majority. Multiculturalism reveals such biases of dominant liberal model of democracy and demonstrates that cultural identities are also a source of discrimination in society. Thus, this issue of culture-based discrimination has received a specific articulation within contemporary theories of multiculturalism.

Feminism is the name of a number of social, cultural and political movements, theories and moral philosophies that are concerned with cultural, political and economic practices and inequalities that discriminate against women. Feminists may disagree over the sources of inequality, how to attain equality and the extent to which gender and gender-based identities should be questioned and critiqued; some of this disagreement may stem from continuing pressure to conform to social norms. Liberal feminists believe the women's liberation movement revolves around the equality of sexes, and that biological sex should not be the only factor in shaping a person's social identity, socio-political or economic rights.

Feminist writers such as multiculturalists also emphasize the principle of difference. They also affirm the politics of difference and maintain that having same rights as men could never be the basis of women emancipation in society. The idea that women embody a distinctive perspective has provided a new justification for group representation and differentiated rights; while affirmative action policies had been defended on the ground of compensating and reversing the effects of social discrimination, radical feminism seeks group representation for women on account of their difference. Thus, in this sense they are similar to multiculturalism as both talk of group representation on account of their difference, hence both pursue the politics of difference. Before elaborating the main traits and relationship between multiculturalism and feminism lets first understand the common feature among them, that is, 'Politics of Difference'.

POLITICS OF DIFFERENCE

In this age of globalization, different cultures and societies are becoming increasingly tightly linked and interconnected, and as societies become increasingly multicultural. These developments bring forth a heightened concern with identity, both regarding recognition of *uniqueness* and recognition of *equality* and of *equal value* (Held 2002). Nations, regions, groups and individuals seek recognition of their unique identity. Struggles for recognition of uniqueness are labelled *politics of difference*. The efforts by groups and collectives to protect and promote their difference and uniqueness must contend with the efforts by individuals and groups and collectives to ensure the recognition of equal rights and equal dignity of every individual being.

The modern notion of identity that views human being as unencumbered self has given rise to the politics of difference. The politics of difference want recognition of their unique identity, their distinctiveness from everyone else. The basic idea behind this is that it is precisely this distinctiveness that has been ignored, assimilated to a dominant or majority identity. The politics of difference wants this distinctiveness to be recognized and, thus, forms the basis of differential treatment so that member of their group can avail certain group-specific rights. The politics of difference challenges established notions of legitimacy based on the premise that state and other political institutions are difference-blind. The politics of difference emphasize on the cultural aspects and the role of societal cultures and other group-based affiliations in shaping identities. In the extension of this, they widely recognize that the state and other political institutions are *not* difference-blind. Rather, the state and other political institutions are seen as heavily biased in favour of certain cultures. The modern liberal thinkers talk of principle of equal respect and equal dignity, which requires that all people be treated in a difference-blind fashion or follow universal valid principles. The believers of politics of difference have a problem with this version as they believe that the pursuit of what are thought to be universally valid principles leads to the reinforcement of certain culture-specific values associated with a hegemonic culture that discriminates against the values promoted by other cultures. The net effect is to weaken not only individuals and groups trust in public policies and political institutions but also their sense of self-respect. Weakened trust and self-respect make groups and individuals who feel oppressed demand changes in institutional arrangements not only to protect group-based difference and foster empathy and solidarity among groups but also to restore a measure of self-respect.

Both multiculturalists and feminists affirm the politics of difference. Multiculturalists affirm it on the basis of cultural difference, whereas feminists assert it on the basis of gender difference. Yet, despite sharing the same concern with multiculturalism the feminist writers feel that multiculturalism is bad for feminism. They feel that limited gains that they have achieved by women movement may be lost if the multicultural agenda is accepted.

FEMINISM

Feminism is committed to the equality of women. This is first of all a normative commitment to the equal worth of women and women's experiences. It is also a political commitment to strive to change the practices and beliefs that have subordinated women and treated them as less than equals. According to Susan Moller Okin, feminism is 'the belief that women should not be disadvantaged by their sex, that they should be recognized as having human dignity with men, and the opportunity to live as fulfilling and as freely chosen lives as men can' (Okin 1998).

Feminists deplore that in virtually all societies throughout history women have been considered inferior to men. They deny that the subordination of women is inevitable. The task of feminist political theory is to understand how equality for women might be achieved. Some feminist political theorists have adopted a traditional liberal political framework and applied it to issues of interest of women. They have tried to explore how justice requires a more equitable division of labour in the household, equal pay for comparable work, security for women against violence, right for women to control their own reproduction and a fair share for women around the world regarding the availability of food and educational opportunities in a family and in society (Held 2002).

The feminist movement has passed through mainly three phases. The first phase is the phase of liberal feminism. During this phase, the liberal feminist fought against existing social prejudices and division of function by demanding equal political right for women. They claimed that women should have the same rights and the same opportunities as that of men. Public offices and institution should be open to women and they must have an equal opportunity to participate in public domain. Nineteenth century appealed to the idea of formal equality to challenge the exclusion of women from political and professional life (Mahajan 2002).

After having received the legal and political rights, the second wave of feminist movement started in which the feminist focused on the special needs of women. They referred to the biological difference between men and women to argue that women require special treatment and special rights. From their perspective, equal political rights were necessary but not enough in the case of women. Women had special requirements such as, on one hand, they need special assistance to overcome the disadvantage they had suffered on account of their subordinate position in the society. On the other hand, as mothers or child bearers they had special claims from the state such as maternity leave, child support and healthcare for their family. Thus, they used the concept of difference to justify special treatment (Phillips 1992).

During the third phase, the feminist thinkers affirmed the 'the politics of difference' and maintained that having the same rights as men could never be the basic of women's emancipation in society. Women would always remain disadvantaged in a framework that expects them to be the same as men in public domain. They wanted women should be included as women. By affirming the politics of difference, they wanted to show that the public world is not neutral and is structured by the dominant group, that is, men (Mahajan 2002). By highlighting the difference between men and women, they wanted to show that public domains are culture specific and these disadvantage women. Thus, they wanted their difference to be acknowledged and reflected in public domain.

The second and the third phase of feminism were phases in which feminist political theorists present a critique of liberal individualism as a major theme. They fault liberal individualism for neglecting the social structures within which a person develops and the relations between persons, for instance, family ties, membership in groups and social connections are part of what constitutes a person as who she is.

To see only abstract liberal agents as the units of political thought as in the social contract theory is a denial of the interdependence that characterizes human life. Understanding the 'embeddedness' of persons in social and historical contexts helps us to see that we should not merely supplement the traditional concept of an abstract rational liberal individual historically thought of as male, with a concept of abstract essential women (Held 2002). Recently feminist scholars have begun to seriously investigate the tangled relationship between gender and cultural identities. Most of the feminist writers agree that cultural identity of the women is been expressed in the realm of the family, through adherence to a set of gender-biased norms and practices, which often subordinate women (Shachar 2000a). Laws pertaining to the family are central to the self-conception of cultural groups. However, these very same laws and practices often subordinate women to such an extent that when their groups' practices are accommodated by the state, women living in cultural groups risk losing their basic rights as state citizens (Shachar 2000a).

CULTURE, GENDER AND GROUP RIGHTS

Most cultures are patriarchal, then, and many (though not all) of the cultural minorities that claim group rights are more patriarchal than the surrounding cultures. So it is no surprise that the cultural importance of maintaining control over women shouts out to us in the examples given in the literature on cultural diversity and group rights within liberal states (Parekh 1996). Most cultures are marked with practices and ideologies concerning gender. Suppose, then, that a culture endorses and facilitates the control of men over women in various ways (even if informally, in the private sphere of domestic life). Suppose, too, that there are fairly clear disparities of power between the sexes, such that the more powerful, male members are those who are generally in a position to determine and articulate the group's beliefs, practices and interests. Under such conditions, group rights are potentially, and in many cases actually, antifeminist. They substantially limit the capacities of women and girls of that culture to live with human dignity equal to that of men and boys, and to live as freely chosen lives as they can.

Advocates of group rights for minorities within liberal states have not adequately addressed this simple critique of group rights, for at least two reasons. First, they tend to treat cultural groups as monoliths – to pay more attention to differences between and among groups than to differences within them. Specifically, they give little or no recognition to the fact that minority cultural groups, such as the societies in which they exist (though to a greater or lesser extent), are themselves *gendered*, with substantial differences of power and advantage between men and women. Second, advocates of group rights pay no or little attention to the private sphere. Some of the best liberal defences of group rights urge that individuals need 'a culture of their own', and that only within such a culture can people develop a sense of self-esteem or self-respect, or the capacity to decide what kind of life is good for them. But such arguments typically neglect both the different roles that cultural groups require of their members and the context in which persons' senses of themselves and their capacities are first formed *and* in which culture is first transmitted – the realm of domestic or family life (Okin 1999).

MULTICULTURALISM

The concept of multiculturalism came to prominence in 1960s and 1970s partly due to the debate surrounding minority rights and feminist movement. Nationalism was an important theme in the first half of twentieth century, which was used to persuade the population within the boundaries of one nation to mobilize against the other or colonial powers, whereas multiculturalism as a concept came up after decolonization and began to make its impact felt in Asia, Europe and America (Watson 2000) The concept of multiculturalism emerged with the growing self-awareness of internally colonized people who started making legitimate claims for recognition in public arena. Thus, the concept of multiculturalism, when looked upon from political and philosophical points, tries to highlight the demands placed by the minority culture for recognition and equal status within national and global boundaries.

The concept of multiculturalism when viewed from positive side will make us realize that it is through its recognition only true legitimacy can be achieved in a democratic society. Multiculturalism involves far more than the passive acceptance of diversity. It sees diversity as a quality to be actively embraced as a source of social wealth and dynamics. It encouraged groups to be open and to interact so that all groups may learn and benefit from each other's heritage. Multiculturalism is about diversity and not division. It is about interaction and not isolation. It is about cultural and ethnic differences within a framework of shared fundamental values that enable them to coexist in a complementary rather than on competitive basis (Mahajan 2002).

Before moving further we would like to distinguish between cultural pluralism and multiculturalism. Cultural pluralism is not a modern phenomenon. In India, people of diverse religions and languages have lived together for several centuries. In some pre-modern societies, difference of religion was even legally recognized and accommodated. The existence of plurality at the societal level doesn't imply that multiculturalism as a value prevailed in these societies. Multiculturalism is concerned with the issue of equality. One of the essential prerequisite of multiculturalism is the coexistence of different communities as equal partners in the public arena. Thus, it is this emphasis on equality that distinguishes multiculturalism from pluralism (Mahajan 2002). Pluralism only indicates the presence of differences and is silent about the public status of different communities.

Multiculturalism is best understood neither as a political doctrine with a programmatic content nor as a philosophical school with a distinct theory of man's place in the world but as a perspective or a way of viewing human life. Its central insights are three. First, human beings are culturally embedded in the sense that they grow up and live within a culturally structured world and organize their lives and social relations in terms of a culturally derived system of meaning and significance. This does not mean that they are determined by their culture in the sense of being unable to rise above its categories of thought and critically evaluate its values and system of meaning, but rather that they are deeply shaped by it and can overcome some but not all of its influences (Parekh 1999).

Second, different cultures represent different systems of meaning and visions of the good life. Since each realizes a limited range of human capacities and emotions and grasps only a part of the totality of human existence, it needs other cultures to help it understand itself better and expand its intellectual and moral horizon. This does not mean that one cannot lead a good life within one's own culture, but rather that, other things being equal, one's way of life is likely to be richer if one also enjoys access to others, and that a culturally self-contained life is virtually impossible for most human beings in the modern, mobile and interdependent world. Nor does it mean that all cultures are equally rich and deserve equal respect, that each of them is good for its members, or that they cannot be compared and critically assessed. All it means is that no culture is wholly worthless, that it deserves at least some respect because of what it means to its members and the creative energy it displays, that no culture is perfect and has a right to impose itself on others, and that cultures are best changed from within (Parekh 1999).

Third, every culture is internally plural and reflects a continuing conversation between its different traditions and strands of thought. This does not mean that it is devoid of coherence and identity, but that its identity is plural, fluid and open. Cultures grow out of conscious and unconscious interactions with each other define their identity in terms of what they take to be their significant other and are at least partially multicultural in their origins and constitution. A culture cannot appreciate the value of others unless it appreciates the plurality within it; the converse is just as true. Closed cultures cannot and do not wish or need to talk to each other. Since each defines its identity in terms of its differences from others or what it is not, it feels threatened by them and seeks to safeguard its integrity by resisting their influences and even avoiding all contacts with them. A culture cannot be at ease with differences outside it unless it is at ease with its own internal differences. A dialogue between cultures requires that each should be willing to open itself up to the influence of and learn from others, and this presupposes that it is self-critical and willing and able to engage in a dialogue with itself (Parekh 1999). According to Bhikhu Parekh, a multiculturalist's perspective is composed of the creative interplay of these three important and complementary insights – namely the cultural 'embeddedness' of human beings, the inescapability and desirability of cultural plurality, and the plural and multicultural constitution of each culture.

MULTICULTURALISM AND FEMINISM

Like multiculturalism, feminist writers also accord positive value to difference. Theories of difference believe that the public world is not neutral and is always structured by the dominant group, that is, in case of feminism the group is men and in case of multiculturalism the group is dominant culture. Thus, both these theories want their different needs to be acknowledged and reflected in public domain.

Yet, despite the shared commitment to the value of difference women groups and analysts are among the most vocal critics of multiculturalism. For feminist theorists, the most striking inadequacy of multiculturalism is that it addresses the issue of inter-group equality but remains more or less indifferent to the concern of intra-group equality. Like liberalism, it discusses the issue of justice with reference to inequalities that exist in the public domain but is silent on the issue of discrimination that occurs in the private domain, or the sphere of family (Okin 1998). Multiculturalism deals with discrimination of minority communities that we witness in public domain but it does not talk about the subordination of some groups within the community. Thus, through a system of special cultural rights for communities, it leaves the private sphere almost entirely in the hands of the community (Mahajan 2002).

Multiculturalism takes note of only one kind of difference, that is, cultural difference. Through this category of difference, it points to cultural discrimination within the nation-state. In this process, it presents each culture as a homogeneous entity with clearly defined practices and norms. Thus, multiculturalism does not talk about the difference that exists within each tradition.

When multiculturalism presents operating practices as being collectively valued, endorsed by community members and sanctioned by tradition, it overlooks the disputes surrounding the community practices. It ignores the fact that tradition is open to interpretation and no culture is static as it keeps on evolving over a period of time. Over a period of time, identity is contested; transformed and redefined by group members through ongoing interaction both inside and outside the identity group and it is this fact that needs to be understood in multicultural discourse. If we have to understand the real problem between multiculturalism and feminism, then we have to distinguish between two different brands of multiculturalism, that is, between strong multiculturalism and weak multiculturalism (Shachar 2000b).

The strong version of multiculturalism calls for a new understanding of multiculturalism in which identity groups are to be granted strong formal legal and constitutional rights so that they may govern their members in accordance with their own customs and views. This concept focuses almost exclusively on the problem of injustice between different cultural groups but doesn't address the problem of injustice within the cultural group. Thus, this concept of multiculturalism is not compatible with feminism.

The weak version of multiculturalism more affectively addresses the intra-group complexities of multicultural accommodation. It acknowledges the potential tension between the accommodation of identity groups and the protection of citizenship rights. They agree on the proposition that a morally adequate treatment of identity group means providing multicultural accommodation without abandoning the protection of individual rights. This type of view is also held by Will Kymlicka who argues that the real test of the multicultural model of citizenship lies in the ability to explain how minority rights coexist with human rights and how minority rights are limited by the principle of individual liberty, democracy and social justice (Shachar 2000b). He believes that in a multicultural society, group differentiated rights should be awarded to different communities but these group differentiated rights should be supplemented with intra-group freedom clause so that those members of the group who don't want to comply by the group norms can opt for other moral laws because the basic essence of multiculturalism is providing safeguard so that individual within a society can have a choice between different traditional values, and this can only be made possible if the individual within a group is given total freedom to opt for other appealing moral traditional values.

In order to create such an environment within a multicultural society, Will Kymlicka talks of 'internal restrictions' and 'external protection' (Brink 2000). According to him, if the state is pursuing multicultural policies, then less emphasis should be laid on 'internal restrictions' and more on 'external protection'. He wants the cultural group to acknowledge and respect the plurality within their own community and not much restriction should be imposed on the members of the community so that they for themselves decide what type of norms they want to practice. The only thing which the state need to do is to provide them with 'external protection', that is, protection from the outside world so as to ensure that if the change has to be brought out in a particular culture, then this change should be from within rather than being imposed by other cultures.

In multicultural societies, minority communities also have a moral responsibility, that is, to initiate a process of internal democratization because they too are asking for special rights in the name of democracy. Thus, if they expect rights to protect their difference, then they must allow space for expression of internal difference. Most of the contemporary multiculturalists talk of diverse communities within the nation-state and consider these communities as homogenous. If multiculturalism has to be made compatible with feminism, then multiculturalists will have to explore the difference and heterogeneity that exist within the community. They will have to challenge the basic assumption about the homogeneity of the community.

At present, most statements on multiculturalism suggest that minority cultural communities need to be protected because individuals value these membership and identities. This is the reason they demand certain special rights for their communities. But over here we need to understand that culture and identities are not static and they keep on changing with changing time. This change within culture and identities happens when different cultures come in contact with each other. In this whole affair, the role of state should only be that of a facilitator who will not impose any cultural values or favour any cultural values but will only see to it that proper civic discourse is taking place within different communities. The task of the state is to provide external protection to different communities so that no culture can impose its values on others and ensure that if there has to be a change, then it should be from within. It is also the task of the state to see that those groups who are demanding special community rights are internally democratic or not, and while giving them special rights, certain rights should be given to those persons within the community who do not want to abide by certain community values so that the community cannot impose their values over them.

Just preserving different cultures is not the sole purpose of multiculturalism. The basic purpose of multiculturalism is to create a diverse society in which the individuals have a choice between different cultural patterns so that new cultural patterns can emerge, and this is only possible when individuals within the community who do not want to comply by group norms are given certain special rights. Thus, in multicultural societies the women within a particular culture should be given freedom of choice, regarding the values that they want to endorse, and then only can multiculturalism be made compatible with feminism.

REFERENCES

Brink, B. (2000). *The Tragedy of Liberalism*. Albany: State University of New York Press.

Held, D. (2002). Globalisation, Corporate Practice and Cosmopolitan Social Standards. *Contemporary Political Theory* 1(1). pp. 59–78.

Mahajan, G. (2002). *The Multicultural Path*. New Delhi: Sage.

Okin, S.M. (1998). Feminism and Multiculturalism: Some Tensions. *Ethics 108*(4), July 1998, pp. 661–84.

—- (1999). *Is Multiculturalism Bad for Women?* Princeton, NJ: Princeton University Press.

Parekh, B. (1996). Minority Practices and Principles of Toleration. *International Migration Review 30*(1), April, pp. 251–84.

—- (1999). What is Multiculturalism? *Seminar*, December, pp. 1–8. Available at http://www.india-seminar.com

Phillips, A. (1992). Democracy and Difference: Some Problems for Feminist Theory. *Political Quarterly 63*(1), pp. 79–90.

Shachar, A. (2000a). Should Church and State be Joined at the Altar? Women's Rights and the Multicultural Dilemma. In Will Kymlicka and Wayne Norman (Eds), *Citizenship in Diverse Societies*. New York: Oxford University Press, p. 199.

—- (2000b). On Citizenship and Multicultural Vulnerability. *Political Theory XXVIII* (1), pp. 64–89.

Watson, C.W. (2000). *Multiculturalism*. Philadelphia: Open University Press, pp. 87–102.

CHAPTER 4

Methodological, Pedagogical Contestations and Complications in Gender Studies

Queering Gender in India

Anup Shekhar Chakraborty

'Gender' in India in particular has conveniently been understood to mean 'women' by overlooking the definitional encapsulations within the ambit of gender. Such understanding largely excludes the other sexual or bodily located identities conveniently categorized as the LGBTIQH. The chapter attempts to unravel and accentuate the less traversed terrain of queer methodologies and 'queering' so as to accentuate the converging, diverging and overlapping folds between and among sexual or bodily located identities. At another level, the chapter attempts to glean the institutionally recognized understanding of gender and unearth the politics of exclusion and inclusions within the same.

SOCIAL SCIENCE RESEARCH IN THE GLOBAL SOUTH

What comes out very strongly in academic deliberations and discussions in the global south is the enabling as well as the disabling aspects of the methods and the pedagogies invented, styled and tailored in the West (Alvares 2011). Ambivalent as it is the postcolonial world exhibits a society that needs to be studied anew with methods homespun and more accommodating to the lived realities of the same (Varghese 2011: 91–98). The global south is faced with multi-level dilemmas. At one level is the problem of adopting, inventing/birthing and acceptable methodologies and at another level is the problem of shedding the methodologies and pedagogies implanted through the colonial encounter (Seidman 1997: 1–20). The first level of the problem reflects the contested nature of the voices in the global south and the plurality of the society. The projected unified face of the south is as diverse and fissured as is the demonized projection of the north in this engagement. The north is often accused to be racist and patriarchy driven, however, experiences from ground zero in India conveys rather strange encounters of patriarchy(ies) and an unusual obsession with 'whiteness'. A casual glance of matrimonial advertisements in Indian newspapers on Sundays would bring out the obsession with 'whiteness' rather strongly cutting across gender, and also a glance at advertisements promoting fairness products would be sufficient to drive forward my arguments that 'if the north is sexist, racist, gendered'; the south is not free from it.

The second level of the fore mentioned problem refers more to the contestation of the dominant methodologies in more or less incoherent unison by the global south (Balakrishnan 2011; Varghese 2011). There is a rather strong fixation to quantification and a doubtful sneer to other methodologies relying on qualitative analysis, biographic approach, use of music, the virtual spaces and so on to substantiate ones arguments. To put it across more simply, there is a discomfort in using what is clubbed as 'mundane' and a clear wedge demarcating what is categorized as 'authentic source' and 'unreliable/mundane source'. Can the global south provide an authentic/indigenous southern methodology based on their unique experiences? Well such a proposition seems unreal keeping in mind the unique positions within and among the global south. Therefore, the urgency to 'detoxify' the south from the toxicities of the north remains a challenged project in the sense that the south cannot ignore the contributions of the north. This dilemma of detoxification is best summed up as 'you may hate it (north), you may love it (north), but you cannot ignore it (north)'.

The terrain of social science and research methods is highly contested (Foucault 1970; Rescher 2003; Rundell 2011) so much that it is always in the process of 'becoming' (Deleuze 1994). The conjoining feature of this area of the study is usually the focus on 'the social', and conceptualizing 'the social' has moved through different phases in academic thinking. Increasingly, it has been argued that there is no one 'social', but many 'socials' operating temporally and spatially in diverse ways and across multiple scales (Baert 2006; Dallmayr 2006; Turner 2001). Social science methods seek to investigate those that cannot be reduced to, and at times contest, traditional forms of data collection methods and in the process capture only in parts the fuzziness of social worlds. Also, such methods often question the place of social science in understanding social lives by challenging the tenants of social science research, such as rigour, clarity and the possibilities of 'knowing' social life. Social research methods in particular when dealing with 'sexuality' may or may not necessarily adhere to any 'scientific' structures of knowledge (Elliot 2001; Stein 1992; Weeks 1986; Wiederman and Whitley 2002). Strategies of data collection need to address this understanding of social worlds, including various forms of observation, visual materials and engagements with auto-ethnography as well as exploring the intersections of humanities and social sciences through art and textual analyses (Moi 1985). However, there is a danger that investigating social worlds in this sense returns us to textual analyses that proclaim the messiness of everyday life, without involving the people and materialities present in the creation of these studies.

Likewise the process of identifying the locational as well as positional sources of sexual or bodily related identities converts the human body into the site for defining and determining sexual orientations through things such as the search for the gay gene or assertions that gay men have larger fingers, the length of the thumb is related to the size of the penis, gay men sway their hips while walking and look at their nails in certain ways, gay men have gender incongruent shapes, gay person can be identified with mannerisms, voice and accent, colour coding related to sexual orientation and so on. The body thus becomes the ready-reckoner for information generation, data analysis and interpretation in order to arrive at the sexuality(ies) of individuals and then 'categorize them accordingly, often, to oppress the studied' (Butler 1993; Turner 1997).

The treatment of the body becomes either pathological or moralistic. The body becomes the site of the problem as well as the source of the problem and therefore exorcized into the hierarchical brackets of hetero-normalcy and if everything else fails a nail be driven into the heart of the studied body so that the body becomes attributeless and segregated into sacred and profane. For example, the mind is more sacred and more evolved than the hands, or the penis is at a higher plane than the vagina, and so on. What goes missing in such engagement with sexualities is that sexualities are not always as clear-cut as one might suppose.

Amidst the mélange of theoretical, methodological and pedagogical contest in the south, there does exist a rather strong discomfort of the south to the dominance of the north, and also the contentious engagement of the south within itself when it comes to 'gender studies'. For instance, in the context of studies related to sexualities the global south seems to present an array of contesting arguments ranging from those who shun the entire sexual liberation movement as the evil effects of the 'west' or 'north' and globalization to those who locate it within the realms of sanskritized sensibilities.

The study of sexualities in India is commonly perceived to be an 'exposing' and contagious engagement and therefore better to be avoided. I use the term 'contagious' in the sense that the attempt to study sexualities or be engaged in it even in the remotest sense is commonly perceived as 'coming out' of the closet. For instance, when I proposed to write a paper on queer theory most of my friends and also persons whom I interviewed asked me questions such as, 'Why are you interested in 'queer'? Are you gay? Are you bisexual? Can you go on a date with me? The treatment is such that one has to 'belong' in order to have the license to investigate or research or study. To put it more precisely you need to be 'queer' to study 'queer'.

GENDER STUDIES, WOMEN'S STUDIES, QUEER STUDIES: AMBIGUITIES AND COMMONALITIES

'Gender' in gender studies is used to refer to proposed social and cultural constructions of masculinities and femininities (Brooks 1997; Butler 1999; Fine et al. 1997; Essed 1996; Walby 1990; Walby 1997; Harrison and Hood-William 2002). Strangely, gender studies in India has conveniently been understood to mean 'women's studies' or 'feminism' (Haraway 1991; Harding 1986; hooks [1984] 2000; Mayberry et al. 2001; Modleski 1991; Rogers and Pemberton 2005; Rose 1986; Shiach 1999; Smith 1987, 1990; Thornham 2000; Wyer et al. 2000) by overlooking the definitional encapsulations within the ambit of gender and largely excluding the other sexual or bodily located identities conveniently categorized as the LGBT or LGBTI or LGBTIQH. In other words, the politics of inclusions and exclusions occurs even within the gender studies circle.

'Gender' is often also used as means of determining sexual identity (Butler 1993, 1999; Seidman 2002). Elsewhere in the broadest sense, gender has been employed by social theorists to denote a distinction between the biological categories of female and male and the socially constructed categories of woman and man (or girl and boy). In this juxtaposition, while sex is assumed to represent a biological difference, gender is used to define those socially constructed feminine and masculine modes of behaviour considered normal and natural for females and males (Millet 1981; Probyn 2005; Simonds and Brush 2005; Taylor and Winguist 2001). Thus, gender varies dramatically across societies and throughout human history.

The analysis of gender involves studying the normative conduct associated with males and females, the relative valuations of masculinity and femininity, and the social processes whereby males and females learn normative behaviours. Gender constructions thus relegate female and male bodies to discrete and often intensely regulated masculine and feminine types. Indeed, feminist studies have exposed the typically rigid constructions of masculinity and femininity. Gender is revealed to involve the management of situated conduct in adherence with normative conceptions of masculinity and femininity. Gender is thus seen as a highly significant dimension for understanding how the body becomes a social fact (Burnette 2006; Kauth 2006). Approaches to understanding the connections between gender and sex, gender differences and gender inequality, vary widely (Connell 1987; Ember and

Ember 2003; Nicholson 1995). Gender has been studied as a central problematic within various branches of feminist social theory, including liberal feminism and radical feminism. Existential feminists were among the first to assert that 'the personal is political'. They gave rise to a notion of identity politics based on the unique social locations of a given individual. The claim to identity was seen as a political assertion rather than a personal claim because identity also brings with it membership in community. In turn, membership demands equality with others in that group, and so those with identities that disrupt the status quo are seen as a threat to the hegemony of the ruling class. Allowing members of a social minority equal claim to social goods would call for a reshaping, often a radical reshaping, of societal values, norms and even sometimes laws (Chafetz 2006; Nicholson and Seidman 1995).

In addition to studying the socially produced differences between masculinity and femininity, sociologists also study how these differences are linked to inequality, power and domination. Feminist sociologists are interested in revealing whether, why and how feminine qualities, practices and accomplishments are socially and historically subjugated or valued, celebrated or negated. Significant work among feminist sociologists has revealed the ways in which gender constructions relegate women into subordinate and unequal social relations with men, thereby instantiating the belief that men 'naturally' possess a superior nature in comparison with females (Butler 1997: 300–316; Gardner 2006). By examining gender relations, feminist sociologists, activists and writers produce strategies to challenge the negative conceptions and invisibility of women's intellectual accomplishments.

The term 'queer theory' was specifically chosen by those in the field over 'lesbian and gay studies' because of the fixed identity and exclusivity the latter term seemed to imply (Lovaas et al. 2007; Phelan 1994; Weed and Schor 1997). One of the goals of those interested in the topics that would become queer theory was to displace many of the commonly held notions about lesbian and gay people and, in fact, to destabilize those categories of identity (Abelove et al. 1993; Burnette 2006; D'Emilis 1992; Kauth 2006; Stein and Plummer 1996; Taylor 1989).

Hence, an area known as lesbian and gay studies would seem contradictory, confining and non-liberating. Such a limited term would also seem to exclude many who have found refuge in queer theory, such as transsexuals, transvestites, sadists, fetishists and others whose sexuality has been labelled deviant (Binnie; Morland and Willox 2005).

Perhaps the most visible break between lesbian and gay studies and queer theory (aside from its greater inclusion) is the move from studying only the lives and experiences of lesbians and gay men to critical studies on heterosexuality, in particular a deconstruction of the binary of hetero/homo (Fuss 1991). Homosexuality is what (the later defined) heterosexuality has to exclude from itself to maintain its boundaries and definition. Queer theory 'reads' the perversity back in and rediscovers the queer that has been sublimated from heterosexuality's consciousness or expelled into its 'other' that is the 'homosexual'. As a profoundly subordinated identity, queers have been 'invisiblized' by heterosexual culture. There are people who have been able to transcend this invisibility by virtue of class, collectivity or vocality, for example, it becomes easy for most elites or celebrities to openly exhibit their sexualities or present them as 'fashionable'/'fashion statements' or as in the case of 'hijra' in India, they become partially included due to their vocality and 'fear' of their vocality (Hall 1997: Chapter 25, 430–460), but in day-to-day life, many queer subjects have faced the necessity of staying in the closet, communicating identity in surreptitious ways or by replicating heteronormative categorization of relations. To secure employment or maintain relationships with family members, for example, queer subjects have effectively walked a tightrope between being 'in' or 'out' and because of this, they have developed specialized reading skills concentrated on reading the identities of others, potentially alike.

Coming back to the relationship between feminism and queer theory, one notices that it is not a straightforward one. At face value, they seem a likely pairing as both at some level attempt to deconstruct identity categories and register difference. Though queer theory has been challenged by some feminist critics because it seems to neglect political theories in favour of a focus on gender and sexual transgression, yet there are many fruitful intersections between feminism and queer theory. In other words, feminism and queer theory share common political interests – a concern for women's and gays and lesbians' rights – and many of the same academic and intellectual roots. And yet, they can also seem like strangers, needing mediation, translation and clarification (Genz and Brabon 2009; Lovaas et al. 2007; Marinucci 2010; Richardson et al. 2006; Weed and Schor 1997).

QUEER METHODOLOGIES: LESS TRAVERSED TERRAIN IN INDIA

It is theoretically and methodologically exasperating to adhere to any specific school of thought about what it might mean to queer methodologies and methods. 'Queer research' can be any form of research positioned within conceptual frameworks that highlight the instability of taken-for-granted meanings and resulting power relations (Nigianni and Storr 2009). Queer inflected perspectives, approaches and conceptualizations have been taken up, disputed and reworked in different disciplinary contexts, reflecting the traditions of knowledge production in those disciplines (Yep et al. 2004). Genealogies of queer theory unveils a wave of agreements, disagreements, constructions and deconstructions over its relationship with and rootedness to philosophy, women's and lesbian studies, second wave and postmodern feminism and gay and lesbian studies (Beemyn and Elianon 1996; Jagose 1996; Seidman 1996; Simon 1996; Sullivan 2003; Tuner 2000). Whatever be one's stance on queer theory's historical lineage, contemporary queer theory remains in continuous conversation with innumerable bodies of scholarship, however contested or collegial such exchanges might be (Nardizzi et al. 2009). What is important for present purposes is how queer conceptualizations have intersected in a general sense with the research design and knowledge production and execution in the social sciences (Wiederman and Whitley 2002)

Looking at the wide range of queer scholarship that has been developed since the early 1990s, it is clear that queer approaches are deeply engaged in questioning the existence and 'knowability' of the social, particularly in various socials normative claims (Baumeister et al. 2006; Butler 1999; Elliot 2001; Lauretis 1991). The entanglements of methods, lives and research move beyond 'explaining' the social, making it clear that queer theorizing and social research fields are mutually constituted. If sexual and gender studies (and broader social theorising) create social fields, then it follows that destabilizing such theorizing, including through queer theorizing, and creating new social methods can create transformative politics through research. This mode of politics is one of the many ways that power relations and associated hierarchical constructions of social lives can be contested through research.

The emergence of queer theory led to an understanding of the identity of the homosexual that is both comparable to and contrastable with the identity of the heterosexual. It also allowed for the homosexual to be taken as a subject in and of itself (Piskett 2003). Queer theory is often seen as a standpoint theory, one that is particular to the viewpoint of sexuality, and most usually homosexuality. Eve Kosofsky Sedgwick's (1990) conceptualization of the 'closet' and 'coming out' as the dividing line between straight and gay is indeed 'the defining structure for gay oppression in this century'. The closet paired against coming out have thus come to respectively represent the secrecy and revelation of almost any 'identity' that is seen as politically charged. In particular, these ideas seek to crystallize the identity of the homosexual. It seeks to insert the social location and viewpoint of homosexuals and others labelled as sexual deviants into the mainstream of social theory (Beemyn and Elianon 1996; Stein and Plummer 1996; Sullivan 2003; Tuner 2000). However, the locational, positional and situational ambiguities become relevant when one looks at the closet and its paired category coming out in the Indian context where being in the closet has been converted to a degree of advantage. On a similar note, male–male bonding is and has been given a special acceptance as 'Yarana', 'Dostana' and 'Launde bazzi' in India. Thanks to Bollywood masculinity in the form of male–male bonding has been given a general acceptance as 'men will be men', a deep friendship that doesn't raise the eyebrows and is socially accepted.

A hybrid methodology (Brannen 1992; Caracelli and Greene 1997; Creswell 2003; Malhotra and Shapiro 1998; Teddlie and Tashakkori 2003) or 'scavenger methodology' (Halberstam 1998; Sedgwick 1993, 2003) recognize not only the messiness of social life, but also the place of the research/researcher in (re)creating it, such research can provide a place for those who otherwise tend to be marginalized, disenfranchised and excluded in the process. Queer theory takes up these realignments and works specifically to unravel the commonly taken-for-granted and normalized connections between sexuality and gender in order to render visible their contingent connections (Beemyn and Elianon 1996; Tuner 2000). Queer theory challenges the normative social ordering of identities and subjectivities along the hetero-sexual/homosexual binary as well as the privileging of heterosexuality as 'natural' and homosexuality as its deviant and abhorrent 'other'. In concert with various feminist, gay and lesbian scholars, many queer theorists argue that normative understandings of sexuality (and gender) are central, organizing principles of society, social relations and social institutions and are designed to preserve this hegemonic ordering.

A growing body of multi- and interdisciplinary scholarship explores desires, practices and identities that defy the dualities of social categories and unsettle the epistemological and methodological assumptions underpinning much of the work on gender and sexualities – that there is a 'man', 'woman', 'lesbian' or 'homosexual' to be studied as the object of research. Queer scholars can argue for the 'playful' possibilities of unstable and indeterminate subjectivities and for transgressive practices that challenge heteronormative sexual and gender assumptions (Sedgwick 1990; Sullivan 2003). While queer scholarship is most often interested in examining the experiences of sexual/gender minorities, some scholars argue for a queering of heterosexual relations as well as including a rigorous analyses of the category of heterosexuality, its disciplinary processes and the heterosexist assumptions embedded in much social science scholarship (Sullivan 2003).

Not everyone is enamoured with queer theories deconstructive tendencies, and critiques have emerged from numerous quarters. Those involved in various forms of identity politics such as second wave women's or gay and lesbian's and trans' movements argue that denying the stability of the subject (women or lesbian) undercuts the ground on which political activism is built by denying the existence of a viable political subject (Giffney and O'Rourke 2009).

Contestations of homonormativity (Giffney and O'Rourke 2009) point out that the homonormative/queer binary often implicit in these critiques problematically neglects how we are all complicit in the reproduction of power relations (Giffney and O'Rourke 2009). Moreover, it can essentialize (and demonize) white gay men who are assumed to experience particular forms of privilege without examining the experiences of those who are presumed to occupy these subjectivities (Giffney and O'Rourke 2009). In rejecting a representational theory of 'truth', certain strands of queer theorizing use various forms of discourse and textual analyses to consider how power relations are constituted and maintained in the production of social and political meanings. With this initial focus on discourse analysis and cultural critique, some scholars argue that queer approaches, while interesting theoretically, are largely detached from the blood, bricks and mortar of everyday life. Trans scholars, for example, argue that using trans people to illustrate the fluidity of gender/sex is problematic and an appropriation of an assumed lived experience that generally does not actually engage with trans people themselves. Queer theorizing arguably does not lead to effective changes around the material inequalities in everyday life (although this could be questioned by the cultural materialist strand of (still textual) queer theory). Such a critique has less purchase in the social sciences where scholars often deploy queer approaches in their examination of the material experiences of their subjects. Further, some scholars contest the supposedly liberating possibilities of queer 'playful', 'fluid' and transgressive practices and behaviours.

Queer theory is opposed to all normative regimes of sexuality; not only heterosexual but also homosexual ones. The term 'queer' is always in transition, attempting to avoid reification as a normative category. Although it is tempting to insist on some kind of 'insider' research, it also comes with a caution given the instability of the category. Queer methodology following Judith Halberstam (1998) can be conceptualized as:

> A queer methodology in a way is a scavenger methodology that uses different methods to collect and produce information on subjects who have been deliberately or accidentally excluded from traditional studies of human behaviour. The queer methodology attempts to combine methods that are often cast as being at odds with each other and it refuses the academic compulsion towards disciplinary coherence.

Queer as a 'situated inquiry' relates to specific ways of knowing particular locations (Haraway 1993). Strangely enough 'queer' rarely recognizes its own locational and spatial pull and how it travels. The global north with its social and historical specificities and contexts has engaged constantly with gendered and sexual lives (Gibson-Graham 1996), and as a result, the study of sexualities has a tilt towards the north in terms of knowledge production and creation (Nardizzi et al. 2009). Queer studies much like the rest of the social sciences and humanities are faced with the dilemma of temporal and spatial dynamics of having been produced elsewhere and not being at 'home' (Halberstam 2005). One can hardly ignore the hegemony of geographies in queer thinking, theorizing and identification (Gibson-Graham 1996). The acknowledgement of the 'situatedness' of queering at the global north accentuates the cleavages in the geographies of queer thinking and also brings into the 'open' micro-spatialities and juxtaposed positions (Culler 1982; Derrida 1974, 1981), which had been tucked in the closets elsewhere such as in the global south.

The first goal of queer methodology is to challenge invisibility, 'normalcy' and stability, which are produced by dichotomous understandings, second, is to resist neo-liberal, assimilation and reverse discourses; and last, is to expose and deconstruct respectability, heteronormativity and homonormativity. Queering social science research in other words calls for 'detoxification', 'alteration', 'mutation' and 'hybridization' of the available of options however limited that maybe.

CONCLUSION

Some Queering Observations

The chapter explores the diverse possibilities and impossibilities of queer and accentuates the limitations and potentials of queer engagements with social science research techniques and methodologies. A queer methodology intentionally does not attempt to reify mobile, unstable 'disorientations'. Instead, it exposes hetero- and homonormativity. A queer methodology reveals the complex plurality of sex, gender and sexuality. Queer methodologies attempt to un-wrap the homo/hetero, man/woman, female/male and insider/outsider binaries embedded in everyday life. By deconstructing these binary notions, it renders the possibilities of calling into being multiple existences previously rendered deviant or invisible. However, one needs to be cautious and resist the slippages (Terry 1995) of solidifying queer approach or methodology. By allowing disorientation(s), contradiction(s) and pluralities to exist within research, 'queer methodology' remains reflexive and at the same time continually challenging its own character. In short, the use of hybridization of methodology in queer research flows from the understanding that a 'magic formulae' does not exist but can be created to serve our purpose of study.

REFERENCES

Abelove, H., Barale, M.A. and Halperin, D.M. (Eds) (1993). *The Lesbian and Gay Studies Reader.* New York: Routledge.

Alvares, C. (2011). A Critique of Eurocentric Social Science and the Question of Alternatives. *Economic and Political Weekly XLVI* (24).

Baert, P. (2006). Social Science and Social Theory. Chapter 2, in G. Delanty (Ed.), *Handbook of Contemporary European Social Theory*. London: Routledge and New York: Taylor & Francis Group, pp. 14–24.

Balakrishnan, P. (2011). A House for Social Sciences: Government Review of ICSSR. *Economic and Political Weekly XLVI* (33), 13 August, pp. 29–31.

Baumeister, R.F., Maur, J.K. and Dewall, C.N. (2006). Evked Culture and Evoked Nature: Co-evolution and The Emergence of Cultural Animals. *Psychological Inquiry*, 17(2) 128–30.

Beemyn, B. and Elianon, M. (1996). *Queer Studies: A Lesbian, Gay, Bisexual and Transgender Anthology.* New York: New York University Press.

Binnie, J. (2004a). Locating Queer Globalization. Chapter 3, in J. Binnie (Ed.), *The Globalization of Sexuality*. London: Sage, pp. 32–49.

—- (2004b). Queer Postcolonialism. Chapter 5, in J. Binnie (Ed.), *The Globalization of Sexuality*. London: Sage, pp. 67–85.

—- (2004c). The Economics of Queer Globalization. Chapter 4, in J. Binnie (Ed.), *The Globalization of Sexuality*. London: Sage, pp. 50–66.

Brannen, J. (Ed.) (1992). *Mixing Methods: Qualitative and Quantitative Research.* Aldershot: Ashgate.

Brooks, A. (1997). *Postfeminism*. London: Routledge.

Burnette, M.M. (2006). Gender, Gender Identity and Sexuality. Chapter 8, in R.D. McAnulty and M.M. Burnette (Eds), *Sex and Sexuality, Vol. 1: Sexuality Today: Trends and Controversies*. London: Praeger Perspectives, pp. 185–201.

Butler, J. (1993). *Bodies That Matter: On the Discursive Limits of Sex*. New York: Routledge.

—- (1997). Imitation and Gender in Subordination. In L. Nicholson (Ed.), *The Second Wave: A Reader in Feminist Theory*. New York: Routledge, pp. 300–316.

—- (1999). *Gender Trouble: Feminism and the Subversion of Identity*. London: Routledge.

Caracelli, V.J. and Greene, J.C. (Eds) (1997). *Advances in Mixed-Method Evaluation: The Challenges and Benefits of Integrating Diverse Paradigms*. New Directions for Program Evaluation No. 74. San Francisco, CA: Jossey-Bass.

Chafetz, J.S. (Ed.) (2006). *Handbook of the Sociology of Gender*. New York: Springer.

Connell, R.W. (1987). *Gender and Power*. Cambridge, UK: Polity.

Creswell, J.W. (2003). *Research Design: Qualitative, Quantitative, and Mixed Methods Approaches*. 2nd ed. London: Sage.

Culler, J. (1982). *On Deconstruction: Theory and Criticism after Structuralism.* Ithaca, NY: Cornell University Press.

D'Emilis, J. (1992). *Making Trouble: Essays on Gay History, Politics and the University*. New York: Routledge.

Dallmayr, F. (2006). Encounters between European and Asian Social Theory. Chapter 29, in G. Delanty (Ed.), *Handbook of Contemporary European Social Theory*. London: Routledge and New York: Taylor & Francis Group, pp. 372–380.

Deleuze, G. (1994). *Difference and Repetition*. New York: Columbia University Press.

Derrida, J. (1974). *Of Grammatology*. Baltimore, MD: Johns Hopkins University Press.

— (1981). *Positions*. Chicago, IL: University of Chicago Press.

Elliot, A. (2001). Sexualities: Social Theory and the Crisis of Identity. Chapter 32, in G. Ritzer and B. Smart (Eds), *Handbook of Social Theory*. London: Sage, pp. 428–438.

Ember, C.R. and Ember, M. (Eds) (2003). *Encyclopaedia of Sex and Gender: Men and Women in the World's Cultures*. New York: Plenum Publishers.

Essed, P. (1996). *Diversity: Gender, Colour and Culture*. Amherst, MA: University of Massachusetts Press.

Fine, M., Wies, L., Powell, L. and Wong, L.M. (Eds) (1997). *Off White: Readings on Race, Power and Society*. London: Routledge.

Foucault, M. (1970). *The Order of Things: Archaeology of the Human Sciences*. London: Tavistock Publications.

Fuss, D. (1991). *Inside/Outside: Lesbian Theories, Gay Theories*. New York: Routledge.

Gardner, C.V. (2006). *Historical Dictionary of Feminist Philosophy*. Historical Dictionaries of Religions, Philosophies and Movements Series No. 64, Maryland: The Scarecrow Press Inc.

Genz, S. and Brabon, B.A. (2009). Queer (Post) Feminism. Chapter 6, in S. Genz and B.A. Brabon (Eds), *Postfeminism: Cultural Texts and Theories*. Edinburgh: Edinburgh University Press Ltd., pp. 124–131.

Gibson-Graham, J.K. (1996). Reflections on Postmodern Feminist Social Research. In N. Duncan (Ed.), *Bodyspace*: *Destabilizing Geographies of Gender and Sexuality*. London: Routledge, pp. 72–91.

Giffney, N. and O'Rourke, M. (2009). *The Ashgate Research Companion to Queer Theory*. Burlington, UK: Ashgate Publishing Ltd.

Halberstam, J. (1998). *Female Masculinity*. Durham, NC: Duke University Press.

— (2005). Queer Temporality and Postmodern Geographies. In J. Halberstam (Ed.), *In a Queer Time and Place: Transgender Bodies, Subcultural Lives*. New York: New York University Press, pp. 1–21.

Hall, K. (1997). Go Suck Your Husband's Sugarcane: Hijras and the Use of Sexual Insult. In A. Livia and K. Hall (Eds), *Queerly Phrased: Language, Gender, and Sexuality*. New York: Oxford University Press, pp. 430–460.

Haraway, D. (1991). *Simians, Cyborgs, and Women: The Reinvention of Nature*. New York and London: Routledge.

—- (1993). Situated Knowledge: The Science Question in Feminism and the Privilege of Partial Perspective. In E.F. Keller and H.E. Longino (Eds), *Feminism and Science*. Oxford and New York: Oxford University Press, pp. 113–126.

Harding, S. (1986). *The Science Question in Feminism*. Ithaca, NY: Cornell University Press.

Harrison, W.C. and Hood-William, J. (2002). *Beyond Sex and Gender*. London: Sage.

hooks, b. (1984, 2000). *Feminist Theory: From Margins to Centre*. Boston: South End Press.

Jagose, A. (1996). *Queer Theory: An Introduction*. New York: New York University Press.

Kauth, M.R. (2006). Sexual Orientation and Identity. Chapter 7, in R.D. McAnulty and M.M. Burnette (Eds), *Sex and Sexuality, Vol. 1: Sexuality Today: Trends and Controversies*. London: Praeger Perspectives, pp. 152–184.

Lauretis, T.D. (1991). *Queer Theory: Lesbian and Gay Sexualities*. Bloomington, IN: Indiana University Press.

Lovaas, K., Elia, J.P. and Yep, G.A. (2007). *LGBT Studies and Queer Theory: New Conflicts, Collaborations, and Contested Terrain*. New York: Harrington Park Press.

Malhotra, V.B. and Shapiro, J.I. (1998). *Mindful Inquiry in Social Research*. London: Sage.

Marinucci, M. (2010). *Feminism is Queer: The Intimate Connection between Queer and Feminist Theory*. London: Zed Books Ltd.

Mayberry, M., Banu, S. and Weasel, L. (Eds) (2001). *Feminist Science Studies: A New Generation*. New York: Routledge.

Millet, K. (1981). *Sexual Politics*. New York: Avon.

Modleski, T. (1991). *Feminism without Women: Culture and Criticism in a 'Postfeminist' Age*. New York: Routledge.

Moi, T. (1985). *Sexual/Textual Politics*. London: Methuen.

Morland, I. and Willox, A. (2005). *Queer Theory*. New York: Palgrave Macmillan.

Nardizzi, V., Guy-Bray, S. and Stockton, W. (Eds) (2009). *Queer Renaissance Historiography: Backward Gaze*. Burlington, UK: Ashgate Publishing Ltd.

Nicholson, L. (1995). Interpreting Gender. In L. Nicholson and S. Siedman (Eds), *Social Postmodernism: Beyond Identity Politics*. New York: Cambridge University Press, pp. 39–57.

Nicholson, L. and Seidman, S. (1995). *Interpreting Gender in Social Postmodernism: Beyond Identity Politics*. New York: Cambridge University Press.

Nigianni, C. and Storr, M. (Eds) (2009). *Deleuze and Queer Theory*. Edinburgh: Edinburgh University Press.

Phelan, S. (1994). *Getting Specific: Postmodern Lesbian Politics*. Minneapolis, MN: University of Minnesota Press.

Piskett, B.L. (2003). *Historical Dictionary of Homosexuality*. Lanham, MD: Scarecrow Press Inc.

Probyn, E. (2005). Body. In G. Ritzer (Ed.), *Encyclopedia of Social Theory*. Vol. 1, Thousand Oaks: Sage, pp. 62–65.

Rescher, N. (Ed.) (2003). *Epistemology: An Introduction to the Theory of Knowledge*. Albany: State University New York (SUNY) Press.

Richardson, D., Mchaughlin, J. and Casey, M.E. (Eds) (2006). *Intersections between Feminist and Queer Theory*. New York: Palgrave Macmillan.

Rogers, M.F. and Pemberton, J. (2005). Feminist Epistemology. In G. Ritzer (Ed.), *Encyclopaedia of Social Theory*. Vol. 1, Thousand Oaks: Sage, pp. 271–275.

Rose, H. (1986). Beyond Masculinist Realities: A Feminist Epistemology for the Sciences. In R. Bleier (Ed.), *Feminist Approaches to Science*. New York: Pergamon, pp. 59–76.

Rundell, J. (2011). Modernity, Enlightenment, Revolution and Romanticism: Creating Social Theory. In G. Ritzer and B. Smart (Eds), *Handbook of Social Theory*. London: Sage, pp. 13–29.

Sedgwick, E.K. (1990). *Epistemology of the Closet*. Berkeley: University of California Press.

— (1993). *Tendencies*. Durham, NC: Duke University Press.

— (2003). *Touching Feeling: Affect, Pedagogy, Performativity*. Durham, NC: Duke University Press.

Seidman, S. (1996). *Queer Theory/Sociology*. Cambridge, MA: Wiley-Blackwell.

— (1997). Introduction: The Contemporary Reconfiguration of Social Theory. In S. Seidman (Ed.), *Difference Troubles: Queering Social Theory and Sexual Politics*. Cambridge, UK: Cambridge University Press, pp. 1–20.

— (2002). *Beyond the Closet: The Transformation of Gay and Lesbian Life*. New York: Routledge.

Shiach, M. (1999). *Feminism and Cultural Studies*. Oxford, UK: Oxford University Press.

Simon, W. (1996). *Postmodern Sexualities*. London: Routledge.

Simonds, C. and Brush, P. (2005). 'Gender'. In G. Ritzer (Ed.), *Encyclopaedia of Social Theory*, Vol. 1, Thousand Oaks: Sage, pp. 304–307.

Smith, D.E. (1987). *The Everyday World as Problematic: A Feminist Sociology*. Boston, MA: North-Eastern University Press.

— (1990). *The Conceptual Practices of Power: A Feminist Sociology of Knowledge*. Boston, MA: North-Eastern University Press.

Spargo, T. (1999). Sexual/Cultural Hybridity in the 'New' South Africa: Emergent Sites of New Transnational Queer Politics. Chapter 5, in T. Spargo (Ed.), *Foucault and Queer Theory: Postmodern Encounters*. Cambridge: Icon Books Ltd., pp. 103–131.

Stein, A. and Plummer, K. (1996). 'I Can't Even Think Straight': 'Queer' Theory and the Missing Sexual Revolution in Sociology. In S. Seidman (Ed.), *Queer Theory/Sociology*. Cambridge, MA: Blackwell, pp. 129–144.

Stein, E. (1992). *Forms of Desire: Sexual Orientation and the Social Constructionist Controversy*. New York: Routledge.

Sullivan, N. (2003). *A Critical Introduction to Queer Theory*. New York: New York University Press.

Taylor, C. (1989). *Sources of the Self: The Making of the Modern Identity*. Cambridge, MA: Harvard University Press.

Taylor, V.E. and Winguist, C.E. (2001). Gender. In V.E. Taylor and C.E. Winguist (Eds), *Encyclopaedia of Postmodernism*. London: Routledge, pp. 148–149.

Teddlie, C. and Tashakkori, A. (2003). Major Issues and Controversies in the Use of Mixed Methods in the Social and Behavioural Sciences. In A. Tashakkori and C. Teddlie (Eds), *Handbook of Mixed Methods in Social and Behavioural Research*. Thousand Oaks, CA: Sage.

Terry, J. (1995). Anxious Slippages between 'Us' and 'Them'. In J. Terry and J. Urla (Eds), *Deviant Bodies*. Bloomington, IN: Indiana University Press, pp. 129–167.

Thornham, S. (2000). *Feminist Theory and Cultural Studies: Stories of Unsettled Relations*. London: Arnold.

Tuner, W.B. (2000). *A Genealogy of Queer Theory*. Philadelphia: Temple University Press.

Turner, B.S. (1997). *The Body and Society*. Beverly Hills, CA: Sage.

Turner, J.H. (Ed.) (2001). *Handbook of Sociological Theory*. New York: Springer.

Varghese, G.K. (2011). Rethinking Social Sciences and Humanities in the Contemporary World. *Economic and Political Weekly XLVI* (31), pp. 91–98.

Walby, S. (1990). *Theorizing Patriarchy*. Oxford: Basil Blackwell.

—- (1997). *Gender Transformations*. London: Routledge.

Weed, E. and Schor, N. (Eds) (1997). *Feminism Meets Queer Theory*. Bloomington, IN: University Indiana Press.

Weeks, J. (1986). *Sexuality*. London: Tavistock, pp. 13–81.

Wiederman, M.W. and Whitley, B.E. (2002). A Preview: The Unique Nature of Sexuality Research. Chapter 1, in M.W. Wiederman and B.E. Whitley (Eds), *Handbook for Conducting Research on Human Sexuality*. London: Lawrence Erlbaum Associates Inc., pp. 1–4.

Wyer, M., Giesman, D., Barbercheck, M., Ozturk, H. and Wayne, M. (Eds) (2000). *Women, Science and Technology: A Reader in Feminist Science Studies*. New York: Routledge.

Yep, G.A., Lovaas, K. and Elia, J.P. (Eds) (2004). *Queer Theory and Communication: From Disciplining Queers to Queering the Discipline(s)*. New York: Harrington Park Press.

CHAPTER 5

Engendering Governance

The Gaps and Possibilities

Aruna Gyati and Kalpana Agrahari

Governance is presumed to be gender neutral. But, in fact, the discourse, procedure, structures and functions of governance remain heavily skewed in favour of men in general, and certain group of men in particular. This unequal sharing of power leads to an unequal sharing of resources – time, incomes and property – between men and women. The consequences of this mal-distribution are evident in the disproportionately high number of women who are illiterate and living in extreme poverty. Redressing these inequalities requires a gendered analysis of the process and structures of governance.

Typically, gender perspectives in mainstream governance literature are limited to an examination of the need for more women in formal political life and strategies to achieve this, without consideration of the need for transformation of the institution of power. Governance is about 'getting institutions right for development' but rarely considers how to 'get institutions right for women in development' (Goetz 1995, quoted in Baden 1999). Outside the family, where the gendering of roles and behaviour is explicit but often assumed to be 'natural', there is a tendency to assume that institutions are neutral with respect to gender. However, familial norms and values are constantly drawn for constructing the terms under which women and men enter and participate in public life and the market place. The public–private split has institutionalized women's exclusion from the public sphere and is also drawn on to reinforce gendered power relations in the public sphere.

In this chapter, an attempt has been made to analyse the gender gap in governance. It also examines various steps that have been taken to engender governance. Accordingly the chapter is divided into three sections. The first section deals with the meaning of the core terms of the study. The second section analyses the gender gap in the governance in its three domains, namely state, market and civil society. The third section, which also includes the conclusion part of the study, examines the various programmes that have been taken for engendering the governance.

GENDER

In its initial use, the word gender was understood as synonym for sex and/or *women*; research on gender is research about women, their sexual role or both. Gender, in this view point, is nothing but a restricted field or domain that is far away from the main problems of sociology. In the new use, gender has been theorized as a basic principle of cultural interpretation and social structure. Instead of being a specialty within a recognized field of knowledge, gender is a norm of subordination and inequality, which can be found in many human processes where differences between men and women exist. A study of gendered governance is a study of men and masculinity as much as it is a study of women and femininity (Basu 2003). This chapter focuses on women's lives with the understanding that these lives operate within a system of gendered understanding and gendered power that must be understood as a whole if the lives of women, and their access to governance, are to be enhanced.

GOVERNANCE

Since the lives of women are deeply and systematically conditioned by a host of social norms and expectations, a productive study of gender and governance must understand governance in a broader way than was customary in some earlier studies. The key aspects of governance so understood were public sector management, accountability, a legal framework and information. Politics as such made no appearance in the account. Thus, the many ways in which democratic citizens determine the shape of their societies were not taken into account. Good governance was equated with 'sound development of management' and was defined as 'the manner in which power is exercised in the management of a country's economic and social resources for development' (World Bank 1992, quoted in Jayal 2003).

Newer accounts of governance have followed a broader understanding of the goals of development. As scholars point out it is definitely not just the effective management of economic resources, as the World Bank believes. *It is about freedom, human rights, public accountability and people's participation'. Governance is now understood* to include a wide range of ways in which the political, social and administrative structure of a society affects the access of its members to basic opportunities and capabilities. As the UNDP accounts of governance adopted in 2002 defines, Governance is the exercise of political, economic and administrative authority to manage a country's affairs. It comprises the mechanisms, processes and institutions through which citizens and groups articulate their interests, exercise their legal rights, meet their obligations and mediate their differences. The newer definitions recognize not only the plurality of actors, namely, state, market and civil society, involved in the process of governance but also the substance of governance (Samuel and Hydén 2011).

Thus, governance is no longer equated with the civil society reform, or with application to public organization of management, but greater emphasis is on participation, decentralization, accountability, government responsiveness and broader concern such as social equality and justice. The importance of defining governance in broader and more far reaching ways than it has traditionally been understood emerges from the myriad forms that women's participation assumes at the local level – private and public, economic, social and political.

THE PUBLIC–PRIVATE DIVIDE

One of the most important factors that have affected nonparticipation of women in the decision making and governance is the private–public divide associated with women and men. Women's place is in private domain associated with household, reproductive work and femininity, whereas the public domain is associated with the political authority, public decision making, productive work and masculinity. Such assumptions have always hindered women to negotiate in the public domain and often they find themselves being either criticized for their inadequacies or patronized by men. The other question is what kind of autonomy women and men should have in the different domains. Although the private domain is associated with women, it is a domain where the family/household is the most complex site where it is believed that there is a male altruistic head responsible for the welfare and safety of all members.

Women's bargaining power at the household is restricted typically due to lack of access and control over resource, no autonomy in decision making, low self-esteem, low skills and education, restricted physical mobility and eventually less power as compared to men. Such non-egalitarian gender relations at the household level get manifested in other institutions of the community, market and the state. Gender relations and the patriarchal structures and attitudes prevailing in both the private and public domain therefore contribute to women's subordinate status and their inability to participate in governance. Other intersecting hierarchies, such as caste, class, ethnicity, religion, and rural/urban locations further complicate gender inequality in governance.

THE GENDER GAP IN GOVERNANCE

The recognition of the plurality of domains in governance – the state, market and civil society suggests that it is a process-based definition and not a structure-based definition of governance, which include a range of organizations as well as the complex relationships between them. Institutions of local government (such as panchayats); civil society organizations (ranging from social movements to nongovernmental organizations, and from co-operatives to civil associations) and private corporations as well as other market institutions are all relevant actors. A gendered perspective of governance therefore should encompass all the three domains and requires looking at participation and decision making of women and men in the different institutions, the gender gap and inequalities in each.

In Politics and Government

Recent feminist scholarship on the state has highlighted the lack of neutrality of state institutions and political processes with respect to gender. Women globally are underrepresented in formal politics at all levels. The underrepresentation of women in high offices in politics and government is well documented. While there have been some women heads of state or government (25 presidents and 30 prime ministers from 1954 to 1999), and the numbers across the world doubled between 1987 and 1996, this represented an increase from 3.4 per cent to 6.8 per cent, which is not an impressive figure. Moreover, 48 (out of 187) countries had no women in ministerial position at all. In fact, in the Asia-Pacific region and Eastern Europe, promotion of women ministers had been under 5 per cent. There is also an unmistakable pattern in the nature of portfolios hold by women; in 1999, the most substantial concentration of women ministers worldwide was in ministries of social affairs, health, women affairs, family/youth/children, culture and heritage, education, environment and labour. Very few ministers hold portfolios related to defence, finance and trade, and only one country had a woman minister of home affairs (IPU 1999: 50–52, quoted in Jayal 2003). The areas such as internal affairs, economic affairs, fiscal policy, defence and international affairs, industrial policy and agriculture remain to be men's preserve.

Further, the women comprise only a small percentage of the membership of political parties. From Austria and Canada to Japan and Korea, between 30 and 50 per cent of members of political parties are reported to be women. In Pakistan, by contrast, women accounts for less than 5 per cent of the membership of any political party. Party leadership reflects the same pattern. In India, women constitute only 9.1 per cent of the membership of executive bodies in the main political parties.

In International and National Bureaucracy

The phenomenon of underrepresentation in legislative bodies tends to be replicated in international and national bureaucracy. A look at the gendered pattern of employment in international agencies (the United Nations, the World Bank, etc.) also suggests the virtual invisibility of women from the top management of these organizations and preponderance – even over-representation – of women at the secretarial and clerical levels. Thus, women constitute 3.6 per cent of decision-making elites in the United Nations, but 85 per cent of the workers at the clerical and support staff levels.

National bureaucracies reproduce many of the biases of political institutions, especially concentration of women employees at the bottom of the pyramid, and the confinement of even senior women officials to the 'softer' portfolios. It has been suggested that this is at least partly because salaries being lower in the public sector than the private sector do not attract men. In Denmark, Finland, Sweden and the Philippines, women account for about 50 per cent of public sector employees, and for a sizeable proportion in many more countries. In Israel, for instance, almost 60 per cent of employees in the civil services and the public sector are women. But, while women occupy 92 per cent of the position in lower levels of the civil service, some of the top positions include no women at all.

In the Judiciary and the Military

Two significant areas, which remain substantially male preserves, are the judiciary and military. The importance of these spheres is self-evident: the first is concerned with upholding and interpreting the law, while the second is an area traditionally close to women on account of the gendered division of violence, stereotyping men as aggressive life-taker and women as peace-loving life-givers. In South Asia, women do not account for more than between 5 and 10 per cent of the judiciary, combining positions at higher and subordinate levels. Though both Bangladesh and Pakistan have established quotas for women in the subordinate judiciary, neither has ever had a women judge at the Supreme Court. Significantly, no women have been appointed to the Federal Shariat Court in Pakistan. India has had precisely 3 women on the bench of the Supreme Court, and presently has about 15 women High Court judges.

Participation of women in national military forces has been increasing. In 1973, women accounted for only 2 per cent of the military in the United States, but by 1991, this has gone up to 11 per cent. In some countries today, women are actively deployed in battle, that is, in roles other than the traditional ones of nursing and housekeeping. Canada and Israel also have comparatively high rates of female participation in the armed forces. By and large, as in state bureaucracies, the concentrations of women is in the lower echelons of the armed forces (with sexual harassment of female soldiers being fairly common); or in defence contracting firms. The incorporation of women in the military is thus done in typically gendered ways, which reinforce instead of interrogating dichotomous gender stereotypes.

In the Private Sector and the Financial World

In business organizations, women tend to be even more marginalized than they are in representative political bodies. The census of the 500 largest corporations in United States (Fortune 500 companies) showed that women held just 12.5 per cent of all corporate officer positions, and 6.2 per cent of the most senior positions, such as chairman, vice chairman, president and chief executive officers. Women of colour were appreciably more disadvantaged of 400 companies for which data is available, coloured women accounted for 1.3 per cent of corporate officers and only six corporate officers of this category were top earners.

A similar census of the 560 largest corporations in Canada found that women held 12 per cent of all corporate officer positions, and only 3 per cent of the highest positions, which included 12 presidents and CEOs. Even in Scandinavian societies, where women's representation in national legislatures reaches or crosses the so-called 'critical mass', women holders of elite positions are few.

These data indicate that women are largely excluded from positions of decision making in business. Given that this is a domain in which immense power is concentrated, and given the consideration traffic between this and the domain of the state, such marginalization is surely significant. The phenomenon of women in positions of political and administrative leadership being given 'soft' portfolios has historically had parallels in the private sector. The sectors such as health and health care, social services hostels and restaurants and education are all considered female domains.

In trade unions, women typically constitute a large percentage of the membership, but are excluded from decision-making roles. Thus, women account for less than 10 per cent of trade union officials worldwide. It is notable that even in countries where women have achieved the 'critical mass' in parliamentary representation, their participation in the leadership of trade union lags. Though the first trade union in India was founded in 1917 by a woman, Anasuyaben Sarabhai, the number of women in the national offices of the major trade unions in the 1990s, ranges from 0 to 3. An important exception has been the Histadrut, the federation of labour unions in Israel, which has adopted a resolution stating that 30 per cent of its leadership must be women. Women already account for 19 per cent of the membership of its Executive Committee, and 25 per cent of its Deputy Chairpersons.

In organizations of markets, women tend to be confined to individuated enterprises and restricted to certain points in the marketing chain or geographical spheres of operation, and gender ideology whereby certain goods or skills are deem to be 'female' and therefore 'inferior'. Women's relative lack of access to formal financial services and relative reliance on informal sector of finance can be understood in terms of gendered transactions costs in credit markets, linked to regulatory frameworks and institutional norms. These confine the majority of women entrepreneurs and 'family workers' to the low profit, high competition informal sphere, where prospects for accumulation are weak.

In Civil Society

'Civil society' encompasses the range of voluntary associations in between the family and the state. It is seen as important in providing checks and balances on the action of the state and the private sector, in empowering the poor and ensuring their effective participation in safety nets and other poverty reduction programmes. It has a key role in responding the state and market 'failure' through voluntary provision of various kinds, and more generally in reducing the transactions costs of economic and social development (UNDP 1997, quoted in Baden 1999).

A general problem with analyses of civil society in the governance literature is that it tends to be portrayed as virtuous, non-conflicting and functional to social development. But clearly there are strong conflicts between interest groups (including gender-based interest groups or groups with strongly opposed gender ideologies) in civil society, such that promoting civil society will not necessarily result in outcomes that increased gender accountability. Examples include welfare organizations linked to conservative religious groups or other groups which may have widespread networks of social provisions (health care, schooling, etc.) involving poor people but which excludes girls and women, or relegate them to narrowly gendered roles.

There are a numbers of ways in which the constitution of civil society reflects gendered divisions, norms and practices. The spaces for women to mobilize in civil society may be relatively restricted, such that they belong to a narrow range of organizations, which are gender-typed, gender segregated or less politically influential. For example, poor women tend to be dominant as members of religious groups rather than, for example, trade unions, political parties and business associations, who have a more direct line into policy processes. Where women are active, this tends to be in mobilizing support among women for organizational objectives, rather than organizing around gender interest. Even women's organizations do not necessarily provide space for the articulation of gender interests; they may in fact promote highly conservative agendas. Explicitly feminist groups are often characterized as elitist, urban based and middle class. There are divisions between organizations focused on lobbying and advocacy and those that are engaged in direct service provision, with the latter sometimes a more immediate demand for poor women.

Myriad organizations are formed around women's practical interests, in response to living in conditions of poverty, but rarely do these fragmented forms of organizations result in the articulation of aggregated gender interests in political movements of a durable nature. The problem is that the weak organizational form in which women mobilized is often not recognized in political systems. Where networks or associations formed by women (e.g. around water use management; rotating credit associations) become formalized, positions of authority may be taken over by men and women's participation declines.

Equally, research to date suggests that in the absence of specific goals of promoting gender equity, there is no necessary correspondènce between management democracy in organizations and institutional comparative advantage. So, NGOs do not necessarily provide a more congenial environmental for the institutionalization of women's interests than state bureaucracies. Promotion of NGOs, or even women's organizations, then, should not be seen as an automatic panacea for improving gender accountability.

ENGENDERING GOVERNANCE

Addressing the gender gap in governance implies not only increasing the visibility of women in governance structures, but also creating an enabling environment for women to participate and contribute effectively to governance in terms of both material and social environments that would have the potential to influence women's ability to turn their ideas into action. Alongside there is also a need to improve certain central capabilities of women in terms of internal preparedness – education, health care and supportive social relationship (kin and family support). Equally critical for women is to seek employment outside their homes and form affiliations with other women's groups and movements.

The main policy response to the underrepresentation of women in the formal structures of politics has been the attempt to enhance representation through quotas, whether in political parties or legislatures. However, the issues of quotas are contentious for at least two reasons: the first relates to the lack of genuine commitment in the political parties to increasing women's representation. There are ways in which the political parties may effectively circumvent the quota by, for instance, putting up candidates in constituencies where the party is weak and unlikely to win anyway; or treating the quota as a ceiling rather than a minimum to be improved upon; or nominating women candidates who would be pliable depending on the male party leadership. Nevertheless, there are exceptions such as the ANC in South Africa, which adopted a self-administered quota of 30 per cent, even if many of the women candidates were clustered at the bottom 15 per cent of the list. Other parties in that country followed the ANC's example, with the result that women comprises 27 per cent of the national legislature.

The second argument relates to the fact that policy outcomes are not necessarily superior (in feminist terms) in countries where quotas have been implemented. The symbolic representation of women, it is argued, is no guarantee of a qualitatively better representation of women's interests. The evidence is clearly mixed, both across countries and across levels of governance (local or national). Thus, for instance, a Nordic woman politician laments that even where women account for 43 per cent of parliamentary representation, politics are still led and shaped by men (IPU 1999: 71, quoted in Jayal 2003).

Where quotas have been successful, as in Scandinavian, two conditions have obtained. Quotas have been the result of pressures from strong women's sections within social democratic political parties, and social democracy itself has attempted to change the public–private relationship through the institution of the welfare state, justifying intervention in the market on behalf of women. On the other hand, the emphasis on formal equality in the erstwhile socialist states of Eastern Europe ensures greater representation for women, but did not succeed in policy terms, because it was largely symbolic.

On the whole, quotas appear to be more efficacious at the local level than the national level. The Indian experience of 33 per cent reservation of women in the new Panchayati Raj Institutions under the 73rd and 74th constitutional amendment of 1992 is not unambiguously positive, but there are undoubtedly signs of a slow, but on the whole cheering, process of empowerment taking place. However, though fewer in number, those who entered politics by competing with men rather than as symbols have tended to behave more independently and are often more sympathetic to women issues. In Israel, without quotas, the number of women participating in local politics has remained stable. This is apparently because the parties believe that the inclusion of at least one woman on every local council is a political necessity.

Some countries have experimented with quotas in the civil service, though with ambivalent results. In 1976, Bangladesh introduced a 10 per cent quota for women in government, but it took two decades for female participation to rise to this level, so that women are still concentrated at relatively lower-level positions. Sri Lanka institutionalized quotas, which, over time, varied from 10 to 25 per cent, but were eventually abolished when the country became a signatory to The

Convention on the Elimination of All Forms of Discrimination against Women (CEDAW). Some women's organizations associated with development have striven to function independently of any political party and to cultivate support from the state through such 'neutral' positioning. While this strategy has enabled women to secure more access to public space and decision making, the confinement of such organizations to 'community development' level has also compromised their capacity to assert themselves in more conventional politicized forum. In fact, the state easily ignores or dismisses them as being concern primarily with (non-politicized) development.

CONCLUSION

The very definition of governance needs to be engendered. Efforts so far have been made to engender the public institutions alone, whereas the private sphere is also an arena of governance, for example, the family where there is an influence of the exercise of social power and modes of governance. The interaction of private and public arenas of governance is important as there is a link between the two (private and public patriarchies) along with the manner in which they are constructed and distinguished has an impact on women. Women need to be empowered to counter their oppression in all spheres from the family to create an enabling environment for effective participation in governance (Jayal 2003).

In most of the countries of the world including India, most efforts at engendering of state institutions of governance mostly represent little more than the gendering of the same elites with reference to the legislature, executive, judiciary, bureaucracy and military. In all spheres, there is a concentration of women at the lower levels of structures of governance, with however little impact on decision-making processes and outcomes. Similarly in case of market and the private sector, women are also marginalized and excluded from positions of decision making in business and the entire corporate sector as a whole. In civil society institutions, the number of women in positions of power and decision making are better as compared to the other domains such as the state and market. However, there is a need for more research and exploration to be done.

REFERENCES

Ashworth, G. (1996). Gendered Governance: An Agenda for Change. Gender in Development Programme (GIDP), New York: UNDP.

Baden, S. (1999). Gender, Governance and the Feminisation of Poverty. Paper Presented in the Meeting on Women and Political Participation: 21st Century Challenges, New Delhi: UNDP.

Basu, A. (2003). Gender and Governance: Concepts and Contexts. In Martha Nussbaum, Amrita Basu, Yasmin Tambiah and Niraja Gopal Jayal (Eds), *Essays on Gender and Governance*. New Delhi: Human Development Research Centre (UNDP).

Beall, Jo (1996). Urban Governance: Why Gender Matters? UNDP Gender and Development Monograph Series No. 1, Development Planning Unit (DPU), New York: UNDP.

Hyden, G. and Samuel, J. (eds) (2011). *Making the State Responsive: Experience with Democratic Governance Assessments.* New York: UNDP.

Jayal, G.N. (2003). Locating Gender in the Governance Discourse. In Martha Nussbaum, Amrita Basu, Yasmin Tambiah and Niraja Gopal Jayal (Eds), *Essays on Gender and Governance*. New Delhi: Human Development Research Centre (UNDP).

Nussbaum, M. (2003). Gender and Governance: An Introduction. In Martha Nussbaum, Amrita Basu, Yasmin Tambiah and Niraja Gopal Jayal (Eds), *Essays on Gender and Governance*. New Delhi: Human Development Research Centre (UNDP).

Tambiah, Y. (2003). The Impact of Gender Inequality in Governance. In Martha Nussbaum, Amrita Basu, Yasmin Tambiah and Niraja Gopal Jayal (Eds), *Essays on Gender and Governance*. New Delhi: Human Development Research Centre (UNDP).

Part II

The Equity Scenario in the Asia-Pacific

CHAPTER 6

Trade Liberalization and Gender Wage Inequality in Thailand

A Macro-level Approach

Bui Thi Minh Tam and Chompoonuh K. Permpoonwiwat

Economic integration and trade liberalization were deemed to bring benefits to many groups in society and economic growth as a whole. Research had demonstrated that trade policies affected women and men differently due to gender inequalities in access to and control of domestic and social resources and decision making. Their impact was also mediated by the different roles that men and women had within societies – in particular, the gendered division of labour. There were concerns on effects of the globalization process on women, their opportunities, jobs and income.

A theory of global economic restructuring and its impact on the quality of women's work suggested that national integration into the world economy through trade liberalization significantly expanded women's access to income. It was the fact that trade liberalization had led to an increase in employment opportunities for women – particularly in the export-oriented sectors. Earning an income externally to the household had led to greater empowerment for women, both in the home and in the wider community. However, trade liberalization had also resulted into unemployment and the restructuring of labour markets – a situation that tended to affect poor and marginalized groups of women more than men. Therefore, it did not necessarily remove barriers to women's advancement or improved the predominance of unskilled jobs held by women.

Literatures showed mixed empirical results. Some studies showed that globalization leads to an increase in subcontracting of women and a decrease in the prices of agricultural goods produced by women and a 'masculinization' of typical female employment, such as garment and textiles. Other studies concluded that trade was beneficial to certain groups of women because it could lead to less employers' discrimination in highly paid manufacturing and service sectors. These mixed results indicated that the effect of free trade on women depended on the industrial composition of liberalizing countries, the liberalization process and initial conditions, among other factors, so the impacts of open markets on women's or men's welfare could not be generalized across countries or even across industries within a country.

The effect of trade liberalization on gender wage gap could be looked at by using a macro as well as a micro-approach. With a macro-approach, Carvallo (1997) used time series analysis to draw conclusions about the impact of trade openness and relative price on wage gap in Chile. Granger causality tests were performed for each pair of wage inequality and openness indicator. Openness measures did not seem to Granger-cause the wage gap, and the result is not conclusive. Exports ratio to GDP increased wage inequality, while reduction in average tariff narrows wage gap. Ahmed and Hyder (2006) measured gender inequality in Pakistan during the period 1973–2005 using GDI (Gender Development Index) composed by the UNDP based on three aspects including income, education and health. Using annual series data with OLS econometric model showing that trade liberalization had a significant impact in reducing gender inequality, and gender inequality was more sensitive to exports than imports to GDP ratio.

A micro-approach often used more sophisticated methods utilizing the earnings function regression to obtain wage residuals and Oaxaca and Ransom (1973) decomposition technique in order to bring more specific findings. Aguayo-Téllez (2011) provided a comprehensive review on the empirical impact of trade liberalization policies and FDI on gender inequality, showing that the existing literature suggested unclear evidence of trade liberalization on gender wage and employment inequality. There was some evidence suggesting a positive effect while there were some papers showing the opposite, making it difficult to claim that trade liberalization and FDI had benefited women.

Black and Brainerd (2004) was among the first to study effects of trade liberalization and increasing international competition on the gender wage gap across industries in the United States from 1977 to 1994. It was found that the residual (after controlling for individual characteristics) gender wage gap narrowed more rapidly in concentrated industries than in competitive industries. It concluded that increased international trade had increased competition in some industries, although trade might appear to benefit women by reducing the ability of firms to discriminate.

Seguino (2000), Berik (2000) and Berik et al. (2004) studied the effects on trade liberalization policy on gender inequality in two newly industrialized economies, South Korea and Taiwan. Using industry-level data from 1981 to 1992, Seguino (2000) reported that as a consequence of trade, gender wage differentials widened in Taiwan but narrowed in Korea where the government intervention prevented excessive capital outflows in industries with a large share of female employees. Berik (2000) used industry-level data from 1983 to 1994 to argue that greater export orientation in Taiwan did benefit women relative wages. With more updated industry-level data from 1981 to 1999, Berik et al. (2004) stated that Taiwanese as well as South Korean women were negatively affected by competition from foreign trade and, therefore, concluded that increased international trade reduced women's bargaining power to achieve wage gains.

In most developing countries, women workers were relatively unskilled and overrepresented in the informal sector. In many Asian countries, women workers were also crowded in the agricultural sector. Under this situation, trade liberalization policies that affected unskilled, informal, or agricultural workers would put women workers in a disadvantaged position. A positive relation between trade liberalization and women's relative wages and/or employment was also found in several Asian countries. Chamarbagwala (2006) uses individual-level data of India for the period from 1983 to 2000 and found that an increased demand for skilled workers, and especially for skilled women, contributed significantly to narrow the gender wage gap. Conversely, with more updated data to 2004, Rodgers and Menon (2008) showed that increasing trade openness in India's more concentrated manufacturing industries was associated with growing residual gaps between male and female workers. At the same time, with declining rents in the concentrated sector, firms seemed to maintain men's real wage gains at the loss of women's wage, leading to an increasing wage gap.

In the case of Thailand, the link between trade liberalization and gender equity has not been studied to a full range. There had been several studies looking at Thai gender wage gap. For example, Nakavachara (2007, 2010) indicated that gender wage inequality had been improved in Thailand, and the main factors contributing to the decline in gender wage gap in Thailand from 1985 to 2005 is women's education enhancement. There was no evidence of a published paper showing study on the effect of trade liberalization on gender wage inequality in Thailand.

The current study examined the change in the gender wage inequality between men and women in the case of Thailand from a macroeconomic level and tried to investigate whether this trade liberalization had any effect on closing the wage gap over time. The chapter was structured in five sections. The next section specified some theoretical framework as basis for studying the relationship between trade liberalization and gender wage inequality. The third section provides some facts on gender inequality and trade liberalization in Thailand and also reviews relevant work in the case of Thailand regarding gender wage inequality. The fourth section describes the data set for an econometric analysis. The last section summarizes findings and suggests directions for further research.

THEORETICAL UNDERPINNINGS

The mechanism through which trade liberalization affected gender inequality, specifically for the unexplained portion of the gender wage gap, could be explained using two mainstream theories. The first was the Heckscher–Ohlin (H-O) trade theory, which was first published by Eli Heckscher in 1919 then clarified and built on by Bertil Ohlin in 1933. The second was Gary Becker's theory of discrimination (Becker 1971). The H-O theorem postulated that a nation would export the commodity whose production required the intensive use of the nation's relative abundant and cheap factor and oppositely import the commodity whose production required the intensive use of the nation's relatively scarce and expensive factor. In the case of developing countries with often more abundant unskilled labour relative to skilled labour, the theorem could be understood, for example, as developing countries would export products using intensively unskilled labour inputs while import more skilled and capital-intensive products.

Trade liberalization could be linked to the Stolper–Samuelson theorem postulating that an increase in the relative price of a commodity (e.g. as a result of a tariff reduction) would raise the return or earnings of the factor used intensively in the production of export good while return of the factor used intensively in the production of import-competing goods would decline. In developing countries, the abundant factor was unskilled labour force and in many cases, on average, women tended to have lower skills than men, it follows that gender wage gap should decrease.

In summary, the mechanism started with trade liberalization changed domestic prices, thus adjusted production and the allocations of inputs as well as the distribution of income between different resources. Similarly, trade liberalization changed relative domestic prices of goods, thus differently affected the employment and wages of different social groups, skilled and unskilled workers, as well as women and men working in the different industries.

The way that relative prices of goods modified firms' incentives and decision on reallocation of production inputs and discriminatory behaviours based on the a well-known theory of Gary Becker (1971) called 'the economics of discrimination'. This theory brought the concept of discrimination on the labour market that entailed the possibility of wage differences among male and female workers that could not be explained by differences in observed characteristics such as education, experience, health and age reflecting productivity differences. In a less competitive environment, it was easier for firms to implement a discriminatory behaviour between male and female or between skilled and unskilled workers. Trade liberalization increases competition among firms as well as with foreign firms and thereby eroded firms' ability to maintain costly discrimination, thus reducing wage differentials.

STYLIZED FACTS ON GENDER EQUITY AND TRADE LIBERALIZATION IN THAILAND

Thailand, a constitutional monarchy with a population of 69 million, had made a significant progress in development, not only in economic growth but also in education, health and social services. Thailand ranked 92 out of 138 countries on the Gender Inequality Index. In the past few decades, women had been a major force in Thai economic development and had played a strong role in supporting society. The participation of women in every field has grown in Thailand. The roles of women and social attitudes towards them had changed. Either growth led to gender equality or gender equality led to growth, or both occur concurrently (Nakavachara 2007). The gender gap in the schooling of boys and girls had virtually closed but there was still a significant gender bias including a widening income gap and an unequal access to resources and social services.

Labour Force Participation, Occupation and Wages

According to data from the National Statistical Office (NSO 2012) female ratio of Thai population has been constant at around 50 per cent for decades. In 2010, women accounted for 50.76 per cent of the total population (32.43 million) and 65.1 per cent of women participated in the labour force compared to over 80 per cent of men. Both male and female labour force participation rates gradually raised during 1970s and 1980s, then began to drop at the end of the 1980s (NSO 2010). Table 1 summarizes several descriptive statistics of labour force participation rates and mean wage in logarithm form of male and female labour as well as the difference between them during the period 1998–2012. There was a large difference in labour force participation rate among Thai men and women (80% versus 64%, on average), and the ratio among males seems to be more stable across the time than female ratio, with higher standard deviation of 1.3 per cent.

Permpoonwiwat (2006) showed that the relatively high female labour force participation ratio indicated at least two possible implications. First, proportionally more Thai women than women in other developing countries endured the higher pressures of working outside the home. Second, more Thai women have the freedom to choose their lifestyle or workplace. Job opportunities are now more accessible to women whose potential and capabilities have been recognized.

Table 1 *Statistics on participation rate and mean wage (1998–2012)*

Variables	*Observation*	*Mean*	*Standard Deviation*	*Min*	*Max*
Male participation rate	59	80.8	0.6	79.2	81.9
Female participation rate	59	63.8	1.3	61.6	66.3
Difference	59	17.0	1.0	15.2	19.1
Male log mean wage	47	9.0	0.1	8.8	9.3
Female log mean wage	47	8.9	0.2	8.7	9.3
Difference log	47	0.1	0.0	0.0	0.1

Source: Author's calculation from Labour Force Surveys (NSO, various years).

The implication might be that most employers had the old paradigm that women produced less productivity than men did; they paid women at lower wage rates than men. In particular cases women were not allowed to work in dangerous or too strenuous conditions. With this limitation, women were basically classified and prohibited to select their jobs at the beginning of entering work. Data on average monthly wage in logarithm showed insignificant difference among male and female workers across the time. Overall, on average, monthly mean wage of male workers was about 7 per cent higher than those of female workers. The largest difference was 14.9 per cent. This fact raises a question of whether there was no considerable gender wage gap in Thailand. A more thorough and deeper looked into the mean wages of workers across sexes but breaking into agriculture and non-agriculture groups reveals a different story though. According to data from the National Statistical Office (NSO 2012), men in the non-agricultural sector received the average wage of 10,875 baht compared with 10,472 baht for women. Even though, with fewer promotion opportunities, women in private sector (non-agricultural sector) also received lower average income and wages than men. According to the Labour Force Survey by National Statistical Office (NSO 2012) the ratio of women's to men's average income from waged employment in non-agricultural sector, including government, state enterprise and private sector employees, was 96 per cent in 2011.

In the past, agriculture was the most crucial component of Thai economy with a high share of agricultural employment of 71 per cent in 1980. The employment structure had changed and the major labour force had moved towards manufacturing and service sector, leaving only 39 per cent employed in the agricultural sector in 2005 (Nakavachara 2007). The declining importance of agriculture and changes in farming systems had reduced the demand for women's labour on farms, while their cultural duty to render service to their parents remains the same. The growth in low technological manufacturing industries relied on a large number of unskilled and poorly educated labour force, typically young, unskilled female labour migrants from poor rural regions. According to the gender statistics by the National Statistical Office, the rural to urban migration of women is higher than men because of more available job opportunities for women to work in the factory or other services in urban areas. Moreover, women's average contributions to household income have therefore increased (from 29% in 1976 to 40% in 2000) (Nakavachara 2007).

Table 2 indicates average monthly wages (in Thai baht) adjusted for inflation of male and female workers responding to the labour force surveys. Three specific years 2001, 2006 and 2011 were selected in order to identify the change over a longer period of time. It was very clear that wage differential is much larger in agriculture sector, compared to those in non-agricultural sector (e.g. 32% versus 10% in 2001). Over the period of 10 years, the wage gap had reduced less than half to 19 per cent in agriculture sector, but has declined sharply by nearly two-thirds to 3.9 per cent in non-agricultural sector. These data implied that there had been not only the change in absolute amount but also the speed to wage gap contraction in different sectors of the economy.

Table 2 *Mean real wage of males and females by sector (in Thai baht per month)*

Sector	*2001*			*2006*			*2011*		
	Male	*Female*	*Different*	*Male*	*Female*	*Different*	*Male*	*Female*	*Different*
Agriculture	2.61	1.97	32.3	3.50	2.75	26.9	5.12	4.28	19.4
Non-Agriculture	7.71	6.99	10.3	8.49	8.03	5.7	10.46	10.07	3.9

Source: Labour Force Survey (NSO, various years).

The above improvement in women's wage income over the decade could be related to their accumulated human capital, especially education and health. At present, girls and boys in Thailand have equal access and opportunities for education. The nine-year mandatory education has mobilized all children and youths to school to complete lower secondary education. As a result, the enrolment rates for both gender at the primary and lower secondary levels have increased significantly. However, Thai women are more likely to pursue further study in higher education compared to men. According to a report on

Thailand Gender-Disaggregated Statistics (Ministry of Social Development and Human Security 2008), 52.3 per cent of person who graduated with a bachelor's degree, 51.75 per cent graduated with a master's degree and 53.40 per cent obtained a Ph.D. degree were women.

In terms of health, the life expectancy of Thai women at birth exceeded that of men. Women's life expectancy in 2010 was 76.08 years, about seven years more than Thai men's life expectancy. However, women's illness rate was higher than men. The estimates and projections issued by Thailand's National Economic Social and Development Board (NESDB 2007) reported the longer life expectancy in Thai women, with more elderly and women living alone. Ageing population is one of the concerns in Thailand, which seems to be continued until 2030. It is predicted that the elderly aged from 60 years and over will account for 25 per cent of the population by the end of 2030. This proportion will be even higher among women than men, increasing a share of old-aged women to 61–66 per cent of the total elderly. This is sometimes referred to as the 'feminization of the elderly'.

Literature Review on Gender Wage Gap in Thailand

To our knowledge, there has not been any published paper specifically studying the link between trade liberalization and gender wage inequality in the case of Thailand, although there had been several studies looking at gender wage gap. There were several studies showing that gender wage inequality has been improved in Thailand. Nakavachara (2007) found that the main factor contributing to the decline in gender wage gap in Thailand from 1985 to 2005 was the education enhancement of women. Women had, in fact, overcome men in education attainment and achievement over the past decades. This fact was also confirmed by Nakavachara (2010), revealing that improvement of female education attainment was one of the most important factors explaining the recent decline in mean wage gap.

Female workers receive lower wages than male workers particularly in the group aged 15–24 and 25–54 years old, and the gap of wage was smallest in the group aged 55–60. The gap tended to be larger in young age groups compared to the older ones. Those gender wage gap in Thailand labour market was investigated by using the conventional wage differential decomposition methods (Oxaca et al. 1973) indicating that the gap was caused by gender discrimination, not because of less productivity (Permpoonwiwat 2004, 2006).

Another study of Maithongdee (2010) on the gender wage differentials in professional occupations in the private sector also applied the Oaxaca decomposition approach but accounting for the selectivity term to avoid selection bias. This has not been done in any research in the case of Thailand. The results reveal that men employees working in professional occupations earned 23.14 per cent per hour in real term more than their female counterparts.

Trade Liberalization in Thailand

Thailand joined the WTO officially almost 20 years ago, on 1 January 1995, and for most of the time the country has followed a policy of export-oriented growth. Such policy lifted up the country with high economic growth during 1990s, before the financial crisis in 1997. The economy had been transformed from a pure agricultural economy into a more industrialized economy with majority of exports attributed to industrial and manufactured goods. Food products used to account for about 19 per cent of total exports but had reduced to less than 14 per cent in recent years. Meanwhile, there had been increasing export share of major manufactured products and machinery, from 33 per cent in mid 1990s to over 44 per cent in 2012 and was at a peak of almost 46 per cent in 2007. On the other side, the main imports had not changed much with crude materials and machinery accounted for a large share, followed by manufactured products

Figure 1 presents the movement of trade openness in Thailand for the period 1998–2012 for three indicators (export and import ratio over GDP and trade openness defined as the ratio of total trade value (exports plus imports) to GDP. From the years before WTO accession, trade openness had almost tripled from a little less than 100 per cent to over 300 per cent in 2012 (prediction). Export and import ratios were around 50 per cent 20 years ago but have grown considerably to 146–148 per cent and 152–160 per cent respectively in 2011–2012. Therefore, Thailand continues to be recognized as an open economy. In 2010, it was the

Figure 1 *Trade openness in Thailand (1998–2012)*

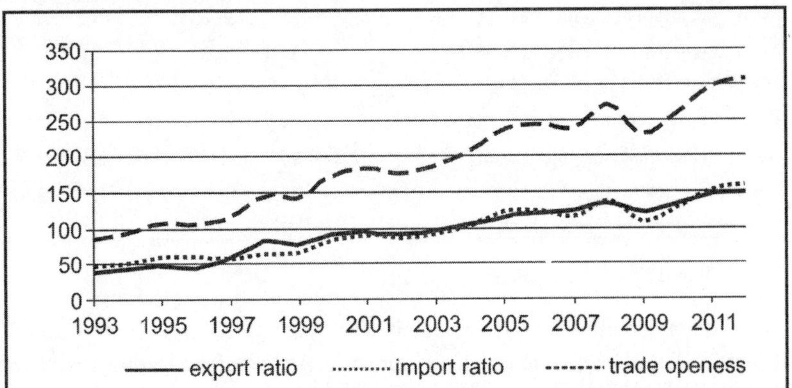

Source: Author's calculation based on the data from the Bank of Thailand.

world's 19 largest exporter and the 17 largest importers of goods, little higher ranks in commercial services (16 and 14 respectively).

Table 3 *Import tariffs in Thailand (1991–2009)*

Indicator	*1991*	*1995*	*2000*	*2005*	*2009*
All products					
Bound rate, simple mean (%)		26.0	25.7	25.8	26.1
Share of tariff lines with *international peaks* (%)	72.8	57.0	46.9	22.1	20.5
Tariff rate, applied, simple mean (%)	37.8	20.9	16.9	10.5	11.2
Tariff rate, most favoured nation, simple mean (%)	38.8	22.9	18.4	11.9	10.4
Share of tariff lines *with specific rate* (%)	22.0	2.0	1.7	1.1	5.2
Tariff rate, applied, weighted mean (%)	31.4	14.6	9.5	5.4	4.9
Tariff rate, most favoured nation (MFN), weighted me	31.4	14.6	9.5	4.8	4.9
Manufactured products					
Share of tariff lines with *international peaks* (%)	74.8	57.3	47.3	20.8	17.6
Tariff rate applied, simple mean (%)	38.8	20.1	16.1	10.1	10.5
Tariff rate, most favoured nation, simple mean (%)	40.6	20.7	16.1	10.7	8.8
Share of tariff lines *with specific rates* (%)	21.9	1.6	0.5	0.5	2.9
Tariff rate, applied, weighted mean (%)	32.8	15.4	10.1	5.9	6.1
Tariff rate, most favoured nation (MFN), weighted mean (%)	32.8	15.4	10.1	6.6	6.14
Primary products					
Bound rate, simple mean (%)		27.0	26.9	26.7	27.2
Share of tariff lines with *international peaks* (%)	56.1	54.9	44.9	29.0	38.6
Tariff rate, applied, simple mean (%)	29.6	26.6	22.8	13.2	15.9
Tariff rate, most favoured nation (MFN), simple mean (%)	32.1	30.3	26.5	16.0	15.7
Share of tariff lines *with specific rates* (%)	22.9	4.9	8.9	4.6	20.1
Tariff rate, applied, weighted mean (%)	25.7	11.3	7.7	2.3	2.9
Tariff rate, most favoured nation, weighted mean (%)	25.7	11.3	7.7	2.7	2.9

Source: World Trade Organization Report 2012.

Fundamentally strong, Thailand has maintained a current account surplus and high level of international reserves. As one of the leading members of the ASEAN group, Thailand is committed to deepening economic integration among members, including removing trade barriers and improving facilitation. It has been pursuing a policy of negotiating free-trade agreement on trade liberalization with a focus on the Asia-Pacific region. There is no comprehensive multilateral agreement on such issues, but many bilateral agreements have been signed.

Since January 2007, Thailand adopted the 8-digit commodity classification code of ASEAN Harmonized Tariff Nomenclature (AHTN categorization) and is applying the code to all imports. Most of applied tariff rates were under a new tariff structure, which is not higher than 10 per cent. Table 3 describes the changes in tariff rates from early 1990s to 2009 for both primary and manufactured products. It could be observed that while there was a significant reduction in tariff for manufactured products, the rates for primary products changed slowly. In fact, some agricultural products were still under a complicated tariff structure with different ad valorem and specific duty rates. However, under the liberalization policy, both import and export controls had been limited to a minimum.

On the sector aspect, Thailand had emphasized enhancing productivity and competitiveness in both the agricultural and manufacturing sectors. Agriculture remained the main sources of employment, and Thailand was a major producer and exporter of several agricultural products, particularly rice and rubber. Agricultural policies varied from one product to another. As for services, policy reforms had been made towards liberalization such as those in insurance and telecommunication sectors.

In the next section, the study further examined whether there was any link between trade liberalization and reduction in wage gap between male and female workers. Our presumption was that Thai economy had not only opened up extensively to international trade, changing export and import commodity composition as said, but also attracted different types of labour or skill in their productions. To implement this task, we applied econometric analysis to see whether more open and liberalized trade helps to narrow down the gender wage gap.

DATA AND THE REGRESSION RESULTS

In order to measure gender inequality, this analysis employed gender wage gap and female versus male employment share. Data were collected from the national labour force surveys, which had been implemented quarterly since 1998 by the National Statistical Office of Thailand (NSO). Therefore, quarterly data from 1998 quarter 1 to 2012 quarter 3 were collected, making up a total of 59 observations.

In order to identify and measure the effects of trade liberalization on gender wage differentials, we first applied OLS regression in a simple and later in a multiple model taking into account the education differences between men and women. There was only the dependent variable in all models, that is, the logarithm difference in mean wages between males and females. Explanatory

Table 4 *Effects of trade liberalization on gender wage differential*

Explanatory variables	*Dependent variable: difference in logarithm of mean wages between males and females*								
	All			*Agriculture*			*Non-agriculture*		
Trade openness	–0.0005***			–0.0001			–0.0005***		
	–5.1			–0.39			–4.31		
Export ratio		–0.001***			0.000			–0.001***	
		–4.85			–0.37			–4.02	
Import ratio			–0.001***			–0.0002			–0.0009***
			–5.09			–0.39			–4.39
R-squared	0.3664	0.3428	0.3653	0.003	0.003	0.003	0.2926	0.2642	0.3003

Source: Authors' calculation from Labour Force Surveys (NSO).

Note: ***, ** and * indicate the level of statistical significance at 1%, 5% and 10% respectively.

variables were incorporated one by one including trade openness, export ratio and import ratio, then later incorporating education variables.

Table 4 presents regression results of simple regressions for the economy as a whole and then by separating agriculture and non-agriculture sectors. Negative coefficients were found in all regressions suggesting a negative relationship between trade liberalization and wage gap. It means that more liberalized trade was associated with less wage inequality between men and women. This finding seems to be quite encouraging, but only in the non-agriculture sector and not in agriculture sector. In the economy as a whole, as well in the non-agriculture sector, this negative relationship was found to be statistically significant at 1 per cent level.

The explanation could come from the fact that in Thailand as in many other Asian countries more women were involved in agriculture activities and working in informal sectors where wages are difficult to measure and to be standardized. In agriculture, it was usually found that women were generally more constrained than men from reaping the benefits from the expansion of agricultural trade. Limited access to productive resources often prevented them from adopting new technologies or from increasing their economies of scale. Another reason was from the international trade aspect as presented above that tariff of agricultural product in particular and of primary products in general has not been changed much and other restrictions in the sector remain.

However, the magnitude of the effect did not seem to be strong. The coefficient of –0.00054 meant that if trade openness increased by 10 per cent, the gender wage gap would reduce by 0.5 per cent on average. Larger effects were found from the export and import ratio. The robustness of those regressions was around 0.36 for the whole economy and 0.3 for non-agriculture, but almost zero as for the agricultural sector.

The result in Table 5 was quite similar to Table 4, except that difference in education attainment between male and female workers was taken into account in order to explain wage difference. At each education level, the difference was measured by subtracting proportion of male graduates to those of female graduates. It was noticeable that the incorporation of such education differences had increased the robustness or the explanatory power of the model considerably. *R*-square is more than 0.7 in non-agriculture sector and 0.3 in agriculture sector. It was interesting to note that while a difference in elementary and secondary education negatively affects wage gap, higher education caused positive effects. This meant that if more men could attain higher education, their wage gap compared to women would be higher as well.

From the above OLS regression, the result was not confirmed especially in agricultural sector. Hence, it was necessary to perform another tests applied

Table 5 *Effects of trade liberalization on gender wage gap*

Explanatory variables	*Difference in logarithm of mean wages between males and females*								
	All			*Agriculture*			*Non-agriculture*		
Trade openness	–0.0002*			0.0006			–0.0003**		
	–1.9			1.3			–2.1		
Export ratio		–0.0004			0.001			–0.0005*	
		–1.61			1.26			–1.81	
Import ratio			–0.0003*			0.0009			–0.004**
			–2.01			1.25			–2.19
Difference in elementary education	–0.025***	–0.026***	–0.025***	–0.073**	–0.071**	–0.0729**	–0.018*	0.0195**	–0.018**
	–3.35	–3.51	3.3	–2.21	–2.18	–2.2	–1.95	–2.11	–1.9
Difference in lower sec. education	–0.016*	–0.175*	–0.017*	–0.03	–0.031	–0.0255	–0.0051	–0.0063	–0.006
	–1.83	–1.89	–1.97	–0.74	–0.75	–0.66	–0.46	–0.54	–0.56
Difference in upper sec. education	–0.015	–0.015	–0.146	–0.131**	–0.13**	–0.1293*	0.0052	–0.0044	0.005
	–1.13	–1.17	–1.15	–2.29	–2.28	–2.27	0.33	0.27	0.32
Difference in higher education	0.0118**	0.0114**	0.0121**	0.0073	0.008	0.0065	0.0152*	0.0147**	0.0157**
	2.33	2.22	2.4	0.32	0.38	0.29	2.41	2.3	2.49
R-squared	0.712	0.7927	0.7994	0.3073	0.306	0.305	0.712	0.7046	0.7145

Source: Author's calculation from Labour Force Surveys (NSO).

Note: ***, ** and * indicate the level of statistical significance at 1%, 5% and 10% respectively.

for time series data, which is called Granger causality test. This type of test could not imply for an actual causal relationship but rather a co-movement or counter-movement of two time series. It could be used mostly for prediction and projection. Granger causality – Wald test showed inclusive results of causality between wage gap and trade liberalization (for all three indicators: trade openness, export ratio and import ratio). For only agricultural sector, the test indicated statistically insignificant relationship. This was a similar conclusion that we also obtained from the OLS regression estimation.

CONCLUSION AND FURTHER RESEARCH POSSIBILITIES

The effect of trade on the gender wage gap and other gender trade discrimination still remains unclear, both theoretically and empirically. Therefore, there was some evidence that women was constrained from moving into more skilled, high-paying jobs created by trade liberalization because they had less access to resources, education and time spent for paid jobs.

The current chapter which was a part of research project on the impact of trade liberalization on gender wage inequality in Thailand looked at this relationship from a macroeconomic perspective. The study was based on a framework incorporating two theoretical pillars: the economics of discrimination initiated by Becker (1971) and the Heckscher–Ohlin/Stolper–Samuelson international trade theory. An overall look on Thailand's labour and wage inequality among sexes did point out a serious problem of gender inequality. Participation rates of males and females in the labour force were in the range of 80–82 per cent and 61–65 per cent respectively during the period 1998–2012. The wage gap between male workers and their female counterparts had been reduced over time from 10.5 per cent in 2001 to 6.7 per cent in 2006 and 3.7 per cent in 2011, on average. From a sectoral perspective, more wage disparity was observed in agriculture than non-agricultural industries, while the speed of gap reduction was faster in the non-agricultural sector. Such observations then could somehow be linked to the process of trade liberalization in Thailand, marked by the WTO accession in 1995, followed by tariffs reduction and/or elimination as well as the removal of other trade barriers. Tariff cut-offs had been more considerable among manufactured products but insignificant among primary products since 1995. Trade openness of Thailand at the same period had risen impressively from 100 to over 300.

Using a macroeconomic approach, our time series model indicated a statistically significant negative relationship between gender wage gap and trade openness, export ratio and import ratio to GDP in overall economy and non-agricultural sector, but insignificant effects in agriculture. This result implied that wage gap tended to be narrower over time as international trade becomes more liberalized. The same conclusion could be made when differences in education among men and women are taken into account. However, the linear correlation did not imply causation. Results from the Granger causality Wald tests for gender wage differential and trade variables offered inconclusive results. Therefore, the question on the impact of trade liberalization on gender wage discrimination in Thailand should be further analysed and ascertained using micro-level evidences. These unconfirmed results in two sectors indicated that the effect of free trade on women was dependent on the industrial composition of liberalizing countries, the liberalization process conditions, among other factors, so that the impacts of open markets on women's or men's welfare could not be generalized across industries within a country. A micro-approach analysis was necessary, especially on the industry basis since trade liberalization process was varied across product items with different industry's concentration. Such kind of industry-level analysis could obtain knowledge on the dynamics of the gender wage differential. Finding out factors affecting those wage gaps would be helpful in suggesting necessary reforms in the labour market and trade policy.

REFERENCES

Aguayo-Téllez, Ernesto (2011). The Impact of Trade Liberalization Policies and FDI on Gender Inequalities: A Literature Review. Background Paper for the World Development Report 2012.

Ahmed, N. and Hyder, K. (2006). Gender Inequality and Trade Liberalization Case of Pakistan. MPRA Paper No. 16252, Munich: Munich Personal RePEc Archive.

Becker, G. (1971). *The Economics of Discrimination*. Chicago: University of Chicago Press.

Berik, G. (2000). Mature Export-Led Growth and Gender Wage Inequality in Taiwan. *Feminist Economics 6*(3), pp. 1–26.

Berik, G., Rodgers, Y.M. and Zveglich, J. (2004). International Trade and Gender Wage Discrimination. *Review of Development Economics 8*(2), pp. 237–254.

Black, S.E. and Brainerd, E. (2004). Importing Equality? The Impact of Globalization on Gender Discrimination. *Industrial and Labour Relations Review 57*(4), pp. 540–559.

Carvallo, R.N. (1997). *Trade Liberalization and Wage Inequality.* Time Series Evidence from Chile; Series de Documenis de Trabajo, Escuelade Ingenieria Commercial.

Chamarbagwala, R. (2006). Economic Liberalization and Wage Inequality in India. *World Development 34*(12), pp. 1997–2015.

Heckscher, E.F. (1919). The Effect of Foreign Trade on the Distribution of Income. *Ekonomisk Tidskrift 21*, pp. 497–512.

Maithongdee, N. (2010). Gender Discrimination and Wage Differentials. (unpublished Master's thesis) Bangkok: NIDA.

Ministry of Social Development and Human Security (2008). Report on Thailand Gender: Disaggregated Statistics. Bangkok: Office of Women's Affairs and Family Development, Thailand.

Nakavachara, V. (2007). *Essays on Labor and Development Economics*. Mich., USA: Pro Quest.

— (2010). Superior Female Education: Explaining the Gender Earnings Gap Trend in Thailand. *Journal of Asian Economics 21*(2), pp. 198–218.

NESDB (2007). Report. Bangkok: Office of the National Economic and Social Development Board, Thailand. Available at www.nesdb.go.th

National Statistical Office (2010–12). National Statistical Office Thailand Reports. web.nso.go.th

Oaxaca, R. and Ransom, M.R. (1973). On Discrimination and the Decomposition of Wage Differentials. *Journal of Econometrics 61*, pp. 5–21.

Permpoonwiwat, C. (2004). Gender Analysis and Equality Plan for CIDA Feasibility Study for LiDAR Surveys for Road Construction in Thailand. Funding by Canadian International Development Agency (CIDA).

— (2006). Gender Impact Analysis and Equality Plan in Male-Dominated Workplace. *Sukothai Thammathirat Economics Journal*, June, pp. 120–146.

Picavet, M. (2005). Thai Women: Key Players in the Country's Economic and Social Development. *ABAC Journal*, September–December, pp. 29–52.

Rodgers, Y.M. and Menon, N. (2008). Trade Policy Liberalization and Gender Equality in the Labour Market: New Evidence for India. Viewed on 15 February 2012, from http://people.brandeis.edu/~nmenon/ruwar_chapter_rodgers&menon.pdf.

Seguino, S. (2000). The Effects of Structural Change and Economic Liberalization on Gender Wage Differentials in South Korea and Taiwan. *Cambridge Journal of Economics 24*(4), pp. 1081–1104.

United Nations Development Programme (2006). *Human Development Report 2006: Beyond Scarcity: Power, Poverty and the Global Water Crisis*. New York: UNDP.

— (2008). Report on Thailand Gender-Disaggregated Statistics 2008. Office of Women's Affairs and Family Development, Ministry of Social Development and Human Security in Collaboration with United Nations Development Programme.

— (2010). *Human Development Report 2010 (20th Anniversary Edition), The Real Wealth of Nations: Pathways to Human Development*. New York: UNDP/Palgrave Macmillan.

World Bank (2001). *World Development Report 2000/2001, Attacking Poverty*. Washington, DC: International Bank for Reconstruction and Development and New York: Oxford University Press.

— (2010). *The World Development Indicators, 2010*. Washington, DC: International Bank for Reconstruction and Development.

World Trade Report (2010). *Trade in Natural Resources*. Geneva: WTO Secretariat.

— (2012). *Trade and Public Policies: A Closer Look at Non-Tariff Measures in the 21st Century*. Geneva: WTO Secretariat.

CHAPTER 7

Women's Political Ambition, Candidacy and Political Participation in Japan

Hiromi Tanaka

GENDER GAP IN POLITICS: WHY JAPAN?

Politics is one of the major areas in which gender imbalances persist. In many countries as well as in the international political arena, it is one of the urgent tasks to increase the proportion of women in national and local decision-making bodies. Nevertheless, the gender gap continues to exist and is retained in most countries in the world. The conventional dominant form of gender prevails and the sexual division of labour, power relations between man and women, consciousness and/or emotional dimension of gender such as gender-based stereotypes and stigmas are deeply embedded in formal, institutional politics. In short, women and politics or gender and politics refer to a deep-rooted structure of gender relations (Connell 1987).

In Japan, the last two decades witnessed more visible increases in the number of female legislators than before. The proportion of women in the House of Representatives of the National Diet was never over 3 per cent between 1949 and 1993 (see Chart 1). The figure, however, increased to 4.6 per cent in 1996, jumping to 7.3 per cent in 2000, 7.1 per cent in 2003, 8.9 per cent in 2005 and 11.3 per cent in 2009. In the House of Councillors, the proportion increased from 8.7 per cent (1983) to 13.1 per cent (1989). Since then, the number of women in the Upper House increased moderately yet more or less steadily: 14.7 per cent in 1992, 13.5 per cent in 1995, 17.1 per cent in 1998, 15.4 per cent in 2001, 13.6 per cent in 2004 and 17.4 per cent in 2007. The proportion of women in the local assemblies (prefectures, cities, towns, special wards), which had been extremely low, even lower than on the national level, also increased in the past two decades, although the increase was again moderate (Chart 2). Particularly in the town assemblies (*chogikai*), there were and remain very few women. Women accounted for less than 1 per cent until 1987 and 2 per cent until 1992. In 2009, it reached 8.1 per cent.

Figure 1 *Women in national parliament, Japan (1950–2012)*

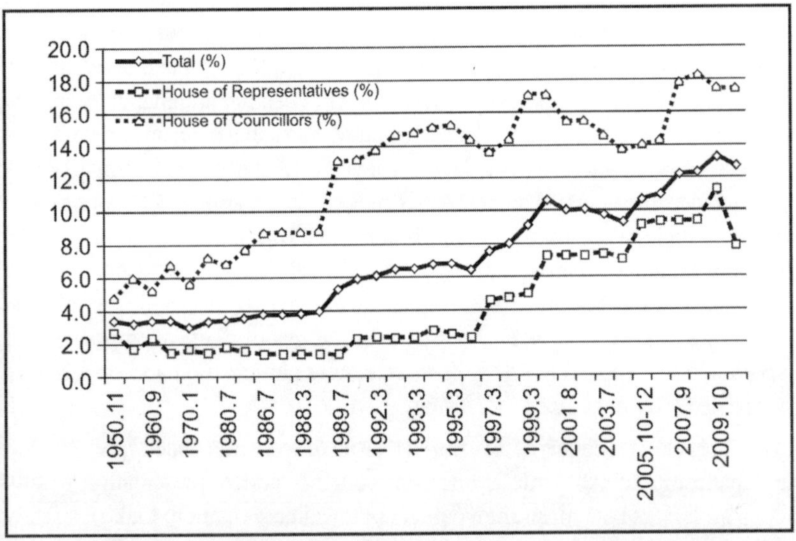

Source: Ministry of Internal Affairs and Communications, Secretariat of the House of Representatives, Secretariat of the House of Councillors.

Figure 2 *Proportion of women in local assemblies, Japan (1976–2009)*

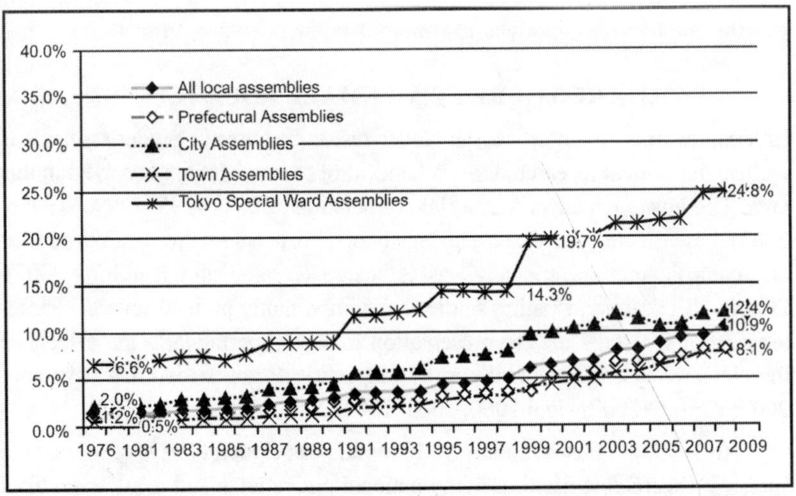

Source: Ministry of Internal Affairs and Communications, The Survey on the Members and Leaders of the Local Public Offices and their Party Affiliations (2006, 2007, 2008, 2009).

Despite all these slight increases in a longer time span, women – who account for about half of the population – are still largely underrepresented in decision-making. This is not a Japan-specific phenomenon, but there is a good reason to look at the case of Japan: Japan is a 'good' example that economic, technological and political/policy development does not automatically lead to a change in the conventional gender structure, particularly regarding women's political empowerment. In fact, Japan stands out in international comparison of such gender imbalance. The country is ranked at 124 among 189 countries in the international ranking of Women in Parliaments conducted by Inter-Parliamentary Union (2013). In the Global Gender Gap Report of the World Economic Forum (2012), Japan, ranked at 101 among 135 countries, does not do well due to its low score the categories of political empowerment (score: 0.0705; rank: 110) as well as economic participation and opportunity (score: 0.5756; rank: 102).[1]

This chapter concerns an unsolved issue of women's underrepresentation in Japanese politics. While studies on women's underrepresentation mostly focus on factors that constrain women's political participation, I take a slightly different angle, namely a perspective that looks at what promotes their participation, more specifically what can stir their political ambition and what can promote their candidacy. To do so, I analysed the political biographies of two female politicians, and in case studies explored how these women became political and eventually made a decision to run for public office, a rare decision for women in Japan. This qualitative methodology enabled me to get insights into the complexities involved in women's political empowerment.

WHY ARE THERE FEW FEMALE POLITICIANS?

In Japan, women and politics is an under-researched area in gender research as well as in political research. Only a handful of researchers are involved in this area. The Fusae Ichikawa Memorial Association[2] (1991, 1995, 1999a, 1999b, 2003) disseminates data on female legislators, but academic research grounded on scientific method and analysis is scarce (Oyama and Kunihiro 2007). Despite this scarcity, existing studies have importantly pointed several characteristics of women's underrepresentation in Japan, particularly the effects of the electoral system, political parties and political traits of women (Iwamoto 2007; Kawato 2007; Ogai 2000, 2003, 2005, 2007).

In 1999, the Fusae Ichikawa Memorial Association (1999b) conducted a survey on women legislators in the national parliaments and local assemblies and interviewed some of these women, as well as representatives of political parties, leaders of women's organizations and officials in charge of gender equality policies. This pioneering study attempts to explain the mechanisms that constrain women's political participation. The study emphasizes socio-cultural factors such as androcentric public consciousness and the gendered division of labour, factors related to political parties (their reluctance of recruiting women), the lack of measures such as a quota system or positive action in politics as well as the lack of foundations or private funds to support women candidates.

Regarding women's underrepresentation in the House of Representatives, Park (2007) reviews existing studies on women's political participation in Japan, the United States and South Korea, and summarizes that four factors determine women's underrepresentation in politics: (1) contenders, (2) selectorates, (3) electorates and (4) opportunity structures. First, when women as contenders run for office, their motivation and resources are key for their election. Second, 'selectorates' or those who select candidates refer to recruitment or selection in party politics such as formal and informal practices and power politics (between internal groupings) within a party. Also the media preferences constitute an important aspect of this second factor. Third, electorates vote for their preferred candidates. Fourth, opportunity structures refer to the electoral system and the party system, affecting all the previous three factors (Norris 1993; Patzelt 1999). Accordingly, women's weak motivation to run for office (e.g. weak political consciousness, heavy burden of family responsibilities in the sexual division of labour, lack of private funds to support women candidates), reluctance of recruiting women within political parties, voters' gender bias or androcentric public consciousness and political opportunities limited for women's political engagement such as the electoral system which is for example advantageous for an incumbent and the lack of a quota system (see Fusae Ichikawa Memorial Association 1999b; Mikanagi 2000).

Constraints caused by the electoral system and the recruitment practices in political parties are stressed in other studies as well (Kubo 1995; Oyama 2003; on the effect of incumbency, see also Oyama 2004).[3] The electoral system was changed several times in Japan. In the post-war election in 1946, 39 women were elected for the House of Representatives. It is assumed that this was because of the electoral system at that time in which voters were allowed to choose two candidates and therefore many voters chose at least one female candidate. After this system was replaced by the proportional representation system in 1947, clearly few women were elected. Recruitment practices in party politics are often cited as another constrain for women's political participation, because women are few and, if they exist, are marginalized within a party.

While these studies focus on institutional aspects, other studies discuss women's underrepresentation in the context of the sexual division of labour in the society. Kawano (1995) examined social backgrounds of female legislators and found that their occupational background was very limited to 'creative' jobs such as teachers and journalists, compared to male legislators, and some were even unemployed in the past (housewife). This suggests that women's limited participation in paid work may be related to that in institutional politics, as the public–private divide prevails in the society overall. Though this is an interesting point, Maeda (2007) found no effect of occupation on women's political participation in his study of the relation between the sexual division of labour and individual political behaviour. Analysing data of the Japanese General Social Survey (JGSS), he found that women who are married and have children are more likely to be politically active and identified that social networks other than kin and occupation (e.g. friends and neighbours) have strong effect on women's political participation. This suggests that in Japanese society where the public–private divide prevails, women might have developed a path towards their political activism totally different from that of their male counterparts. Namely, Maeda's study implies that the division of labour promotes the formation of gender-specific social networks, which may uniquely constrain *and* promote women's political participation.

All these studies concern women's underrepresentation and discuss its reasons. While every point mentioned appears important, there is at least one clear deficit in research. Namely, it is not clear why and how some women become political, while a majority of women remain not active in politics, some are engaged in the public office. In existing research, women's weak political consciousness (Mikanagi 2000; Pharr 1981) and the importance of political experience are mentioned (Gertzog 1995; Park 2007). But these studies done by political scientists tend to overlook the importance of politicization, the process by which one develops political consciousness and eventually political ambition to become a legislator. Such process is vital for individuals to engage themselves in political activities. When and how this process occurs depends on individual biographies, but experience of political activities appears to be significant. Experience of activities in a political party, electoral campaigns and the government (e.g. as a bureaucrat, a minister) may be an important step towards the politicization. In the case of women, Kawano (1995, see also Gertzog 1995) mentions the importance of a women-specific political path through marriage. This means that women who were not politically active can be politicized because they married politically active men. This is an interesting point that looks at family as a place of resources for women's political participation, though Kawano did not adequately analyse in which way women become politicized through marriage. However, it is known in Japan that this path through marriage is effective particularly when a woman succeeds her husband's constituency. What is not fully clear yet is how marriage can be a resource in cases of women married to husbands who are not politicians.

A STUDY OF FEMALE LEGISLATORS IN TOKYO

In the previous section, we reviewed and discussed studies about women's political participation and underrepresentation. Before examining the process of politicization of female legislators in Japan, we will explain the data I use for the analysis.

Data come from our study about married female legislators in the local assemblies in Tokyo.[4] We conducted qualitative interviews with seven female legislators in the local Tokyo assemblies in 2010; two of them were members of the Tokyo Metropolitan Assembly and five were members of three Tokyo Special Ward Assemblies (Chiyoda-Ward, Koto-Ward and Setagaya-Ward). In this chapter, I conduct biographical analysis of only the members of the Metropolitan Assembly because of space limitations.

In interviews, we asked them to tell us about how they became a legislator including their previous political activities. We also asked them about the division of labour between their partners and themselves and their communication with their husbands when they decided to run for office. For example, we were interested in learning whether their partners were for or against the idea of their candidacy, if any, what kind of support they received and/or in which they negotiated with their partner.

In the analysis, I identified and focused on two themes that emerged in data: (1) politicization of the respondents and (2) gender equality in private life. First, regarding politicization, previous studies point out that women tend to be reluctant and less politically ambitious in running for office than men. Fox and Lawless (2003; see also Lawless and Fox 2005) found a clear gender difference in political ambition in their study on an eligible pool such as lawyers in the United States. They asked potential candidates such as lawyers who are most likely to run for office ('eligible pool') about their political ambition, because there is an assumption that there are few women eligible for candidacy and thus there are few women than men among electoral candidates. Their finding suggests that there are eligible women, but there are not many women as men who have enough political ambition to run for office. In case of female legislators, they need to become politically conscious and develop political ambition so that they can make a decision to run for office at all. To examine this politicization or when and how they become politicized, it is important to look at their biographies. Second, regarding gender equality in private life, we drew on studies by Burns et al. (1997, 2001), which found that women who actively engage in social and political activities tend to have egalitarian relationship with their husbands or partners and thus be able to use such relationship as a resource for their participation in public life. In this regard, it is also interesting to see whether this finding generated from a study on women's political participation in the United States can apply to the case of Japan. These two points served as a guiding framework for analysis.[5]

'HOW I BECAME A LEGISLATOR': CASE STUDIES OF TWO FEMALE LEGISLATORS IN TOKYO

Both Ms. A and Ms. B were elected for the Metropolitan Assembly for the first time in 2009. They were both married around the time of the 2009 election, and at the time of the interview, they have so far taken different paths as a woman, a wife, a mother and a political activist. They represent two very different cases in terms of family structure, gender roles at home and political experience. There are, however, several commonalities across these cases, as our analysis below shows.

Case 1: Ms. A and the Seikatsusha Network (Net)

Ms. A is 54 years old. She decided to run for election at least six months before the 2009 election. She had lived for 18 years in her district, with her husband, a university professor of economics, and two children. She became a fulltime housewife when her husband got a tenured position at a university. It was her decision that she wanted to be involved more in childcare. She also wanted to make friends with other mothers. Since then, she has been solely responsible for domestic work. Her friends and acquaintances asked her to run for office. Prior to this, she had no experience running for election, but she was active in communal activities.

As a housewife, she was not interested in politics or any civil activities including PTA. Yet she experienced a turning point in her life about seven or eight years ago, when her second child entered junior high school. Experiencing a transition in her relationship with her son and her involvement in childcare, she suddenly felt the necessity to start something new. At the same time, she was interested in forming new social relationships not as a mother or someone's wife. One day, she noticed an article in a municipal newsletter on an upcoming symposium on the city's dialogue with citizens about its future. She went to this symposium. Afterwards she joined various working groups within and outside the city administration. Such was the very beginning of her public engagement in the area of communal activities.

Running for office gradually became an option for her. She developed certain ambivalences through her communal activities. Despite having much fun and a certain sense of achievement gained through these activities, she faced some difficulties in getting broad support (e.g. from companies) and enough funding for activities and got demoralized. Still, she could not imagine becoming a legislator. She turned down a few offers to run for office. Soon, however, she changed her mind. In 2008, the Seikatsusha Network (Net)[6] asked her to run for office. This time it was different. Her encounter with Ms. C, at the time a legislator from the Net, gave her a new impression of politics. She liked Ms. C's non-authoritative way of work. She also liked other members of the Net (mostly mothers and wives) and a core principle of the Network, that is, the idea of rotation called the agent (*dairinin*) system.[7] The district in which Ms. A ran for election is an area in which the Net has a strong organizational base. The Net has kept a seat in this district since 1985. Eventually Ms. A succeeded Ms. C and became the fourth *dairinin* in this district.

Her decision to run for office was made only after she talked with her family. Support from her husband was particularly important. He assured his support if she 'thinks it is a plus for her'. He also encouraged her by saying 'it is a rare opportunity for you' to be asked to run for office. Her children did not protest either. The overall support from her family seemed to be fostered during the period of her communal activities. Her family did not appear to see her political transition from an active citizen to a would-be legislator as something special.

In election, Ms. A received much support from her husband as well as the Network. He commented on her speech and gave her mental support. Also, he gave advice on the basis of his expertise and knowledge as an economist.

Case 2: Ms. B and the Communist Party

Ms. B is also in her fifties. She married her husband about 20 years ago, the same year she ran for office for the first time. It was a ward assembly election. Two years later, she gave birth to her first child. Two months later, she went back to her work as a legislator. She always wanted to pursue her economic independence. She wanted to marry only after she achieved such independence. She met her husband through activities of the Communist Party. Her husband proposed marriage by saying 'I want to support your legislative activity'. He therefore took all the responsibility for domestic work.

Ms. B started working on disability issues during high school. Upon graduation, she went on to vocational school to obtain a certificate in childcare. She became a nursery school staff for children with disabilities. She joined the Communist Party in her mid-twenties. She felt it was tough to achieve something in her activities on disability issues on the individual level and thought it was necessary to be a part of an organization in order to cause a fundamental social change.

When she first ran for office in the late 1980s, it was not her decision. The party asked her to do so. She agreed more than a year before the election year. She had lived and worked in the district. Her main resources came from her party. Though it was her first election as a candidate, she had worked for elections of her peers from the party before. This was very helpful. Nevertheless, her lack of experience was the most difficult problem she had. She also had some financial problems and worried about the possibility of losing an election and how she might earn a living in case she was defeated. Fortunately, she was elected in her first run. She finished six terms altogether (22 years). Then she transferred from a ward assembly to the metropolitan assembly for the upcoming metropolitan election in 2009. Again, the party prompted her.

When Ms. B was asked to run for office for the first time, she declined this request. She joined the party without any ambition to become a politician. Eventually she changed her mind. She felt stuck in her non-legislative activities. Suddenly it became an option for her to run for election. She thought she could improve the working conditions of social workers and promote the interests of people with disabilities if she became a legislator.

Since her husband married her to support her activity as a legislator, he always supported her election. He not only did household chores and childcare, but also assisted with her campaign activities, for example, by putting up posters.

WHAT DETERMINES WOMEN'S DECISION TO RUN FOR OFFICE: IMPORTANCE OF POLITICIZATION AND AMBIVALENCE OF GENDER EQUALITY

Ms. A and Ms. B are both in their fifties and are wives and mothers. As 'political women', they show different levels of experience. Ms. A became politically aware rather late in her middle adulthood. She began to get involved in communal activities, after her second child entered a junior high school. She was already over 40. Ms. B began her social work for the disabled during high school as a volunteer. She later became a social worker. She was in her early twenties when she became a member of the Communist Party. Though there is a difference between just being a party member and running for office or working as a lawmaker, one usually needs to have a certain level of political consciousness to enter a political party.

Ms. A and Ms. B are also different in their perception of gender roles. While Ms. A accepted traditional gender roles and became a fulltime housewife willingly, Ms. B delayed her marriage until she became independent economically and mentally. Ms. B never thought of becoming a homemaker. She eventually married a man who was willing to take charge of household chores. On the contrary, in the case of Ms. A, the sexual division of household labour remained largely unchallenged despite her political engagement. This suggests that traditional gender roles at home may or may not be undermined through women's transition from the private to the public sphere and their eventual involvement in public life. In other words, at least in Japan, gender equality at home may not necessarily contribute to women's political participation, unlike what Burn and her colleagues argued in their study on the United States.

Apart from these differences, the political biographies of Ms. A and Ms. B show an interesting commonality with regard to their decision to run for office. Both were already active in local politics, when they were first asked to run for office, and both of them declined at first. Neither of them had any political ambition to run for office. To develop political ambition, two factors were important for both Ms. A and Ms. B: Support from spouse and perceived limits in their non-legislative political activities.

Both felt that they received significant support from their husbands. Our analysis, however, found that which type of support they received varied. The husband of Ms. A contributed to her campaign mainly by sharing his knowledge and expertise as an expert of economics. The husband of Ms. B supported her by playing a central role in the practical aspects of her election as well as continuing to do domestic work during the campaign. After the election, he also executed his role as a 'legislator's spouse' by going to local events and building social relationships with the local people for her. This is not the case with Ms. A's husband.

Both respondents also felt the need to go beyond the domain of their previous, non-legislative activity. To achieve something beyond the 'limits' of non-legislative political activities and cause effect on social and political change, they started to think about running for office and working as a legislator as an option for them. This suggests a 'lagging' nature of politicization of Japanese women and the importance of non-legislative political activism, as a kind of preparation, for Japanese women's decision to run for office.

CONCLUSION

This chapter concerns women's underrepresentation in the parliament. We look at the case of Japanese female legislators to examine how they become politicized and decide to run for office. We confirmed the importance of politicization, particularly the development of political consciousness through non-legislative activities process as a kind of preparation for women's decision to run for office. Politicization can be seen as a key factor for women's decision to run for office. In our analysis of biographical data of female legislators, perceived limits of previous non-legislative political activity for social or political change played a significant role. What contradicts previous studies is that egalitarian marital relationship is not a necessity for married women's political participation. In case of those who used to be fulltime housewives, the sexual division of household labour may not change through their candidacy.

In other words, gender equality at home is not a prerequisite for women's involvement in public life. This may be an ambivalent finding for those who are committed to promote gender equality in the society, because, for many, 'more women in the parliament' means or at least has meant for long 'more gender equality'. However, this may not be surprising, if one considers the fact that not all women in the parliament behave or act for gender equality. This has become clear as female legislators increased in number, though still few. Gender imbalance in the parliament remains a key issue in gender equality policies. At the same, it is our urgent task to discuss women's political participation in the context of such ambivalence.

NOTES

1. Japan's score and rank for the category health is 0.9869 and 34 respectively. See World Economic Forum (2012: 11).
2. An organization established by Fusae Ichikawa (1883–1981), an independent politician served as a member of the House of Councillors for many years (1953–1971, 1974–1981).
3. Some studies (e.g. Oyama 2007) reaffirm the regional or local manifestation of these structural and institutional constraints. Apart from that, there are several innovative initiatives taken on the grassroots level to overcome these constraints on the local level of politics. Iwamoto (2001) examined various initiatives including the campaign of 'Let's send women to the assemblies' in the 1999 local assembly election. Ogai (2003) examined women's mock assemblies introduced in several prefectures.
4. It was a joint study with Naoko Shima and Tokuko Ogai. The study was partially funded by a group research grant program of the Tokai Gender Institute (applicant: Naoko Shima).
5. I analysed data in a conventional way of qualitative content analysis. For method of analysis, see Ritchie and Lewis (2003).
6. Net is a local party or a political group that exists in Tokyo and some other prefectures such as Kanagawa and Chiba. It emerged out of the *Seikatsu*

Kurabu, consumer cooperatives that operate independently on the prefectural level. The Net started sending women members to the local assemblies in the 1990s.

7. According to this principle, each agent should have three terms or 12 years at maximum. In other words, each agent should not be re-elected more than two times. This principle was introduced in the Net to increase the level of political participation among ordinary citizens by sending as many people as possible. Such a re-election limitation is rare in Japan.

REFERENCES

Burns, N., Schlozman, K.L. and Verba, S. (1997). The Public Consequences of Private Inequality: Family Life and Citizen Participation. *The American Political Science Review 91*(2), pp. 373–389.

—- (2001). *The Private Roots of Public Action: Gender, Equality, Political Participation*. Cambridge, MA: Harvard University Press.

Connell, R.W. (1987). *Gender and Power*. Stanford: Stanford University Press.

Fox, R.L. and Lawless, J.L. (2003). Family Structure, Sex-Role Socialization, and the Decision to Run for Office. *Women and Politics 24*(4), pp. 19–48.

Fusae Ichikawa Memorial Association (2003). *Josei Sansei Shiryoshu 2003 Nenban: Zen Chiho Gikai Josei Giin no Genjo* (Local Assemblies Handbook of Data on Japanese Women in Political Life 2003). Tokyo: The Fusae Ichikawa Memorial Association.

Fusae Ichikawa Memorial Association (Ed.) (1999b). *Josei no Seisaku Kettei Katei Sankaku ni kansuru Kadai to Taio ni tsuite no Chosa: Sangiin Dai San Tokubetsu Chosa Shitsu Itaku Chosa Hokoku Sho* (A Study on Challenges of and Measures for Women's Participation in Policy Making: A Research Report for the House of the Councillors, the Third Special Research Unit). Tokyo: The Fusae Ichikawa Memorial Association.

Gertzog, I.N. (1995). *Congressional Women: Their Recruitment, Integration, and Behaviour*. 2nd ed. Westport, CT: Praeger.

Inter-Parliamentary Union (2013). Women in Parliament: World Classification. Available at http://www.ipu.org/wmn-e/classif.htm (accessed on 5 May 2013).

Iwamoto, M. (2001). Nen Toitsu Chiho Senkyo ni okeru Josei no Yakushin: Mutoha o Chushin ni (The Advancement of Women in the Unified Local Elections of 1999). *Seisaku Kagaku 8*(3), pp. 21–38.

—- (2007). Kuota ga Ronjirarenai Nihon Seiji no Fushigi: Josei no Seijiteki Daihyo wa Sekai de Donoyoni Ronjirarete iruka (No Discussion of a Quota System as a Wonder of Japanese Politics). In S. Kawato and H. Yamamoto (Eds), *Seiji Sankaku to Jenda*. Sendai: Tohoku Daigaku Shuppankai, pp. 177–210.

Kawano, G. (1995). Erito Josei no Haishutsu Ruto ni Kansuru Kosatu: Shugiin Giin o Jirei toshite (A Study of Recruitment Route of Elite Women: The Case of

Members of the House of Representatives). *Kyoiku Shakaigaku Kenkyu* (Journal of Educational Sociology) *56*, pp. 119–137.

Kawato, S. (2007). Nihon ni okeru Josei no Seiji Shinshutsu (Women's Political Advancement in Japan). In S. Kawato and H. Yamamoto (Eds), *Seiji Sankaku to Jenda*. Sendai: Tohoku Daigaku Shuppankai, pp. 245–263.

Kubo, K. (1995). Josei Sanseiken Jitsugen 50 Nen: Chiho Gikai eno Josei no Shinshutsu Jokyo o Kenshosuru (50 Years of Women's Suffrage: An Analysis of Women's Advancement in the Local Assemblies). *Toshi Mondai 86*(7), pp. 83–96.

Lawless, J.L. and Fox, R.L. (2005). *It Takes a Candidate: Why Women Don't Run for Office*. New York: Cambridge University Press.

Maeda, Y. (2007). Seibetsu Yakuwai Bungyo to Seiji Sanka (Gender Roles and Political Participation). In A. Nagai and S. Matsuda (Eds), *Taito na Fufu wa Shiawase ka*. Tokyo: Keiso Shobo, pp. 97–118.

Mikanagi, Y. (2000). Jenda no Seijigaku (Political Research of Gender). In K. Kaku and H. Maruyama (Eds), *Nyu Poritikusu no Seijigaku* (Political Research of New Politics). Tokyo: Minerva, pp. 95–115.

Norris, P. (1993). Conclusions: Comparing Legislative Recruitment. In J. Lovenduski and P. Norris (Eds), *Gender and Party Politics*. London: Sage, pp. 309–330.

Ogai, T. (2000). *Chiho Gikai ni okeru Josei Giin no 'Keisei' to Ishiki no Henyo: Seikatsusha Nettowaku no Dairinin no Jirei yori* (The 'Formation' of Woman Politicians in the Local Assemblies and Changing Consciousness: The Case of Dairinin of the Tokyo Seikatsusha Network). Dissertation, Ochanomizu University, Tokyo.

—- (2003). Josei Mogi Gikai toiu Josei Seisaku: Onnatachi no Keiken no Seijika Katei (Women's Mock Assemblies as a Women's Policy: The Process of Politicization of Women's Experiences). *Nenpo Seijigaku*, pp. 113–137.

—- (2005). *Jenda to Seiji Sanka* (Gender and Political Participation). Tokyo: Seori Shobo.

—- (2007). Josei Giin no Yukosei ni Kansuru Ichi Kosatsu: Josei Giin Kenkyu no Genjo to Tenbo kara Mieta Mono (An Analysis of the Validity of Women Politicians: The Status-Quo of Research and Its Future). In S. Kawato and H. Yamamoto (Eds), *Seiji Sankaku to Jenda*. Sendai: Tohoku Daigaku Shuppankai, pp. 211–243.

Ogburn, W.F. (1922). *Social Change with Respect to Culture and Original Nature*. New York: B.W. Huebsch.

Oyama, N. (2003). Seito, Toha no Josei Kohosha ni Oyobosu Eikyo: 2003 Nen Do Fuken Gikai Giin Senkyo no Bunseki kara (Impact of Political Parties and Party Affiliation on Women Candidates). *Tokai Daigaku Kiyo Bungakubu 80*, pp. 35–53.

—- (2004). Josei to Senkyo Kankyo: Kohosha Tokusei, Chiiki Tokusei, Senkyoku Tokusei no Bunseki (Women and Electoral Environments: Features of Candidates, Regions, and Districts). *Tokai Daigaku Kiyo Bungakubu 81*, pp. 17–35.

— (2007). Josei no Seiji Sankaku o Sokushin, Sogaisuru Kozo, Seidoteki Yoin (Structural and Institutional Factors that Promote or Constrain Women's Political Participation). *Tokai Daigaku Kiyo Bungakubu 88*, pp. 1–26.

Oyama, N. and Kunihiro, Y. (2007). *Seiji Arina ni okeru Jenda Kozo no Kenkyu (Kadai Bango 16510203) Heisei 16 Nendo—Heisei 18 Nendo Kagaku Kenkyuhi Hojokin (Kiban Kenkyu (c) Kenkyu Seika Hokokusho* (A Report on the Achievements of a Study on Gender Structure in the Political Arena, Funded by the Scientific Research Fund, 2004–2008).

Park, I.K. (2007). Josei Shugiin Giin no Seiji Hoju. *Kokuritsu Josei Kyouiku Kaikan Kenkyu Janaru* (Journal of the National Women's Education Center of Japan). 11 August 2007, pp. 95–102.

Patzelt, W.J. (1999). Recruitment and Retention in Western European Parliaments. *Legislative Studies Quarterly 24*(2), pp. 239–279.

Pharr, S.J. (1981). *Political Women in Japan: The Search for a Place in Political Life*. Berkeley: University of California Press.

Ritchie, J. and Lewis, J. (2003). *Qualitative Research Practice: A Guide for Social Science Students and Researchers*. London: Sage.

World Economic Forum (2012). *The Global Gender Gap Report 2012*. Geneva, Switzerland. Available at http://www3.weforum.org/docs/wef_gender gap_report_2012.pdf (accessed on 4 May 2013).

CHAPTER 8

Women and Expression in Japanese Society

Harumi Hosono

THE HISTORICAL POSITION OF JAPANESE WOMEN

The grammatical system of Western languages identifies genders and is consistent with the dichotomy between the genders. That distinction has also been applied to the standards of value, placing women in an inferior status and as a remote position from God in the spiritual world. Many societies in Asia also give inferior status to women regardless of their religious differences with the West, although their cultural backgrounds may be different from each other.

To give an overview, Japanese spiritual culture is grounded with the ideology of ancient Japanese polytheism, with external influence from Buddhism and Confucianism. Geographically, Japan consists of large and small islands, exposed on its eastern side to the sea, located on the far end of the region and under the influence of culturally advanced regions to the west. It is fair to say that Japan established its own cultural system by processing outside influences and maturing them internally, with little external dissemination.

There were a number of female emperors in ancient Japan, particularly between the end of the sixth century and the end of the eighth century. It is said that they assumed the positions due to a lack of male successors despite their ineligibility for politics (Araki 1999; Yoshe 2002). The empresses, who are the emperors' wives, were also involved in politics with their husbands and had a say to a certain extent (Araki 1999).

The ancient Japanese idea of religion was polytheistic rather than monotheistic devotion to a supreme god. A myth compiled as a chronicle in the eighth century refers to the Sun Goddess as the supreme ancestral deity of the Imperial Family. The idea thought to have taken root at this time is far removed from the view that women were shameful or inferior. There is a conflict between the Imperial system and the Confucian principles, and it is assumed that the introduction of the myth into the Imperial Family chronicle was a complicated process. No historical consensus was formed in Japanese society about the gender of the divinity, but it can be pointed out that the reference of the goddess suggests that women were not excluded from the concept of maintaining order and the social establishment.

It is against this backdrop that Buddhist and Confucian views of women being inferior were introduced. This probably led to the view of men being superior developing around the ninth century, leading to the establishment of a society that views women as inferior by the tenth or eleventh century, and the marital system of men visiting women changed into one in which women move into male households (Sekiguchi 1993).

By this time, there was no rule by a woman emperor as before. Instead, uxorial nepotism was established with an emperor having many wives who were ranked by the financial and other contributions of their families in aristocratic status. The system is vividly described in *The Tale of Genji* written by a woman named Murasaki Shikibu in the eleventh century. Concepts that indicate the inferior position of women began to prevail around that time: the teaching that women to follow their fathers, husbands and sons after their husbands died; the idea that women cannot be reborn into the five sublime existences in Buddhism due to their five defects and a rule that gives husbands the right to leave their wives if they commit one of the seven failures: being disobedient to their fathers-in-law, sterile, talkative, committing theft, being lewd, jealous or having a serious disease. The three ways of obedience and the seven failures are based on Confucianism, while the idea of the five failures comes from Buddhism.

Japan had no history of being invaded by other countries and had very limited contact with the rest of the world as it passed from the ancient period to the mediaeval and early modern times.

When Japan embarked on foreign diplomacy in the late nineteenth century, it adopted the restructured, modernized emperor system but both the Sun Goddess and the emperor were seen as representing the people's parent with no identified gender (Tanasawa 2007).

To sum up, women's status in Japan remained inferior throughout the periods referred to in the literature, but it declined gradually.

WOMEN'S CHARACTERS AND LITERATURE

Now, I would like to discuss the situation in Japan relating to women's expression of their feelings and situations in written language instead of the spoken language. Like in other parts of East Asia, kanji characters were introduced to Japan from China, a culturally advanced nation, and everyone in power learned kanji during the period from around the fifth to the seventh century. This contributed to the significant centralization and the strengthening of the state system. In the eighth century, a chronicle was compiled to justify the emperor authority system, which had been consolidated through civil war.

Kanji is quite ideographic, with each monosyllable character representing one word. They are sometimes called *logograms*. This system is suited for writing Chinese, which is an isolating language with no inflection. Nevertheless, the Japanese and Chinese are linguistically quite different: Japanese is an agglutinative – or multiple morphemes – language, while Chinese is an isolation language. Therefore, using kanji in Japan in those days meant writing a composition in Chinese, which is a foreign language. What is characteristic of the written language in Japan is that original phonetic characters based on kanji were gradually developed for the Japanese language from around the ninth and tenth centuries. Also around that time, two kinds of phonetic characters, namely hiragana and katakana, came about spontaneously. This made it possible to put spoken Japanese into writing and led to the development of diverse forms of expression in Japanese such as myths, legends and poetry. Later, it became common to write Japanese in a various mix of the three characters – kanji, hiragana and katakana. This led to the development of a wide variety of expression in written language, featuring kanji-dominated writing (male writing) and hiragana-dominated writing (female writing) as well as a mix of both. This is likely to have contributed to the high literacy in Japan to a certain extent, as I will discuss later.

It is believed that hiragana and katakana began to be used widely in the tenth century or later. Hiragana, derived from kanji, was presented in a calligraphic style with curved lines. The soft, elegant appearance was seen as feminine, and the script was widely used by women. There are probably few such examples in the rest of the world.

In those days, kanji originating in China and all-kanji passages were given a special status as the formal written language – as opposed to everyday Japanese – and was basically supposed to be the characters and language for men. It should be pointed out that 'woman's hand' does not mean that hiragana was used only by women but that women were allowed to share it with men, whereas kanji was only for men. Kana was used in private situations such as when writing letters and poems to friends and family, and between couples, and therefore was used both by men and women. The double culture in education – with kanji and kana given different roles for men and women – was to continue right up until modern times.

It is not the case, however, that women did not use characters before that time. In ancient Japan, women were not completely excluded from politics, as I mentioned earlier. With no phonogram in the writing system at the time, women in high positions were able to use kanji and all-kanji passages. Not only Chinese-based political documents but also many Japanese poems in kanji remain from that period.

As I stated earlier, male-dominant society had been established by around the tenth or eleventh century and this coincided with the period in which hiragana was used widely. It may also be linked to the descriptions such as 'a man's hand' and 'a woman's hand'. It is significant that women were not excluded from the world of characters. Also, it should not be overlooked that there were many cases in which women were exposed to political developments as the empress or a lady-in-waiting at the inner palace and were able to write about them in a woman's hand. They were in a position to be involved in, or observe, the men's world and had the means for expression. This led to women contributing many works to Japanese literature, including tales, diaries and short poems.

To recap some of the features of the Japanese language I have discussed so far: it is as an original language that can be written with characters; Japan is a geographically coherent island nation; the introduction of foreign languages was not very active; there are dialects but their regional differences are not too wide and they do not deviate from the Japanese language.

EDUCATION

The literacy rate in Japan was already at the highest level in the world in Edo period, even before modernization began. In the last years of the Edo period in the mid-nineteenth century, it is said that the literacy rate of the warrior class was nearly 100 per cent and about half of the common men were able to read and write in Edo where the government was located. The number is almost 100 per cent today. It is not 100 per cent because there are people who are unable to learn characters due to mental disability and other reasons and not because of poverty. In today's Japan, poverty is not directly linked to literacy but is closely connected to the disparity in access to higher education and employment opportunities.

In the last half of early modern times, since the eighteenth century, literacy education became accessible, not only to the ruling class but relatively wealthy tradesmen and the common people, thereby laying the groundwork for educating Japanese people prior to the modern education system established in the Meiji period. At that time, the warrior class was given Confucianism-based education in kanji and all-kanji passages on the principles of ruling, while the common classes were mainly taught to read and write hiragana. A two-tier education in line with the two kinds of characters of kanji and hiragana is also observed here. By that time, dualism between kanji and hiragana had developed into dualism between sophisticated characters and plain entry-level characters. Education in kanji and all-kanji passages was given by an organization established in each province, or han, to educate the sons of the warrior class. There was no such system for the common people, but private schools were spontaneously created to give them basic education in reading, writing and arithmetic (on abacus), or the 3R's. The 3R's became an essential education particularly in cities, as the merchant class grew wealthy in early modern times. Aside from the warrior class, the literacy rate remained low, particularly among the common classes in farming, mountain and fishing villages, and it differed widely among regions and lifestyles.

Those private schools also taught girls, and many of them were able to read and write. In the warrior class and the former nobilities, women were not educated in kanji or all-kanji passages like men, or in reading, writing and arithmetic like in the common classes, but were given an original form of education based on the classic materials in women's literature from the tenth century. In the upper class, education for men in kanji and all-kanji passages and for women in Japanese passages both used classics as the subject matter to teach spiritual ideologies and normative culture. This was in contrast to practical education offered to the common classes. It was the standard at the time to give women a subordinate status in both the upper and common classes.

Starting in the Meiji period, a centralized education system was designed and implemented across the nation as a cornerstone for promoting modernization in Japan. Active discussions were made about which language should be used in primary education and about what kind of standards should be established on the use of characters, but English or any languages other than Japanese has never been the main language for education. This seems to have come about because primary education was already established on a significant scale and the system of writing Japanese characters was already in place, as I discussed earlier.

In modern times, men compete to pursue Western studies in Western languages, and also extend enlightened views and education to women. Men of culture who learned Christianity and Western studies discussed expanding women's rights in female enlightenment magazines. Kitamura Tokoku, an activist in the movement, wrote a love letter to a woman who was to be his wife later that he would respect her character and views; and Shimazaki Toson, a novelist, ardently talked to his niece how a woman in the new age should live. But the former later treated his wife coldly and the latter impregnated his niece. They advocated the extension of women's rights but their acts trampled on women's rights, and there were discrepancies between their words and deeds.

This indicates that men in those days were rushing for modernization and understood Western individualism only theoretically and superficially.

I happened to see material that said the literacy rate in some north area in India is under 80 per cent and is higher than the national average and among the highest in the country. I would like to ask for your advice on whether the data is correct or not, but I imagine that the situation is quite different from Japan in terms of dialects, characters, the influence of English and other aspects. There are specific circumstances due to social, cultural and linguistic conditions, and they should be recognized in developing a more effective style of education.

WOMEN'S EXPRESSION AND PRESENTATION OF THEIR INTENTIONS

I said earlier that hiragana was available to women in Japan in old times. I would now like to introduce *The Tosa Diary* by Kino Tsurayuki. He is a man of culture and said to have written the first substantial composition in hiragana in the early tenth century. In it, he claims to be a woman and says at the opening that she will write a diary that is supposed to be only written by men. It sheds light on a multi-layered paradoxical issue concerning gender. In the early tenth century, hiragana was created alongside kanji. Tsurayuki had also compiled a poetry anthology called *The Kokin Wakashu* in hiragana by order of the emperor. He effectively brought hiragana, whose use was limited to private purposes, under the spotlight to parallel kanji with the authority of the emperor. It was also around this time that characters and passages were categorized either as a man's hand or a woman's hand. In this sense, his remark seems to indicate that he took pride in establishing a culture with a woman's hand to equal the world of a man's hand. Many women writers appeared later in the history of the literature and he effectively led them both as a man and as a woman. A woman's hand did not remain in the world of women but developed as a way to express a world that cannot be expressed with a man's hand.

Murasaki Shikibu is believed to have written *The Tale of Genji* about a thousand years ago. It touches on the issue of lineage backed by her profound knowledge of history and keen observation of the political world, even though it is fiction. It presents a view of history that is probably greater than a history book. It states that fiction can describe the truths of human beings better than a history book that only presents facts, putting forth a view of literature that still stands today. It is essential to be able to read kanji and all-kanji passages with a good understanding of the content to create such a tale, but it was detestable for a woman to show off her knowledge of kanji at the time, as their social status had declined from the early ancient period, and it is said she pretended not to know even the simplest kanji characters in her *Murasaki Shikibu Diary*. Women lost opportunities to be actively involved in the important spheres of the community, including politics, but were able to maintain their positions and talents to observe those activities.

Another area of women's expression in hiragana at the time was a fixed form of verses called waka, which had existed from the early ancient times. Waka at the time, however, used rather emotional expressions in describing inner voices and emphasized the description of lament, rather than a resolution to their situation, as well as the sense of solidarity, or 'a-wa-re', in sharing lament. They could not overcome their situation even if they were able to describe their delicate feelings through waka. Hiragana is a phonogram linked to sounds in the first place and was therefore suited to express the suppressed inner voices of women such as grief and resignation. So, were those women able to express anything using their characters? They may have been able to gain an objective viewpoint to understand their situation and develop critical viewpoints through writing. Nevertheless, they often resorted to euphemism and poetic lyricism instead of direct expressions, thereby contributing to the establishment of the social consensus on the value of 'not saying' and the development of a culture where they controlled their speech and preferring not to express anything. Under this form of expression, kabuki, which is a culture of the common class, plays offering catharsis by describing grief in stressful situations and remained popular until early modern times.

My discussion so far has been mainly focused on expressions in a written language and now I would like to move on to the issue of expression in voices. As I mentioned earlier, being talkative was one of the reasons that would justify a man leaving his wife. A duty to follow has been set as the top virtue of women to just follow since the view of male supremacy was established in Japanese society. Both Buddhism and Confucianism reinforce the view and there also seem to be many societies with such a standard outside Japan, particularly in Asia. Akiko Jugaku tried to overcome this situation and picked up the elements in the Japanese language that enforce feminine qualities. She presented guidelines for women in farming villages that allows them to say 'no' and to speak out strongly when they have to even to someone whom they find it tough to do so, encouraging a new awareness about expressing their feelings. She wrote about her own personal experiences (Jugaku 1979).

In Japanese society, the value of not talking remains a virtue both among men and women. This comes in many forms, such as not talking because they must not because there is no need to say anything, because they do not know how to say something, because they do not feel like saying anything and so forth. This thinking is widespread and deep-rooted, regardless of the reasons

(Ujiie 1996). As far as we can tell, the standard of respecting modesty and being obedient was in Japanese society at least until pre-modern times, and it was almost a taboo to express your intention using words. In modern times, intellectuals introduced Western individualism but the Japanese style of modesty retained a high moral position revealing a gap between accepted views and personal feelings.

In Japanese society, both men and women have been described in many writings, plays and other forms of art as controlling themselves to be silent rather than openly expressing their dissatisfaction, and having given up showing their anger, replacing it by holding grudges, instead. In general, Japanese people have been accustomed to expressing themselves by turning inward rather than expressing themselves outwardly. Elite military officer and novelist Mori Ogai, who studied in Germany by government order in the early Meiji period, couldn't become accustomed to the Western view of self and described his attitude towards various things as resignation in his essay *Yo ga tachiba*. Karel van Wolferen talks about Japanese people's attitude towards politics and power and finds their passive acceptance of something 'shikata ga-nai' or inescapable (Wolferen 1994). If Japanese people still have underlying sense of resignation and harbour doubts about reforming the existing situation, it will be necessary not only to improve their skills of expression, but also to identify what they can change through conveying thoughts and feelings. In this way, they can determine their stance towards self-expression.

Calling attention to the importance of communication has been a relatively recent development in the history of Japanese culture, and it seems we are coming to a time when we need to learn how to express ourselves appropriately and effectively.

OUTSTANDING ISSUES

It is crucial for women who are in an inferior position in society to have an opportunity to raise their voices to overturn the status quo. Nevertheless, they are often subjected to punishment for such actions. It is not easy for women to speak out to begin with, and they sometimes have to risk their own lives in doing so. In many cases, these silent women do not recognize the need and the significance of expressing their views.

Here's a recent example of women protesting against unfavourable treatment, one that drew wide public attention: 15 of Japan's top female judokas filed a joint complaint with the Japanese Olympic Committee against their coaching staff and the coaching system. They said they were subjected to violent coaching method and harassed with abusive words during the training for the Olympics. They complained to the All Japan Judo Federation, but the situation did not improve and so they filed a complaint with the JOC. The names of the 15 athletes have not been announced, due to concerns that their rights may not be fully guaranteed. A woman, who is a former Olympian, said their names should be made public, but withdrew her remark shortly afterward. This indicated a deep-rooted problem. That is, there is still a prevailing notion among the people in Japanese athletic communities and at schools and other organizations that they have to consider the feelings of their superiors when they decide what to do, and that they have to prepare for punishment if they raise objections.

Looking to the future, it is imperative to find ways that will enable women to have their say, without hesitation, in spoken words or written languages, or even online, so they can make meaningful improvements to their lives.

REFERENCES

Araki, T. (1999). *Kanosei to shiteno jotei* (Women Emperor System in Possibility). Tokyo: Aoki Shoten.

Jugaku, A. (1979). *Nihongo to onna* (The Japanese Language and Women). Tokyo: Iwanami Shoten.

Sekiguchi, H. (1993). *Nihon kodai kon-inshi no kenkyu* (The History of Ancient Japanese Marriage System). 2 volumes, Tokyo: Hanawa Shobo.

Tanasawa, N. (2007). *'Kokutai no hongi' dokkai: Seiyo no sekaisei, Nihon no tokushusei* (Reading about '*Kokutai no hongi*': Globalism in the West and Particularity in Japan). Published in *France kara miru Nihon gender-shi* (Modern Japanese History from France), Tokyo: Shin-yo-sha.

Ujiie, Y. (1996). *Gengo bunkagaku no shiten: Iwanai shakai to kotoba no chikara* (A Point of View from Socio-Linguistic in Japanese: The Silent Society and the Power of Words). Tokyo: Ohfu.

Wolferen, K. (1994). *Ningen o kofuku ni shinai Nihon to yu shisutemu* (The System Called Japan that Does Not Make People Happy). Tokyo: The Mainichi Newspapers Publishers.

Yoshe, A. (2002). *Kodai josei-ron no kako to gennzai* (The Discussion about Ancient Women Emperor System in Past and Present). Published in *Tenno to oken wo kangaeru, Vol. 7: jenda to sabetu* (The Study about the Emperor Authority: Gender and Discrimination). Tokyo: Iwanami Shoten.

CHAPTER 9

Cultural Myths and the Reduction of Human Potential in Development

The Case of the Thai Kathoey

Kittikorn Sankatiprapa

> I do not actually choose to be a show girl. When I was young, I wanted to be a teacher. I saw the children played together and I wanted to play with them … *Apart from a cabaret show ... other jobs are what the society does not allow us to do ... .*
>
> —Voice of a Thai Kathoey in Cabaret business

It is believed that the Thai 'Kathoey' or Thai male to female transgender (MtF) represents a woman's spirit trapped in a male body. Being Kathoey is still considered abnormal and is not included in the mainstream gender discussions in Thailand. Across the world some feminist theories and human rights movements have strived to deconstruct gender, and have shown that the accepted two gender category is unnatural, which means our fixed perception of a two genders – male and female – is not the truth. Still, so far, in many places gender diversity and gender variants are not actually embraced, and the discourse of binary sex still prevails and is deeply implanted in many cultures.

Through the network of socio-cultural power, the Thai Kathoey has been positioned as atypical/abnormal. The myths perpetuated about them have resulted in an unfavourable impact upon their lives and well-being. It is still not largely accepted that they have equal rights and freedom to control their lives, and can live as equal citizens in society. It is inevitable that living happily is possible only for a very few of them. That is because their life is extremely complex and their sexual identities are interwoven with other dimensions such as class, social status, race, ethnicity, economic power, education within a defined social context. Therefore, we need to document and examine their experiences using qualitative research methods to understand the specific situations or discursive context each Kathoey faces. This chapter intends to present Kathoey voices that are hidden in the mainstream of heterosexual discourse. In addition, it is necessary to debate how far the social labelling and the cultural perception of the Kathoey reduce their resilience and potential as a human resource. It is vital to look at the private life and inner world of the Kathoey so as to articulate and aggregate their demands as a sexual minority group.

KATHOEY AND EMPLOYMENT ISSUES

Employment and access to work is just as important for the Kathoey as for other persons because it provides economic independence and ensures dignity. Most modern societies and governments have made legal and constitutional provisions to accord equal rights and liberties to all citizens irrespective of their intersectional identities (class, race, ethnicity, sex, etc.). Unfortunately, across the world marginalization of certain groups still continues. While the marginalization due to race, ethnicity, social identity, physical handicaps and especially womanhood has been strongly contested, the marginalization of transgenders such as the Kathoey in Thailand has remained almost unnoticed.

Traditionally in all Asian societies transgenders have been seen as 'abnormal' and relegated to being social outcastes. Alternate sexualities or sexual choices have been considered taboo, and even designated as criminal. Given this backdrop, Asian societies continue even now to be suspicious of and unwilling to accept any person(s) that they as deviant. The Thai Kathoey, like most other transgender groups in Asia faces open social exclusion, economic discrimination and psychological alienation. The main instrument for fighting such marginalization and socio-economic exclusion is education and employment for the marginalized. In the case of transgenders in almost all Asian countries employment opportunities have been greatly limited due to mythical stereotyping of their identity.

So far there is neither official data/census on LGBTIQ jobs and employment in Thailand, nor on the total number of MtF. However, in line with the estimation of the trans-women community, the MtF figure is 1:300 (Winter 2012). It is commonly seen that many of the Thai Kathoey work in the area of the beauty-business, entertainment and show business, as well as in leisure and hospitality services, including sex services. Stereotyping has resulted in the belief is that they are good (only) at these areas of work. Thus, it is assumed that these jobs are most suited for them. There is no scientific proof of any such limited natural capacity/inclination among transgenders. Rather, it is the socio-cultural myths about the Kathoey have played an important part in limiting their life opportunities.

Heterosexual ideologies/norms and practices are behind the Kathoey's plight. Being under constant pressure regarding their identity as 'the other', who does not conform to the mainstream sexual culture, causes many of them to eventually alter their looks and bodies to fit in with the dictated norm. By constructing a female appearance/body and exaggerated femininity, they have created a social space for generations. Therefore, consumption of hormones, plastic surgeries, etc. is common in the Kathoey community to assist in constructing female identities (Sankatiprapa 2007). Hence, it is a costly exercise to become a perfect Kathoey, both in terms of health and money. But, the new look comes with a sense of pride and a feeling of self-confidence. Moreover, it is believed that society as a whole accepts them more readily because of these changes. It paves a way for creating a social identity and social acceptance.

It was revealed that peer-support is strong in Kathoey groups. This helps them in getting on with a female transgender's life and learning the norms and practices of the group, especially regarding how to reconstruct themselves and how to behave in an acceptable format. Some of them have succeeded despite odds in acquiring education. Most of them have faced the dilemma of ostracism from their own family, community and education institutions. The harassment and abuse is both in a simple form (verbal) and in complex (violent) form such as bullying, physical assault/violence, and unfair disciplinary rules. Those Kathoey who enter tertiary education, especially at university level, have invented unique practices amongst themselves. Peer support is provided under the umbrella of 'sotus' system, where senior Kathoeys regulate or lead the junior year to behave or to manage themselves according to freshman rules and manners perceived to be acceptable to a Kathoey community. The seniors may have their own social network, peer groups, either small or large, to provide support.

Most Kathoey are excluded and alienated from heterosexual society. Their sexual identity has caused their marginalization in social space starting from childhood. Within their own families, there is insensitivity and ostracism, including various excuses such as 'Kathoey should not have a school education because one day they might get AIDS and die'. Some parents believe that sending a Kathoey to a monastery will help them to become a 'man'. Some are ignored, or even worse are beaten up by family members, especially by the father to turn them to manliness. Arguments regarding their children's sexual identity and behaviour often take place in a family. Whatever the reasons, often the only outcome is that they run away from home. This study suggests that initial family acceptance is the most initial and important part in the positive construction of a Kathoey life.

The Kathoey children face a very common risk of being exploited and abused especially sexually by men. Mostly people do not detect/perceive such abuse because they assume that sexual abuse and harassment happen only between men and women. The myth of the Kathoey blinds common perception and sensitivity, thus even parents often do not see what the child is undergoing (Sankatiprapa 2007). Failure of the family to protect them from abuse, including sexual assault and harassment, leads to lack of concentration and emotional trauma, and eventually lack of education. Combined with poverty this can also lead to total illiteracy and dereliction.

Lack of education combines with other problematic dimensions of identity crises due to gender, economic status, social class, ethnicity, etc. Consequently, they may choose to join what is called a 'sanctuary'

(a place or a type of work that they are comfortable with and trust that it is a safe place to live their life in). Classic examples of this are the work in a cabaret show or a beauty salon. Besides being in a sanctuary space, they can earn some money, express themselves, group with friends and sisters, as well as feel safe from the public gaze.

In Thailand, it is perceived that there are increasing numbers of Kathoey sex workers (KSW) especially in tourist areas. However, further survey is needed to determine an accurate number. It is clear that the stigmatized social environment and limited job opportunities influences many Kathoey to fall into this trap. Without any job opportunities, they believe that perhaps it is better off entering this business, even though it might come with risks and the deterioration of health. The stigma-sickness slope (Figure 1) was used by Winter to show that the health of the average Asia-Pacific transgender would

Figure 1 *Stigma–Sickness slope*

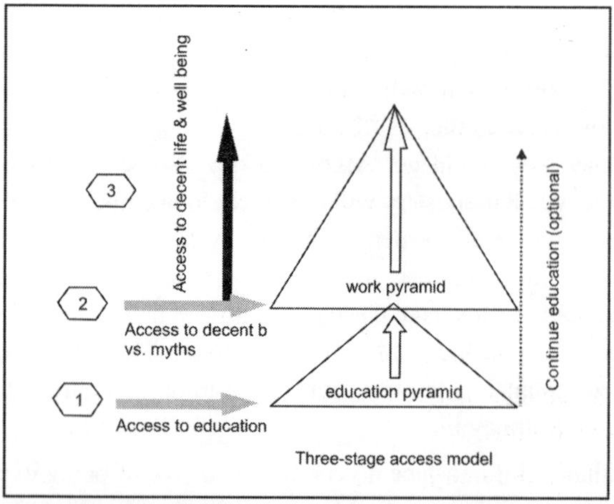

Source: Winter (2012: 13)

become a worrisome issue in the near future especially due to the vulnerability to sexually transmitted diseases (STD) at a young age (Winter 2012).

Society views the Kathoey as sexually perverted, sexually active with many partners, presenting a hyper-feminine body and role, having entertaining characteristics, and comical. This agrees with the beliefs stated by Winter (2012) that they are perceived as unnatural, mentally sick, sexually deviant, deceptive or immoral. He added that the common element of these beliefs is that the trans-woman is actually a man and a trans-man is actually a woman. Moreover, transgender persons are stigmatized across the Asia-Pacific region. These stigmas push transgender people to become a marginalized group in society and face many troubles in their life as the Stigma–Sickness Slope diagram given below shows.

It is very likely that the transgender persons who are engaging in sexual services are at high risk. Kathoey sex workers could jeopardize their sexual health with multiple partners for commercial sex. From a macro-perspective, the root of such a problem again originates from the limited scope of life opportunities available to them.

So far, the Kathoey remains an object of heterosexual knowledge/myth, and in the face of society's ignorance must internalize their problems. Society has perpetuated the mythical discourse on Kathoey through cultural and social institutions, both formal and informal. Literature, Theatre, and Media have for long transmitted the stereotyped images/messages. Therefore, a falsely constructed truth about the Kathoey is fixed in the Thai people's mind. The power of heteronormativity is immerse, and will remain so unless people start to question these norms.

EDUCATION AND COMPETITION IN THE JOB MARKET

MtF's employment is a major issue to be discussed in this chapter. As mentioned earlier, the hegemonic heterosexual ideology made both the Kathoey and the general people think that Kathoey are only good at some specific jobs. In addition, their characters fit in with the beauty and entertainment business. Also, traditionally it was said that they are 'si-san', which means they bring colours to people's life. Most of the time, if they appear in a movie scene, a TV show series, a music video or a comedy show, they typify extreme characters and a comical aspect. This depiction is often unacceptable to the Kathoey community. For example, a Kathoey's comment on a character in one show echoes that, 'it's like a crazy person, who would wear/act like that!' It can be said that Kathoey myths are perpetuated partly by themselves (without realization) and partly by the public.

MARGINALIZATION OF KATHOEY AND ITS IMPACT ON HUMAN CAPITAL

The human capital theory (Becker 1993) argues that education is the key to enhance people's capacity and to aid people in climbing the socio-economic ladder. The more the people invest in education, the more the returns they receive. The life of a Kathoey is not linear as in the theory. Striving upwards through the education pyramid is not beyond a Kathoey's capability provided they have societal and family support. Some are successful in education, and even get to the top of the class proving their educational ability, including their extracurricular capacities.

Life after graduation is not easy for the Kathoey. In the process of job recruitment, people are judged not only objectively for their competence, observable manner and behaviour, but also by several subjective biases and social attitudes such as those on gender. In the figure given below a three-stage access model describes the complexities at each stage of such struggle for equal opportunities and access to work.

Each access has conditions, and it interrelates to others. To be able to reach optimum well-being, Kathoey will have to strive harder than others for it. Gaining access to a decent job, invariably results in reaching a minimum level

Figure 2 *Three stage access model*

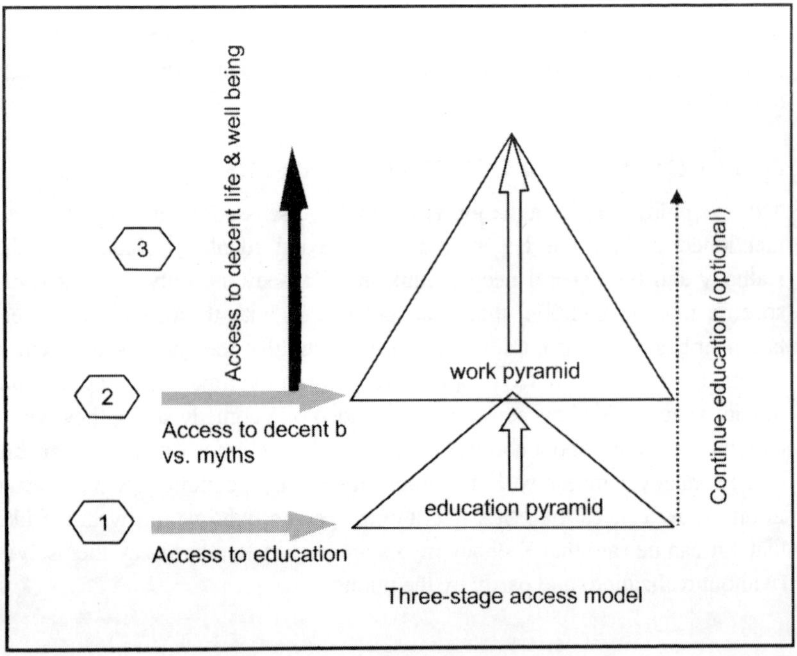

of a quality life. Even though the process may be the same for everyone in society, generally a Kathoey has to face many more difficulties. The degree of seriousness in discrimination reflects on the level of insensitivity and lack of empathy regarding sexual diversity among those who regulate the recruitment. For instance the labelling of Kathoey by the military as 'mentally ill' persons has serious ramifications. Despite the fact that many do not wish to be a soldier, the label stigmatises them.

Presently, the situation has improved to some extent as there is an on-going negotiation with the military by those concerned on LGBTQ rights and advocates as well as Kathoey activists. Consequently, the rules are more relaxed, and they are being treated more humanely. Even after this, the problem of unemployment is not totally eliminated. Many Kathoey adopt an 'Ab-man' strategy, which means to disguise as or to pretend to be a man by painstakingly adopting the social characteristics and behaviour of men, that is, wearing an accepted male haircut, dressing as a typical male, wearing no make-up, speaking in a heavy voice, etc. so as to get a job. Some can do it, but some cannot, especially when they have to cut off their hair. Thus, the strategy is only an alternative that is a big trade-off with their perceived sexual identity. Consequently, many of them have to turn to a stereotyped job available in the job market for Kathoey. Entering the same old rut traps them in the vicious Kathoey cycle of life.

Therefore, it is imperative to closely examine Kathoey accessibility to work and the problems they face. The exclusion from the job market and work, as well as a constant mental harassment is a socio-economic phenomenon. This is in addition to their striving to attain their gender identity directed towards the female and femininity. Accounts narrated by Thai Kathoey regarding obstacles in employment were obtained so that the problem could be analysed.

REVEALING KATHOEY VOICES THROUGH CASE STUDIES

Qualitative methodology frames this study. It is believed that subjective understanding of Kathoey can lead to what lies behind the phenomena. Their life stories are collected as texts for a thematic analysis. Some selected texts are drawn from my previous works on Kathoey sexual harassment and sexual literacy. This together with new texts was collected between 2010 and 2013. Through an association and a friendship established during working on a doctorate dissertation and other related researches afterwards, it has supported me in continuing cooperation with people in transgender community. Rapport has been rapidly built along with a co-construction of new and accumulating knowledge gaining from conversations and their lived stories, one after another, which have touched upon the topic in some ways.

Adding to this, qualitative data from specific interviews in the area of job and work were collected. The emphasis was on those who were educated at the level of a vocational certificate or a high vocational certificate, and a bachelor degree. The reason was that an education at these levels was good enough for getting access to a competitive job market. Key texts from conversations with eight Kathoeys were transcribed verbatim, using people with disability services. The age of respondents was ranging from 20 to 40 years old. During the time of data collection the respondents were working in a number of fields, including the beauty business, a government office, fashion business, a non-governmental organization, the entertainment business, a factory employee and in cleaning services.

Data collection was arranged in cooperation with some trusted 'gate-keepers' who helped in connecting with the key respondents. Discussion on issues/qualitative interview of discrimination relating to 'work', especially at an access stage, was emphasized. Most interviews were face to face, supplemented by a few on phone at late night when a respondent was available. Many of the respondents were interviewed more than once, especially when there was a need for further details and clarification. The length of a conversation was between 90 and 160 minutes, or more, for each person.

Relating to ethical issues, the personal data of respondents is all protected. Anonymous names have been assigned to the respondents. Respondents agreed to disclose their experiences and agreed to be recorded. If they could not be recorded, hand written notes were taken.

THEMATIC ANALYSIS OF KATHOEY EXPERIENCES RELATING TO EMPLOYMENT AND WORK

Ethnographic Evidence

Everyday lived stories of eight Kathoeys were recorded regarding their interaction with potential employers, employers, superior staff, co-workers and colleagues. Transgender myths interfere in this area of life. Social practices play an important role in securing the established gender norm. Social myths and practices under the hetero-social order play a strong role in perpetuating the social power network, therefore only a very small space is available for sexual diversity. Dominant themes which emerged from the Kathoey's lived experiences are—disruption of education at an early stage, negative conditionality for job recruitment, repetition of a negative 'relevant job' discourse, perpetuation of prevailing stereotype, harassment and stigmatization of Kathoey in work places.

Blocking of Education at an Early Stage

In a modern society, it cannot be denied that education is a pathway to social and economic prosperity. However, the success stories or normal stories mostly do not figure the achiever as of abnormal/'the other'/third sex. A conventional story never includes a Kathoey.

Case Study: Rita and Endoo

The stories of Rita and Endoo combine in illustrating this theme. Rita, an Isan Kathoey or a Kathoey in the poorest north-eastern region of Thailand, talked about herself as a child. Rita had her education only at Pathom 6 level (12 years old). After that she had to quit the school and stay home as she was led to believe that her family could not afford it. Every time some former classmate passed by her house on the way to school, she had to try to look the other way or pretend to do something else, because she felt shame and degraded inside. She was not told clearly of any reason why she could not go to school. However, the one thing that she realized was that her brothers and sisters all continued their education. Only she alone was denied a chance. Once she grew up, she ran away from a temple where her father sent her with a hope to changing her sexual orientation. After that Bangkok became her destination. With low education, she took up many different jobs just for her subsistence. From a plate cleaner in a restaurant to a beer bar, to customer services and from being a partner to a foreigner, to becoming an inmate in a prison for drug charge, she passed through all these experiences (Sankatiprapa 2007).

She got HIV, from a gang rape incident that happened in prison. However, she strived to survive after all the sickness and poverty that she faced. The last job she got was of an AIDS volunteer in a local hospital. She questioned that if she had acquired a higher level of education, would she have ended up like this? Her question was never answered.

Endoo was once a top-grade student when she was young. She is now around 30 years old. She was once a show girl, a prostitute and then a makeup artist. The memory that Endoo had regarding her lack of education was of the words of her mother, 'you are a Kathoey … studying means nothing … wasting money. Even if you get a higher education, society cannot accept it'. Actually Endoo's family had no trouble with finance to support their children. Her elder sister, elder brother and younger brother, all had a university education. It was a conviction in her community that if a Kathoey finishes an education, they would never get a job, or they would certainly die of AIDS. Her family embraced and reproduced this belief. Thus, this forced her to leave her hometown with 1,200 baht (40 dollars) in her pocket to follow her own path. Nowadays, she sends her earnings to her parents, sometimes in the form of money and sometimes gold, which has led to her getting accepted by them! It is said that it is a kind of proof that she has done well with her life.

Case Study: Benja

The situation is even worse for those who do not have a Thai national identity card. It is a rare case, but it presents the problematic intersection between poverty and education, in addition to being a Kathoey. Benja, a Kathoey from a poor family, is an example. Her mother had so many children that she could not raise them all. So, Benja was sent to be raised by a kind monk at a temple. At that time, she still had a boy 'look'. She had a school education when the monk was alive. However, when he died, his son took further care of her instead. She worked in a rice field for him. Many times she asked about an identity card, but there was no response. So she grew up without the Thai identity card and with a low education background.

She was good at making artificial flowers. To maintain her life in her adulthood, she worked in the informal sector to craft them, as it did not require any document for the job. Later on she was infected with HIV from a relationship. She could not get access to the free pills unless she had the card. She went to the district office where she was born to ask for one, but she was refused even from submitting her official request to the authority. The head of the village and the people in the community tried to help her by giving verbal verification to confirm her identity but the attempt failed. Even her mother could not do anything as the officer raised a question regarding the delay in asking for the issue of an identity card.

She was extremely depressed and talked to no one. As a poor and uneducated Kathoey, going to the government office was hard enough already. The lower the self-esteem, the more the lack of confidence she had. She did not dare to disclose the symptoms of her sickness to make them sympathize as it would stigmatize her. This was until her old friend, who was also a Kathoey, came to lend a hand. They went to the district office together and again their request was refused. Finally, a mutual friend learned about it, and sympathized. A phone call was made to the district office to ask about the case, and on that day they went again to the office. She and her friend heard the officer who had refused her application speak out aloud that, 'from now on, the request has to go through the entire process!' This was after the officer knew of the call. After a while, she also heard that it was made difficult so that it would be easier to get some bribe from desperate persons! Benja did not have any money and she was very sick. In the end, she got her identity card as a consequence of efforts by a network of friends. It was too hard and she was tired as family members were called to verify her identity from everywhere. She also had to find financial support for their travelling. They were all questioned in a way that could be described as too tough! Finally the identity card was in her hands, once she looked at it said to herself 'This is how the ID looks like!' However, it was extremely late. Two days after getting the first ever identity card in her life, she died as she was seriously ill. According to the doctor, there was a chance of 20 per cent but her old mother gave up. At her funeral, her friends wondered why so many people came including the questionable district officer, whereas when she was alive he intimidated her and did not seem to care.

Problems in Job Recruitment

> There are two choices for us; blending smoothly in the society … just resent to it … for applying and getting a job … or stubborn … to be … then must work in another route, and there are limited choices … . Then, I have to cut my hair … have to apply for a job … have to be a man.
>
> —Voice of Thai Kathoey in a Private Company

Gender discrimination limits Kathoey's access to job. Having school and university education does not seem to be a lot of trouble for Thai Kathoey especially when they dress according to their sex (anatomy). Even though there are some certain boundaries that they cannot cross, they survive the social and academic life in educational institutions. Some classmates, teachers and lecturers can understand and tolerate them, but some cannot and express their adverse attitudes, such as bullying, verbal attacks, insulting looks, not allowing the Kathoey to sit in an examination room if she does not wear a uniform relevant to a heterosexual gender or wearing makeup. Once they graduate from a higher education college or a university, they then experience a worse real life situation.

Case Study: Meena and Dasy

Meena graduated from a university in the north of Thailand where she was respected by her lecturers and other students as she had outstanding performance. Others students highly respected her and voted for her to be a student president. Meena convinced her parents to accept her sexual identity. She received good grades in her study in the field of business and for general graduates such grades would get a decent job right away. Meena intended to find a job to make her parents proud of her, 'Once I graduated, I just wish to get a job. It will be my pleasant start. I want my parents to be proud of me. They had to be patient and support me financially till I finish my first degree …'

It was extremely hard for her to get a job. One attempt after another and she failed. Many Kathoeys realize that they are more likely to be hired by a private company than by a governmental organization. About some, such as her·seniors, who had their own survival strategy, she added that, 'I do know that my seniors just cut their hair short, if they are going to sit for a test to be included in the government roster as a teacher … . They all cut it short. I remember.' Meena preferred to work fora private company. Normally, in an application form, she put her picture taken with long hair. However, her title was 'Mr'. She recalled one interview by a big transnational company. That day she wore a neat black suit and a skirt as well as a heel. The selection committee was composed of six male staff and one elder. When Meena went in, she started to greet them politely, 'Sawaddee ka, di chan Meena na ka (Hello, my name is Meena)'. They all flipped through her application and looked at her face. The older one commented that she had got good marks and he was impressed. Then the questions went on without touching upon the issue of sexual identity. Nonetheless, she had noticed at the beginning that when she walked in they all had laughed at her. 'I wore light makeup … they just know … when they glanced at my name … Mr … no … I could see confusion on their faces. They looked at each other. I knew what they were talking about.' When the result came out, those who succeeded were men or women. She noticed that even her friend, a gay who adopted the appearance and manners of a handsome man could not get the job. She was so disappointed, but she did not give up.

Meena's mother encouraged her to apply for a vacancy in a banking institution. She did not quit that easily. One day she had a call inviting her to an interview. She agreed to go. She was quite surprised to see that she was the only Kathoey there. While walking towards an interview table, she was observed from head to toe by a lady's eyes until she sat down. If a look could kill, Meena would die many times. Meena understood that the person was a manager. When the person viewed her application, she asked, 'Are you Sao Pra Phet Song (the second type of woman)? Are you not a female?' 'Yes', Meena answered while she saw the lady's subordinate's face turned pale. Meena understood immediately that those who had done the first screening of the application were not thorough enough or had not even looked at it. Perhaps they selected her only from seeing the picture in it. Meena thought to herself, 'I won't survive this!' They asked her more questions about work which gave her hope that she might succeed. Nevertheless, time passed from hope to despair. Nothing came up. In fact, she gave up when she walked in and saw other candidates. She realized that it was tremendously hard for her to find a job. She failed many times, and it was just because of her sexual identity.

Dasy, a 30-year-old state employee, revealed her harsh experiences. Dasy graduated in economics. For her getting a job was very important as her father had died, and she wanted to help her mother. She applied for many jobs but was unsuccessful. She was distressed and asked herself of the reason behind it. It was the same old story of her unwelcome sexual identity, although she was quite a neat person. However, when she was a student, she had a good reputation and noticeable profile in her outside class activities as well as her university's projects. She then went straight desperately to the head of an organization and told him that she wanted to apply for a job. The person was kind enough to listen, she requested him to give her opportunity to prove herself for six months. Surprisingly, he agreed because of her profile. Since then she has been employed as a staff in that organization.

RECOUNTING A 'RELEVANT JOB' DISCOURSE

Case Study: Tida

Once a Kathoey successfully gets a job, it does not mean that life will become normal. Society does this to safeguard heteronormativity and at the same time control Kathoey. Tida's case showed that she had been working in a number of business organization. Entering the career was not a problem as she could overcome her identity crises and took on a male look to acquire a job. Tida talked about her decision to adopt 'ab-man' strategy for her job application 'patient, be patient, my family said.' I then went to the hairdresser. I wanted to have a job … had to apply for a job, had to be a man.

Tida had more advantages as she had both a bachelor's degree from abroad and good language skills. Even though the private sector seemed to be quite open in comparison to the government one, the organization's rules were influenced by the view of the organization's head. A rigid view about sexual orientation of the management could be troublesome for a Kathoey. She recollected a story of her Kathoey colleague in one of the previous company who quit the job because she crossed the line of 'de-facto' dress code. 'I saw one Kathoey in a woman dress …' lerd (excellent), but after a while, at noon she changed to a trouser … and then she quitted the job. Finally, Tida came to a conclusion that the big boss had 'Kathoey-phobia'.

> The big boss (male) … he doesn't like Kathoey … you can ask everybody, they all know … no Kathoey … if … happens to have one and she shows that she is … (There are no written rules) but it is prohibited for a male to have long hair. He doesn't want to speak to a gay, promotion … job assignments (to kathoey) is rare … prefer to give assignments to general individuals instead … Being a Tom (boy) is better respected … .

Actually the issue was not of dress but a gender identity. If she could not abide by the organization's rules, which safeguarded heteronormativity, she had to leave. It was a matter of similarity and difference. A sexual minority person can be controlled via the so-called 'organization rules' without any reference to the person's ability and competency in their work. The organization regulations were based on an intolerant heterosexual order.

In a public space, Kathoey's job opportunities are quite limited. Within a workplace itself, their scope of work is classified by what is believed to be appropriate for them. One Kathoey who is a government employee confirmed that even when she was an executive secretary and she did all the jobs for her boss, she could follow him to public events only when there were no other seniors around. 'I can accompany my boss for a certain function, but if the event is to be with high rank staff, I am exempt from it'. A Kathoey's job is also defined by the way society views them. This makes Kathoey a mere dummy of their social meaning and consequently affects their excellence.

Tida remembered that her Kathoey hairdresser tried to convince her to go abroad to earn money and believed that it was a good opportunity. She was asked, 'What are you doing? … You are so tall! You should go to … (A name of a country in Southeast Asia) … so much money you can earn …! (ie. from becoming a prostitute abroad (author)'. Tida thought about the person's words and questioned, 'I am a Kathoey, is this the only work I can do?' This reflects the common phenomena when a Kathoey cannot find a job or a good job, and seems to have no alternative to becoming a prostitute. In addition, many of them are concerned with finances as they have to collect enough money to do a plastic surgery to achieve their female gender identity.

So accessing a good job is essential not only for sustaining their life, but also for creating their own female beauty/identity. Meena is sadly reminded about some newly graduate Kathoeys she heard of. 'They all graduated with a good grade in their bachelor degree, but now they all are in … (A name of a country in Southeast Asia)'.

Prevailing Stereotype of Kathoey in the Working Environment

To allow Kathoey to work happily and productively, there has to be an encouraging environment in the workplace, where difference among people is respected. Whether diversity, especially sexual diversity is embraced or not is important for a tolerant organization to emerge. Tida's experiences would highlight the issue. Tida, a 30-year-old business graduate, worked with few companies. The most recent one was a foreign company that accepted her regardless of her sexual identity. The company's policy was focussed on women, in which MtF was included. Personal competency seemed to be the first priority when recruiting her. However, she felt that the working environment somehow adopted Kathoey myths. Thus, the discourse of 'proving oneself' existed both in a Kathoey mind and in the employer's effort to verify whether she was competent enough in his/her view. Tida recalled that she had to work harder than other male and female colleagues, 'double even triple' to prove herself. Moreover, at the beginning she was not trusted enough by the boss. The type of work she got also could not compare to herr heterosexual colleagues.

In the office, Tida interacted with many people internally and externally. Outside the office, customers showed their respect to her and treated her professionally. Conversely, the people inside did have a certain attitude towards Kathoey. For instance, her woman boss called her to help with the make-up under the popular belief that a Kathoey is good at make-up. Other assumptions that were brought up included that a Kathoey is always funny while she was quite serious about her job. The conviction that a Kathoey liked to overtly present herself sexually, and a Kathoey liked to chase guy, and was easy to have a sexual relationship with.

Once Tida went to ask her female colleagues for feedback on how she looked in a dress. However, the feedback was an unpleasant one! 'Wearing like this (a short skirt) is too much for a woman, but not for a Kathoey'. Another incident took place in the office coffee room where she sat with a female and a male manager. Suddenly, the female co-worker took the male's hand in hers and said 'Here, that is a man'. The scene did not stop there and his response was awfully rude.

Beyond that sexual abuse and assault can also take place while a Kathoey is working. Some male customers have a mistaken idea that Kathoey likes to be harassed sexually. One Kathoey expressed her feeling on the inappropriate manner of a male customer towards her. The man tried to touch her sexual organ and she was upset. She angrily shouted that, 'I don't like it; I don't want to be touched like this!'

CONCLUSION

Demystifying Kathoey Discourse: Moving Beyond Hetero-hegemonic Sexual Culture

Access to education is the very first stage of accessing well-being. It is viewed as the most important step for many, including Kathoey, to build up their life. However, it is comparatively difficult for Kathoey to study further after graduation. Obviously, gender bias played an important part in such cases as of Meena and Dasy. Written rules become irrelevant in the face of bias and discursive practices by recruiters. Kathoey who are realistic, or who understand that it is not the time to challenge the hegemonic power, recreate male identity to beat the bias. Nevertheless, confusions and questions that trouble their mind continue. Access to a decent job is still a big problem for Kathoey, especially those who dress as a female. Both the type and the scope of work seem to be extremely limited. For a relatively poorly educated Kathoey, working in a female-oriented job and entertainment business seems to be a good option. For a well-educated Kathoey, the scope for work is within the business sector. Rigid gender rules and roles are taken more seriously in a formal government organization than in a private one. Therefore, very few competent Kathoey can be seen in government organizations.

There may have some arguments that there is a sign of change. For example, in Tida's case, at last she did not have to be a man to enter her job. However, the sexual culture in the organization could not keep pace with the idea. Kathoey life stories showed personal experiences each of them faced in the process of acquiring, attaining and maintaining their job, which reflects the consequences of society's exclusion of this minority group. It is essential to stop the negative information and value flows through media, TV series, comedy shows etc. so that a positive attitude and discourse is initiated and widely circulated in society.

Discursive practices have caused people to be unaware and insensitive to the truth about transgenders. The consequences of the continuation of Kathoey myths jeopardize their future and well-being as equal members in the society. To bring the Kathoey into mainstream Thai society, by creating a healthy livelihood and lifestyle for them is not an easy task, as it will have to face resistance from both society at large, and also the Kathoey themselves. Breaking centuries old socio-cultural taboos, myths and corrupt practices is always a herculean task. The Kathoey society and groups also have their own beliefs, practices and some vested interests which they seek to continue. Besides, the Kathoey have so internalised the myths and the related way of life that they will resist sudden change or reform.

Letting Kathoey have an education is only a starting point. In order to be self-reliant, employment plays a crucial role. This argument is not based on the romanticized idea that all Kathoeys are competent and have desirable characters. But, in today's world, the basic human right to have equal access to opportunities cannot be denied. Women have fought for such opportunities for a long time and have successfully achieved considerable success. For the Kathoey, there is a long struggle ahead before securing similar access However, multipronged efforts to ensure education, training, and job opportunities can be the initial remedy to the problem of Kathoey marginalization. This must be combined with sensitizing socio-economic institutions to be tolerant on the sexual diversity issue.

REFERENCES

Becker, G.S. (1993). *Human Capital: A Theoretical and Empirical Analysis, with Special Reference to Education*. 3rd ed. Chicago: University of Chicago Press.

Sankatiprapa, K. (2007). *Kathoey Sexual Harassment: It's Significance in Hetero-sexual Discourse*. Unpublished Development Education Dissertation, Bangkok: Srinakharinwirot University.

Winter, S. (2012). *Lost in Transition: Transgender People, Rights and HIV Vulnerability in the Asia-Pacific Region*. Bangkok: United Nations Development Programme.

CHAPTER 10

Gender Issues in the Organizational Attitudes and Behaviour of Japanese Care Workers

Ikushi Yamaguchi

More than a quarter of a century has already passed since the establishment of the Equal Employment Opportunity Law for Men and Women in Japan in May 1985. Moreover, 18 years have passed since the establishment of the Revised Equal Employment Opportunity Law for Men and Women in 1997. Yet, although men and women are equal in terms of the law, there remain some problems in fairness regarding the treatment of female workers in Japanese companies. For example, the distribution ratio of female workers in managerial positions was only 8.7 per cent in 2011, according to the research of the Ministry of Health, Labour and Welfare (2012).

Perceived (un)fairness or (in) justice is related to workers' organizational attitudes and behaviour (e.g. Beugre 1998), which influence the quality of care in care facilities. If female care workers are unfairly treated in Japanese care facilities (special nursing homes for the aged in the present study) where female workers are the majority (according to the research of the Ministry of Health, Labour and Welfare [2010], the distribution ratio of female care workers in welfare facilities was 69.1% in 2009), a good quality of care is not expected. Then, the present study explores the differences between the organizational attitudes and behaviour of male and female care workers in Japanese care facilities.

Since this study is based on both qualitative and quantitative research and the objective of the present study is to explore gender similarities and differences in organizational attitudes and behaviour, specific hypotheses to be tested are not constructed. Instead, research questions on the relationships between sex and organizational attitudes and behaviour of Japanese care workers are proposed.

ORGANIZATIONAL ATTITUDES AND BEHAVIOUR

This section reviews the concepts of organizational attitudes and behaviours that can shed light on perceived organizational justice, organizational commitment, job satisfaction and burnout as a background to the comparison between male and female Japanese care workers. Regarding organizational justice, voice, interactional justice and perceived organizational justice are examined. Folger (1977) introduced the concept of voice, which is a chance to express one's opinion that can influence the results of decision making as a process of control, into the field of studies on organizational behaviour. However, procedural justice such as voice does not consider the importance of the roles played by decision makers (Bies 1987; Bies and Shapiro 1988; Folger and Cropanzano 1998; Folger and Konovsky 1989), psychological aspects of justice (Tyler 1989), and interpersonal communication between managers and workers (Bies and Tyler 1993). Justice theory focusing on those aspects is called interactional justice. There are two dimensions of interactional justice (Bies and Moag 1986): informational justice, which includes the provision of adequate explanations and accounts of the decision-making procedures to outcome recipients by decision makers, and interpersonal justice, which is communication with a respectful and sincere attitude. For example, Yamaguchi (2007) revealed that in Japanese companies, female workers felt much more dissatisfied with the provision of information and opportunities available to them for expressing their opinions as compared to their male counterparts. This suggests that gender is related to organizational justice.

Regarding organizational commitment, Allen and Meyer (1990) and Meyer and Allen (1991) identified three types of commitments; i.e. affective, normative and continuance ones. Among them, affective commitment is assumed to be most necessary to raise the quality of care work because an affective commitment is an attitude of fondness and loyalty to an organization. Such attitudes motivate care workers to exploit their energy, efforts and time to service in their facilities. The quality of their service will deteriorate without affective commitment. Organizational commitment in the present study represents affective commitment. A spirit of service is required for care work and care workers. Care workers are expected to devote themselves to offering their services in their care facilities. This attitude is reflected in the concept of affective commitment of care workers. As long as organizational commitment leads to the quality of care, it is desirable that there is no difference in the organizational commitment of male and female workers. Therefore, it is worthwhile to explore whether gender relates to organizational commitment.

Job satisfaction indicates how happy workers are with their job and daily work life. Masterson et al. (2000) measured the degree of employees' job satisfaction with the variables of 'Compared with most jobs, this is pretty good' and 'I am happy with this job'. Job dissatisfaction is one of the main reasons workers quit jobs (e.g. Likert 1961; Thierry and Koopman-Iwema 1984; Vroom 1964). According to the research conducted by Ministry of Health, Labour and Welfare (2009), care workers have a higher turnover rate than the average rate of whole industries in Japan. The research also suggests that this high turnover rate may be attributed to the high ratio of female workers. This implies that gender has something to do with job satisfaction.

According to Maslach and Jackson (1981: 99), burnout is 'a syndrome of emotional exhaustion and cynicism that occurs frequently among individuals who do 'people-work' of some kind'. According to them, there are three dimensions of burnout: emotional exhaustion, depersonalization and personal accomplishment. Care workers are engaged in 'people-work', and they can experience emotional and psychological problems such as burnout. Several previous studies have examined psychological malaise, including burnout, for workers at hospitals and care facilities (e.g. Elovainio et al. 2001; Spell and Arnold 2007). In Japan, Ohue et al. (2010) and Yajima (2011) found that female nurses in general hospitals and female school teachers reported significantly higher emotional exhaustion than their respective male counterparts. This implies that there are also gender differences in Japanese care worker regarding burnout.

Methods

Based on the above discussion, the following research question was framed: Are informational and interpersonal justice, voice, perceived organizational justice, organizational commitment, job satisfaction and burnout similar or different between male and female workers in Japanese care facilities? A Survey was carried out.

Respondents

The questionnaires were sent to 100 care facilities on the list of council members of the Council of Senior Citizen Welfare Services in a prefecture in Japan in June 2008. These 100 organizations represented the care facilities that belonged to the council in that prefecture at that time. We sent the questionnaires to the council, which distributed 10 questionnaires to each of the 100 care facilities. Reminders were sent to the care facilities only once. A total of 538 completed questionnaires were returned (response rate: 53.8%). The obtained results are shown in Table 1.

Table 1 *Means, standard deviations, correlations, and reliabilities*

	,Ž	*M*	*SD*	*1*	*2*	*3*	*4*	*5*	*6*	*7*	*8*	*9*	*10*	*11*	*12*	*13*	*14*
1. Sex	532	0.28	0.45														
2. Age	501	32.6	10.93	–.146**													
3. The length of service in the facility	489	4.81	3.89	–.097*	.407**												
4. The length of service as a care worker	495	6.15	4.08	–.103*	.428**	.739**											
5. Employment types	493	0.96	0.19	0.053	–0.03	.119*	0.045										
6. Informational justice	523	3.9	1.1	0.047	0.002	0.055	0.063	0.041	–0.88								
7. Interpersonal justice	520	4.13	1.2	0.082	–0.064	–0.082	–0.04	0.06	.762**	–0.93							
8. Voice	519	4.1	1.21	.095*	0.028	–0.023	0.078	0.027	.520**	.671**	–0.91						
9. Perceived organizational justice	507	4.01	1.1	.093*	–0.063	–0.068	–0.078	0.018	.703**	.748**	.567**	–0.91					
10. Organizational commitment	529	4.2	1.09	0.07	.149**	0.022	0.021	–0.06	.555**	.571**	.487**	.562**	–0.83				
11. Job satisfaction	526	3.97	1.16	–0.005	.184**	–0.062	0.012	–0.078	.414**	.430**	.409**	.478**	.609**	–0.82			
12. Emotional exhaustion	530	4.37	1.14	–0.065	–.184**	0.006	–0.086	.095*	–.254**	–.248**	–.263**	–.290**	–.330**	–.429**	–0.84		
13. Depersonalization	511	3.01	1.12	–0.027	–.106*	0.073	0.01	0.062	–.299**	–.295**	–.270**	–.364**	–.383**	–.468**	.652**	–0.87	
14. Personal accomplishment	518	3.98	0.93	0.063	.124**	–0.031	0.017	–0.035	.342**	.336**	.338**	.352**	.564**	.656**	–.293**	–.288**	–0.81

Note: SEX: male = 1, female = 0; Employment types: full-time = 1, part-time = 0; Alpha coefficients (Cronbach's α) are on the diagonal in parentheses. $^{*}p < 0.05$. $^{**}p < 0.01$

Measures and Analyses

Sex is an independent variable, and the data are a dummy variable (0 = female and 1 = male workers). Control variables include age, average length of service in the facilities, average length of service as care workers and a dummy variable of full- or part-time workers (0 = part-time, and 1 = full-time workers). Dependent variables include informational and interpersonal justice, voice, perceived organizational justice, organizational commitment, job satisfaction and the three dimensions of burnout. Because all the respondents were Japanese care workers, the original English items were translated into Japanese. The subjects were asked as to what degree could they agree with the question items on a six-point Likert-type scale from 1 (strongly agree) to 6 (strongly disagree). The scores were inverted.

For informational and interpersonal justice, voice and perceived organizational justice, the researcher developed question items for Japanese care workers, referring to the questionnaires on and the definitions of those concepts that were developed and presented by Shapiro et al. (1994), Colquitt (2001), Moorman (1991), Bies et al. (1988) and Bies and Shapiro (1988). The researcher also developed other original questions according to the definition of the concepts. There were four questions on informational justice, four on interpersonal justice, four on voice and six on perceived organizational justice. As a result of exploratory factor analysis (EFA) with maximum-likelihood method (ML), only one factor was extracted with eigenvalues of 2.61 (65.12%) and factor loadings ranged from 0.75 to 0.88 (Cronbach's $\alpha = 0.88$) for informational justice, with eigenvalues of 3.16 (78.13%) and factor loadings ranged from 0.86 to 0.92 ($\alpha = 0.93$) for interpersonal justice, with eigenvalues of 2.87 (71.73%) and factor loadings ranged from 0.80 to 0.88 ($\alpha = 0.91$) for voice and with eigenvalues of 3.83 (63.89%) and factor loadings ranged from 0.61 to 0.90 ($\alpha = 0.91$) for perceived organizational justice.

For organizational commitment, the questions were made for Japanese care workers with reference to Bies and Tyler (1993). There were three questions on organizational commitment. As a result of EFA with ML, only one factor was extracted with eigenvalues of 1.89 (63.04%) and factor loadings ranged from 0.64 to 0.91 ($\alpha = 0.83$).

For job satisfaction, the question items were partly adapted from Masterson et al. (2000) and Adachi (1998). The researchers also developed other original questions according to the definition of the concepts. There were three questions on job satisfaction. The results of EFA with ML showed that only one factor was extracted with eigenvalues of 1.89 (62.89%) and factor loadings ranged from 0.67 to 0.89 ($\alpha = 0.82$).

For burnout, there are 17 questions in the Japanese version of the Maslach Burnout Inventory (MBI) that Tao (1995) developed for Japanese workers in Japanese human service industries by referring to Maslach and Jackson's (1981) MBI (Tao and Kubo 1996). Because both MBI and the Japanese version are established questionnaires and have been repeatedly used in many studies, EFA was not conducted. However, since this study is specific to Japanese care workers, some terms were slightly adjusted. There were three dimensions: emotional exhaustion (five items: α = 0.84), depersonalization (six items: $\alpha = 0.87$) and personal accomplishment (six items: $\alpha = 0.81$).

Multiple regression analysis was conducted to explore if sex was related to the organizational attitudes and the behaviour of care workers. Sex as an independent variable, other demographic variables as control variables, informational and interpersonal justice, voice, perceived organizational justice, organizational commitment, job satisfaction and burnout as dependent variables were entered into the model.

RESULTS AND DISCUSSION

Similarities and Differences in Organizational Attitudes and Behaviour from Quantitative Research

As shown in Table 2, the models for informational and interpersonal justice and perceived organizational justice did not fit the data well. Adjusted R^2 of those models was not significant, and sex, length of service and employment type (full-time or part-time) did not explain the variances of organizational justice (i.e. informational and interpersonal justice and perceived organizational justice), except for the voice of care workers. On the other hand, demographic variables including sex explained the variances of voice, organizational commitment, job satisfaction and burnout. Therefore, in this section, only the relationships between the demographic variables and these organizational attitudes and behaviour will be presented and examined.

SIMILARITIES AND DIFFERENCES IN VOICE BETWEEN MALE AND FEMALE CARE WORKERS

Demographic variables including sex explained 2 per cent of the variance of the voice of care workers. Controlling for other demographic variables, sex influenced voice of care workers ($\beta = 0.14, p < 0.01$). Thus, male care workers are provided significantly more opportunities to express their opinions in their workplace than their female counterparts. One possible reason for this may be in differences in the ratio of group leaders between the male and female care workers in the present study. Out of the 362 female care workers, 74 (20.4%)

were leaders and 42 (11.6%) sub-leaders, whereas out of 140 male care workers, 40 (28.6%) were leaders and 21 (15%) sub-leaders ($\chi^2(4) = 12.97, p < 0.05$). Even though female care workers are the majority in care facilities, the ratio of male leaders is higher than that of female leaders, and voices are provided more for the former than the latter. This situation is a gender problem that needs to be improved.

Apart from the gender issue, an interesting finding here is that the workers who had worked longer in their current facility indicated lower voice ($\beta = -0.13, p < 0.10$), whereas those who had worked longer as care workers showed higher voice ($\beta = 0.18, p < 0.05$) in their facilities. This suggests that care workers tend to often transfer workplaces in Japan, and the opinions of workers who have experience as care workers are valued.

SIMILARITIES AND DIFFERENCES IN ORGANIZATIONAL COMMITMENT BETWEEN MALE AND FEMALE CARE WORKERS

Demographic variables including sex explained 4 per cent of the variance of the organizational commitment of care workers. However, sex did not relate to the organizational commitment of care workers ($\beta = 0.08$, n.s.). The spirit of service and attachment to care work and organizations did not differ by sex. The organizational commitment of Japanese care workers did not indicate a gender problem. The characteristics of human service jobs were strongly reflected in the participants' work attitude. As mentioned earlier, care workers are inclined to devote themselves to offering their services in care facilities because of a strong attachment to their job and organization. Indeed, the mean score is 4.20 (SD = 1.09), and hence, their commitment to organizations is rather high regardless of sex.

The age of care workers affected their commitment to facilities. For controlling other demographic variables, age influenced the organizational commitment of care workers ($\beta = 0.21, p < 0.001$). According to the data, younger care workers had a lower organizational commitment than their older counterparts. It is reasonable that if workers belong to the organization, they form a deeper attachment to their facilities and the residents. This is true for both male and female care workers.

SIMILARITIES AND DIFFERENCES IN JOB SATISFACTION BETWEEN MALE AND FEMALE CARE WORKERS

Demographic variables including sex explained 5 per cent of the variance of the job satisfaction of care workers. However, the job satisfaction of care workers was not affected by sex ($\beta = 0.05$, n.s.). Both male and female workers were satisfied with their job to the same degree. Thus, there is no gender problem concerning job satisfaction. Although the mean score ($M = 3.97$, SD = 1.16) is not as high as that of organizational commitment, it is moderately high; that is, both male and female care workers like their jobs.

The age of care workers and length of service in the facility positively and negatively affected their satisfaction with job ($\beta = 0.26, p < 0.001$, and $\beta = -0.14, p < 0.10$), respectively. Although growing older makes care workers more satisfied with their jobs, staying in the same facility lowers their job satisfaction. This suggests that care workers tend to transfer workplaces before feeling satisfied with the job in the facilitation and continue to be engaged in care work at different facilities. Job dissatisfaction is a main cause of workers leaving jobs (e.g. Likert 1961; Thierry and Koopman-Iwema 1984; Vroom 1964), as mentioned earlier, and care workers have a higher turnover rate than the average rate of whole industries in Japan, according to research conducted by the Ministry of Health, Labour and Welfare in 2009.

Indeed, the mean score of the length of service in their current facilities ($M = 4.81$ years, SD = 3.89) is much shorter than that for their entire career as care workers ($M = 6.15$, SD = 4.08). On the other hand, continuing the job as their career suggests their satisfaction with the work.

SIMILARITIES AND DIFFERENCES IN BURNOUT BETWEEN MALE AND FEMALE CARE WORKERS

Demographic variables including sex explained 6 per cent, 3 per cent and 4 per cent of the variances of emotional exhaustion, depersonalization and personal accomplishment of care workers, respectively. When other demographic variables were controlled, female workers felt more emotional exhaustion and depersonalization than male workers ($\beta = -0.11, p < 0.5$, and $\beta = -0.09, p < 0.10$, respectively), while the former felt less personal accomplishment than the latter ($\beta = -0.08, p < 0.10$). These results may be related to the relationships between voice and each of the three dimensions of burnout. Some research suggests the relationships between voice and organizational attitudes and behaviour (e.g. Holbrook 1999).

Indeed, as shown in Table 1, voice was negatively correlated with emotional exhaustion and depersonalization and positively correlated with personal accomplishment, and male care workers were provided with more voice than their female counterparts. This means that because male workers have more opportunities to express their opinions and influence the process of decision making (i.e. voice) than their female counterparts, they feel a sense of personal accomplishment. Lind et al. (1997: 779) stated, 'Voice works to enhance one's feeling of identity with and security within a group in two ways.

First, the opportunity to speak gives one an opportunity to participate actively in the life of the group. Being listened to indicates that one's membership in the group is valued by others'. This situation can mitigate care workers' burnout of emotional exhaustion and depersonalization and enhance their personal actualization. Thus, the burnout of Japanese care workers reflects a gender problem in Japanese care facilities.

FINDINGS AND SUGGESTIONS FROM QUALITATIVE RESEARCH

In this section, some suggestive statements that were collected through the interview research are introduced to confirm the results of the quantitative research. Although the objectives of the research were not directly related to gender issues, data on 'voice' were collected. Because voice is much related to care worker burnout and reflects the gender issues of Japanese care workers, as discussed in the previous section, selected statements from the interviews on voice and organizational attitudes and behaviours will be introduced.

In the early September of 2012, semi-structured interviews totalling 1,415 minutes were conducted with 32 Japanese care workers at 10 care facilities in Tokyo, Japan. Interviews were undertaken at two facilities per day, one in the morning and the other in the afternoon. The interviewees were each interviewed for about 30–90 minutes.

Examples of Statements

Out of 32 care interviewees at 10 facilities, 12 interviewees (approximately one-third) at 8 facilities mentioned 'voice'. Out of them, 3 female and 11 male interviewees provided us with information on a system, a function and a problem of upward communication. Some of the summaries of their statements on voice and organizational attitudes and behaviour (OB) in pair for each interviewee are introduced as follows:

A Female Director (A)

<Voice> We have established a system of appeal with reconsideration if workers cannot accept the results of the performance appraisals.

<OB> The contents of work lead to workers' satisfaction. Participation in briefing sessions every year also can raise the job satisfaction of care workers. Mutual support among workers is natural in this facility. The turnover rate was 8.6 per cent – much lower than the average rate (17%) in this industry last year. Workers are not reluctant to do new and innovative things, saying 'Let's start as a first step'.

A Female Chief (B)

<Voice> My subordinates seem to be unwilling to appeal and directly communicate to me. Sometimes I try to take into account their opinions by asking questions. I indirectly hear some information and opinions through other persons.

<OB> Three workers quit in June without telling their colleagues why. Our job has no accomplishment since the residents don't recover and are growing weaker: I don't really feel that the results are good. I don't feel very satisfied with my daily work life, although I am pleased when I am told 'thank you' by the residents and their families. However, it does not lead to a satisfying job. When what I figured out as a good way to do jobs goes well, I feel happy, but the feeling doesn't last long.

A Female Floor Leader (C)

<Voice> I felt that upward communication from me was not much considered (When I was a floor leader). Although the communication was not top down and we could make complaints, I wondered if managers listened to them.

<OB> I don't know the turnover rate of this facility, but there were quite a number of workers who quit the job because they were fed up with this work. There are also workers who had to leave the office with a heavy heart because their family members relocated to another city. However, it seems to me that the latter reason is more common than the former. Other reasons are dissatisfaction with their superiors and exhaustion with the night shift.

A Male Director (D)

<Voice> An upward communication system is one of the assignments leaders worked on this year. Early this year, they stated that they should collect the opinions of general care workers, such as what they think about, what problems they face, and what complaints and questions they have. Although they have started to talk with the general care workers, few opinions and ideas have been offered and gathered.

<OB> Certainly, worker motivation is low. One of the reasons is that there are some workers who have been employed here for a long time and are satisfied with the present condition, such as a stable salary. They rarely express ideas for improvement and innovation when I interview them. This is one of our unmanageable problems.

Economic situations can also be one of the reasons for low motivation, and there are many other reasons such as organizational climate, less mutual support, and turnover of colleagues to better workplaces. So, I made a project plan for this year and assigned some tasks to workers as a goal, although I am not sure if that it will be successful. We also had an in-house training session, but … . For example, the building was constructed 20 years ago and needs to be renovated, and although we should think about something innovative, few managing staff consider it, and hence, the subordinates under those staff members are not motivated to do so. I encourage workers to join and participate in a presentation session of care practices in order to help them find some topics on care works. Organizational commitment is not low, maybe because we have had various kinds of events concerning the establishment of this facility, explained the mission, and offered a training session for that.

A Male Section Manager (E)

<Voice> When I was a chief, I received information from workers and understood it, and then selected what should be reported to my superiors (i.e. a section manager). I thought that only critical information should be reported to my superiors. Considering a superior's burdens, I wondered if I should inform him/her of whatever happened at the work sites.

<OB> I think that the turnover rate is relatively low. I have not seen that workers suddenly quit here. Maybe because of the organizational climate of this facility, workers steadily work hard on their assignments. I have to be careful about not working as much as expected. The other workers don't show frivolous attitudes.

A Male Social Worker (F)

<Voice> Although I am relatively younger than the others in this facilitation, I am able to speak up and be listened to regarding whatever I want to say. I am thankful for being in a situation and climate where I can express my opinion and improve things.

<OB> Trainees are employed by this facility, which is a desirable recruitment. Cohesiveness among workers has been nurtured, and the organizational climate is better than before. The turnover rate was higher in the past. The reason for the low turnover rate at present is the feeling new employees have that people here have them on their mind. There is a person who fondly watches them. When we are

short of hands at some events, the workers are willing to come in to the office, and are also willing to participate in training sessions for self-enlightenment, which reflects their high organizational commitment. For example, when some residents pass away on the weekend, the workers inform their colleagues.

A Male Chief (G)

<Voice> I think I talk to my superiors rather frequently, although I don't know if my superiors think my communication with them is sufficient. Some of my subordinates are not good at expressing their complaints and dissatisfaction to upper managers, and thus I inform the upper managers of their opinions for them. If I receive opinions on more formal matters concerning, for example, tasks from my subordinates, I will listen to them first. If the opinions are reasonable, I will consider reforming measures.

<OB> Since I was promoted to a chief, I have not had enough time to talk to the residents, and hence have not been able to get information from them. I feel more pressure and stress in working in this position than the previous year. The turnover rate is not very high in this facility compared to three other facilities in a corporate group. However, this job has a low salary and not much future prospects. Some workers change jobs, and even male workers get married to quit the job.

SUMMARIES OF THE FINDINGS FROM THE QUALITATIVE RESEARCH

Directors of facilities, both male and female, seem to make efforts to collect opinions from their subordinates and promote upward communication. Male middle managers also seem to hope that they can hear the opinions of their subordinates. However, two female interviewees in leadership positions (a chief and a floor leader) stated that they are not satisfied with upward communication. This suggests the possibility that female care workers perceive the provision of voice to be less than their male counterparts, which is not contradictory to the results shown in Table 2. Thus, it seems that the lower position the workers are in, the lesser voice they are provided.

The investigation of the relationships between voice and organizational attitudes and behaviours in the qualitative data showed that positive and negative opinions on voice are compatible with those on organizational behaviour and attitudes. Workers who perceive low voice describe negative organizational attitudes and behaviours: a female chief (B), a female floor

Table 2 *Results of multiple regression analyses*

Independent/Control variables	*Regression Coefficients (β) for dependent variable*					
	Voice	*Organizational Commitment*	*Job Satisfaction*	*Emotional Exhaustion*	*Depersonalization*	*Personal Accomplishment*
Sex	.14**	0.08	0.05	–.11*	–.09†	.08†
Age	0.04	.21***	.26***	–.24***	–.20***	.23***
The length of service in the facility	–.13†	0.01	–.14†	0.1	0.1	–.12†
The length of service as a care worker	.18*	–0.05	.02	–0.08	0.02	0.04
Employment types	0.01	–0.08	–0.06	.09†	0.06	–0.05
Adjusted R^2	.02*	.04**	.05***	.06***	.03**	.04***

Note: SEX: male = 1; female = 0; Employment types: full-time = 1; part-time = 0

*$p < 0.05$
**$p < 0.01$
***$p < 0.001$
†$p < 0.10$

leader (C) and a male director (D). A female director (A), a male section manager (E) and a male social worker (F) stated that voice is sufficiently provided, and their organizational behaviours and attitudes are positive. The relationship between voice and organizational attitudes and behaviours that was found by analyses of the statements is compatible with the results of the analyses of the quantitative data, shown in Table 1: voice was significantly positively related with job satisfaction, organizational commitment and personal accomplishment, and negatively related to emotional exhaustion and depersonalization. Two female interviewees indicated negative situations for both voice and organizational attitudes and behaviours.

CONCLUSION

This study explored gender issues in the organizational attitudes and behaviours of Japanese care workers using both quantitative and qualitative research. In the analysis of quantitative data, the variances of informational and interpersonal justice and perceived organizational justice were not explained by demographic variables, including sex. Gender was not related to organizational commitment or job satisfaction but to voice and the three dimensions of burnout. The results suggest that female workers are in more disadvantageous situations than their male counterparts in Japanese care facilities. The above findings were confirmed by the analyses of qualitative data.

The majority of workers in Japanese care facilities are female. Nevertheless, female care workers do not have working conditions as good as male care workers. This may be related to the value of masculinity (Hofstede 1980). People in high-masculinity-oriented cultures like Japan tend to separate social roles between males and females, and male workers have enjoyed higher and advantageous positions and status in Japanese organizations. Since there are more female workers than male workers in Japanese care facilities, management should consider systems and practices that can provide female workers with opportunities to exert their competencies and skills in care work. This is indispensable for improving the quality of care in Japanese care facilities. Management should develop environments in which more voice should be provided to female workers. Management should also promote them to higher positions and allow them to participate in decision making.

Finally, some limitations are mentioned. First, this chapter was written on the basis of two different research investigations: we conducted research at different times and for different respondents and organizations. Ideally, we would conduct research on care workers in the same organizations. Second, we did not consider any organizational variables in examining the data. Some of the interview data suggest that the characteristics of organizations, such as a facility size, may influence management and the organizational attitudes and behaviours of care workers. Third, it would also be useful to compare the interview data from the same organization. We had interviews with one to five interviewees at one facility, but it was beyond the scope of the present study to consider individual and organizational differences. With these limitations, the present study can contribute to the field of gender studies, care management and organizational behaviour in that the relationships among them were explored and examined in detail.

ACKNOWLEDGEMENT

This study was conducted with the support of the grant-in-aid for Scientific Research (C), No. 19530567. Representative: Ikushi Yamaguchi, 2007–2008) for quantitative research and of the grant-in-aid for Scientific Research (B), No. 24330177 (Representative: Ikushi Yamaguchi 2012–2016) for qualitative research from the Ministry of Education, Culture, Sports, Science, and Technology of Japan.

REFERENCES

Adachi, T. (1998). Job Satisfaction of Sales People: A Covariance Structure Analysis of the Motivational Process (Japanese written). *The Japanese Journal of Psychology 69*(3), pp. 223–228.

Allen, N.J. and Meyer, J.P. (1990). The Measurement and Antecedents of Affective, Continuance and Normative Commitment of the Organization. *Journal of Occupational Psychology 63*, pp. 1–18.

Beugre, C.D. (1998). *Managing Fairness in Organizations*. Westport, CT: Quorum Books.

Bies, R.J. (1987). The Predicament of Injustice: The Management of Moral Outrage. In L.L. Cummings and B.M. Staw (Eds), *Research in Organizational Behaviour*. Vol. 9, Greenwich, CT: JAI Press, pp. 289–319.

Bies, R.J. and Moag, J.S. (1986). Interactional Justice: Communication Criteria of Fairness. In R.J. Lewichi, B. Sheppard and M.H. Bazerman (Eds), *Research on Negotiation in Organizations*. Vol. 1, Greenwich, CT: JAI Press, pp. 43–55.

Bies, R.J. and Shapiro, D.L. (1988). Voice and Justification: Their Influence on Procedural Fairness Judgments. *Academy of Management Journal 31*(3), pp. 676–685.

Bies, R.J. and Tyler, T.R. (1993). The 'Litigation Mentality' in Organizations: A Test of Alternative Psychological Explanations. *Organization Science 4*(3), pp. 352–366.

Bies, R.J., Shapiro, D.L. and Cummings, L.L. (1988). Causal Accounts and Managing Organizational Conflict: Is it Enough to Say it's Not My Fault? *Communication Research 15*(4), pp. 381–399.

Colquitt, J.A. (2001). On the Dimensionality of Organizational Justice: A Construct Validation of a Measure. *Journal of Applied Psychology 86*(3), pp. 386–400.

Elovainio, M., Kivimaki, M. and Helkama, K. (2001). Organizational Justice Evaluations, Job Control, and Occupational Strain. *Journal of Applied Psychology 86*(3), pp. 418–424.

Folger, R. (1977). Distributive and Procedural Justice: Combined Impact of 'Voice' and Improvement on Experienced Inequity. *Journal of Personality and Social Psychology 35*, pp. 108–119.

Folger, R. and Cropanzano, R. (1998). *Organizational Justice and Human Resource Management*. Thousand Oaks, CA: Sage.

Folger, R. and Konovsky, M.A. (1989). Effects of Procedural and Distributive Justice on Reactions to Pay Raise Decisions. *Academy of Management Journal 32*(1), pp. 115–130.

Hofstede, G. (1980). *Culture's Consequences: International Differences in Work-Related Values*. Beverly Hills, CA: Sage.

Holbrook, R.L., Jr. (1999). Managing Reactions to Performance Appraisal: The Influence of Multiple Justice Mechanisms. *Social Justice Research 12*(3), pp. 205–221.

Likert, R. (1961). *New Patterns of Management*. New York: McGraw-Hill.

Lind, E.A., Tyler, T.R. and Huo, Y.J. (1997). Procedural Context and Culture: Variation in the Antecedents of Procedural Justice Judgments. *Journal of Personality and Social Psychology 73*(4), pp. 767–780.

Maslach, C. and Jackson, S.E. (1981). The Measurement of Experienced Burnout. *Journal of Occupational Behaviour 2*, pp. 99–113.

Masterson, S.S., Lewis, K., Goldman, B.M. and Taylor, M.S. (2000). Integrating Justice and Social Exchange: The Differing Effects of Fair Procedures and Treatment on Work Relationships. *Academy of Management Journal 43*(4), pp. 738–748.

Meyer, J.P. and Allen, N.J. (1991). A Three-Component Conceptualization of Organizational Commitment. *Human Resource Management Review 1*, pp. 61–89.

Ministry of Health, Labour and Welfare (2009). *Seisaku report: Kaigoshokuin shoguukaizen koufukin nitsuite.* Viewed on 30 December 2012, from http://www.mhlw.go.jp/seisaku/2009/12/03.html

—- (2010). *Kaigo jinzai no kakuho to shoguu nokaizensaku nitsuite.* Viewed on 29 December 2012, from http://www.mhlw.go.jp/stf/shingi/2r9852000000sj2d-att/2r9852000000sj4y.pdf.

—- (2012). *Heisei 23 nendo koyo kinto kihon chosa*. Viewed on 3 April 2013, from http://www.mhlw.go.jp/toukei/list/dl/71-23r-07.pdf.

Moorman, R.M. (1991). Relationship between Organizational Justice and Organizational Citizenship Behaviours: Do Fairness Perceptions Influence Employee Citizenship? *Journal of Applied Psychology 76*(6), pp. 845–855.

Ohue, T., Moriyama, M. and Nakaya, T. (2010). Byoutou ni kinmusuru kangohshi nioite seisato gender type no dochiraga stressor to burnout nochikaku ni eikyou suruka. *Hiroshima University Hokengaku Journal 9*(1), pp. 7–14.

Shapiro, D.L., Buttner, H.E. and Barry, B. (1994). Explanations: What Factors Enhance Their Perceived Adequacy? *Organizational Behaviour and Human Decision Processes 58*, pp. 346–368.

Spell, C.S. and Arnold, T. (2007). A Multi-Level Analysis of Organizational Justice: Climate, Structure, and Employee Mental Health. *Journal of Management 33*(5), pp. 724–751.

Tao, M. (1995). Burnout – Human Service Stress. "Jyujisha Niokeru Soshiki." *Shakai Shinrigaku Kenkyuu* 4(2), pp. 91–97.

Tao, M. and Kubo, M. (1996). *Banauto no riron to jissai.* Tokyo: Seishinshobo.

Thierry, Y. and Koopman-Iwema, A.M. (1984). Motivation and Satisfaction. In P.T.D. Dreth, H. Thierry and C.M. De Wolf (Eds), *Handbook of Work and Organizational Psychology*. New York: John Wiley & Sons, pp. 131–174.

Tyler, T.R. (1989). The Psychology of Procedural Justice: A Test of the Group-Value Model. *Journal of Personality and Social Psychology 57*(5), pp. 830–838.

Vroom, V.H. (1964), *Work and Motivation*. New York: John Wiley & Sons.

Yajima, H. (2011). A Relationship between Perceptions of Teachers about Helping Characteristics of School Consultants and Teachers' Burnout (Japanese written). *Bulletin of Living Science 33*, pp. 67–77.

Yamaguchi, I. (2007). Shokuba no communication kankyo to kouseikan no danjo ninshiki hikaku. *Human Communication Studies 35*, pp. 93–107.

Yamaguchi, I. and Yamaguchi, M. (2009). Kaigohokenshisetu niokeru chimu komyunikeshon. Working Paper, pp. 1–121.

CHAPTER 11

New Initiatives in Building a Violence Free World for Women

An Indian Perspective

Poonam Bawa and Ram Chandra

All patriarchal societies have created differential norms and practices, structures and institutions, images and perceptions for determining the role of woman. In this process, women have been subordinated to men through denial of dominant areas of expression, creativity and acquisition of power. India is a striking example of a rapidly developing nation, which despite modernizing in many other spheres remains, paradoxically, still retains many of the ills of patriarchy in all spheres of life. The power relationship between men and women remains asymmetrical in this process. Apart from institutionalization of specific spheres of work of men and women, there are several social and cultural practices, which further empower men and create inequality between sexes both in rural and urban India.

Independent India has adopted some unique measures to promote equality and development of women. It has one of the most forward looking constitutions, and has enacted a number of legislations to protect the interests of women and to encourage their participation in national development. Not only this the Constitution grants equality to women in all spheres and also empower the state to adopt protective measures for neutralizing the cumulative social, economic, educational and political disadvantages of women and for making special provisions for promoting their growth and development. Article 39 of the Directive Principles of State Policy concerns women directly includes directives for provision of an adequate means of livelihood; equal pay for equal work both for men and women, and protection of health and strength of workers – men, women and children. Similarly Article 42 provides for just and humane conditions of work and maternity relief (Constitution of India 1950).

In India, since independence, a number of laws have been enacted in order to provide protection to women. These include the Dowry Prohibition

Act 1961, The Equal Remuneration Act 1986, The Hindu Marriage Act 1956, The Hindu Succession Act 1956, The Muslim Women (Protection of Rights on Divorce) Act 1986, the Commission of Sati (prevention) Act 1987, Protection of the Women from Domestic Violence Act 2005, etc. (Kumar 2006). But, the implementation of these laws faces many challenges and remains incomplete.

In spite of all the constitutional measures taken by the Indian government, the reality is that girls and women still face inequality. This remains true for many third world countries where they do not even get a fighting chance to lead healthy, productive lives. Instead, they are devalued as human beings from the day they are born, and even before birth. In Asian countries where a preference for sons is strong, girls are often aborted or killed as infants. Nobel Laureate Amartya Sen estimated that in 1990, 100 million women less than that projected by demographic studies were alive. Abortion, infanticide and other practices harmful to girls were clearly implicated in the numbers of 'missing women' (Ghosh 1999).

In the Indian context, a very strong gender bias is entrenched in the cultural heritage of Indian society. The role of the patriarchal family is crucial. Ironically, the family is the place where most deep-rooted discrimination finds expression. It is a society that idolizes sons. Sons are considered ritually and economically desirable. They are desirable not only to light the funeral pyres of their Hindu parents, but also to ensure continuation of the lineage and family name (Chattopadhyay 1983).

AS A CONCEPT

Gender inequality refers to the obvious or hidden disparities among individuals based on gender. Gender bias, refers to the gender hierarchies in society. In reporting gender inequity, India has the 10th rank out of 128 countries all over the world. And, this problem is increasing. The world in which we live is characterized by deep unequal sharing of the burden of adversities between women and men. Gender inequality exists in most part of the world, from Japan to Morocco, or from Uzbekistan to United States of America.

However, inequality between men and women can take very many different forms. Indeed, gender inequality is not one homogeneous phenomenon, but a collection of disparate and interlinked problems. The issue of gender inequality is one that has been publicly reverberating through society for decades. The problem of gender bias in employment is one of the most pressing issues today. In order to examine this situation, one must try to get to the root of the problem and must understand the sociological factors that cause women to have a much more difficult time getting the same benefits, wages and job opportunities as their male counterparts.

GENDER DISPARITY: INDIAN PERSPECTIVE

Women have always played a crucial role, whether visible or not in Indian society and history. In Indian tradition a woman is formally regarded and depicted as an honourable and dignified personality. She is a venerated as goddess, in many forms. Women have been the subjects of authors and poets, and the objects for artists and sculptors, depicted as the symbol of beauty and love. Traditionally, the Indian woman has been called the foundation stone of the family and society in general. She creates life, nurtures it, guards and strengthens it. In her task as mother, she plays a vital role in the development of the nation. She is the transmitter of tradition, the instrument by which culture is preserved (Chattopadhyay 1983).

Paradoxically, it is also true that despite all these assertions in public life, Indian society has not yet given woman her due. One of the most serious impediments to women's development is the phenomenon of increasing violence against them. This constitutes a serious violation of women's human rights. Violence against women is one of the most significant phenomena of marginalization of women in the development process. Gender violence manifests itself in various forms: female foeticide, infanticide, sexual abuse, incest molestation, sexual harassment at work and on the streets, marital rape, domestic violence in the form of wife-assault and woman battering. Of all the forms of violence that women face, domestic violence remains the least reported and largely suppressed. Recently urban India has been hit by a surge of increasing crime rates against women and also, by rising civil society awareness of its ramifications.

VIOLENCE AGAINST WOMEN: A LIFELONG CURSE

For women, violence is a phenomenon that starts at conception and carries on through their entire life span. In India, pre-birth selection and consequent infanticide is a common occurrence and the preference for a male offspring widespread. This gender bias becomes manifest even when the child is in the mother's womb and attains the form of foeticide and infanticide if the girl child is born. The reason is socio-economic, that is, the patriarchal community considers the female child as a liability to family and society.

Female Foeticide

Of all demographic groups, the girl child is perhaps the most socially disadvantaged. At every stage of her life cycle from conception to adulthood, she is vulnerable to human rights abuses. A life time of systemic gender bias for the girl begins in the mother's womb itself. Gender discrimination-linked abortions have become rampant, after middle-class and upper-class families go for amniocentesis. The boon of the medical field became a curse (Kalyani and Shiv Kumar 2001).

Debates over the woman's right to choose to abort, versus the foetus's right to be born are entering Indian discourse, focussing on the continuum between a prenatal death sentence by virtue of sex and the woman's lack of reproductive autonomy. In India, statistics about sex-selective abortions begin with the dramatic figure of about 10 million such abortions being performed over the last quarter century and end with the horrific count of 3 million female foetuses being aborted annually. Both the right of the girl child to be born and the long-term consequences for women and society are the issue here.

It is necessary to protect the rights of the girl child – particularly her right to be born, her right to remain alive, her right to protection from neglect and abuse and her right to a secure family environment. Despite adequate legal provisions, so far there is no fool proof way of preventing the complete misuse of foetal sex determination through amniocentesis or ultrasound tests to ensure this right.

Female Infanticide

Female infanticide is a most inhuman, uncivilized, barbaric tragic event that is taking place silently in India especially in the states of Tamil Nadu, Bihar, Gujarat, MP, Maharashtra and Rajasthan. The killing of girl babies is frequently practiced in Thar Desert area of Rajasthan, particularly among the Bhati Rajput families. The infant is killed through manual strangulation or through administration of opium. She is killed immediately after birth – either drowned in a tub of milk or fed *afeem* (opium), or simply smothered with a pillow (Venkatachalau and Srinivas 1993).

In India, the sex ratio is skewed dramatically in favour of men. The chief reason is the high number of females who die before reaching adulthood. Tribal societies in India have a less skewed sex ratio than other caste groups. This is in spite of the fact that tribal communities have far lower income levels, lower literacy rates and less adequate health facilities. Many experts suggest the higher number of males in India can be attributed to female infanticides and sex-selective abortions (*Encyclopaedia of Indian Women* 2005). Continuity of the dowry tradition has been one of the main reasons for sex-selective abortions and female infanticides in India. Fear of sexual abuse of the girl child is also a major cause for female infanticide (*The Hindu* 2012).

BARRIERS IN EDUCATION FOR GIRLS

While gender discrimination exists in providing care to the girl child in the areas of health, nutrition, education and distribution of work during early childhood years, this gets further heightened with the advent of puberty. More drop-out of girls after middle school education is due to the fear of sending girls alone to the school as they are afraid of their safety and chastity. Hence, they want to be sure that the girls are 'safe' at home till they get married at the earliest opportunity, so that the 'burden' clan be passed on to her in-laws. To remain chaste amidst temptation is like walking on fire. If 'anything happens' to a girl, she has no other option except to commit suicide. Hence, the parents are anxious to get their daughters married off as soon as they attain puberty.

INEQUITY IN ACCESS TO HEALTH AND NUTRITION

Education is not the only area in which girls are being neglected. In places where family resources are scarce and discrimination strong, girls get inferior food and their health care. In many countries, girls are breast-fed for shorter periods than boys. A study in India revealed that 51 per cent of boys were breast-fed, compared with 30 per cent of girls (Kalyani and Shiv Kumar 2001). Girls in many parts of the world are not taken to health centres, have lower rate of immunization and receive less nurturing than their brothers.

Moreover, a girl's poor health is likely to be passed on to the next generation when she becomes a mother, especially if she is uneducated. A United Nations study of 115 countries found that a mother's literacy was more closely correlated with life expectancy at birth than was any other factor. And a mother's education has a greater effect on lowering infant mortality and improving family health than does a father's education. The advantages of educating mothers are indisputable. Women with schooling tend to delay marriage and childbirth and have fewer children. They also provide their children with better health and nutrition.

The maternal mortality in India is the second highest in the world. Only 42 per cent of births in the country are supervised by health care professionals. Most women deliver babies with help from women in the family who often lack the skills and resources to save the mother's life if she is in danger. According to UNDP Human Development Report (1997), 88 per cent of pregnant women (aged 15–49) were found to be suffering from anaemia.

Domestic Violence

Domestic violence is the most serious violation of all basic rights that a woman suffers in her own home at the hands of members within her own family. A recent study of National Family Health Survey and National Crimes Records Bureau has revealed that almost every six hours, somewhere in India, young married women is being burnt alive, beaten to death or force to commit suicide. At least 20 per cent of married women between the ages of 15 and 49 have experienced domestic violence at some point in their lives (National Crime Records Bureau [NCRB] 2012). Domestic violence has not only serious consequences for the health and well-being of the individual women, but it also serves to maintain their subjugation as a class. What is most alarming and painful is that domestic violence occurs within the framework of intimate relationships in a situation of dependency, making reporting and access to legal aid and other support services difficult.

FAMILY PLANNING

The average woman in rural areas of India has little or no control over child bearing. Women, particularly in rural areas, do not have access to safe methods of contraception. This has major implications for empowerment and health. The public health system emphasizes permanent methods, such as sterilization, or long-term methods such as IUDs that do not need follow-up. Sterilization accounts for more than 75 per cent of total contraception, with female sterilization accounting for almost 95 per cent of all sterilizations (GOI 2006).

SANITATION

In 2011 a 'Right to Pee' (as called by the media) campaign began in Mumbai, India's largest city. Women, but not men, have to pay to urinate in Mumbai, despite regulations against this practice. Women have also been sexually assaulted while urinating in fields. Thus, activists have collected more than 50,000 signatures supporting their demands that the local government stop charging women to urinate, build more toilets, keep them clean, provide sanitary napkins and a trash can, and hire female attendants. In response, city officials have agreed to build hundreds of public toilets for women in Mumbai, and some local legislators are now promising to build toilets for women in every one of their districts (New York Times 2012).

Violent Crime Against Women

Police records in India show a high incidence of crimes against women. The National Crime Records Bureau had reported in 1998 that by 2010 growth in the rate of crimes against women would exceed the population growth rate (NCRB 1998). Earlier, many crimes against women were not reported to police due to the social stigma attached to rape and molestation. Official statistics show a dramatic increase in the number of reported crimes against women. Over 32,000 murders, 19,000 rapes, 7,500 dowry deaths and 36,500 molestation cases are the violent crimes reported in India against women (NCRB 2012). While Madhya Pradesh is worst off among the states, the national capital New Delhi continues to hold on to its reputation of being the most unsafe city in India. Delhi takes the top slot for crimes ranging from murders and rapes to dowry deaths and abductions (NCRB 2012).

TYPES OF GENDER CRIME

Acid Throwing

A Thomas Reuters Foundation survey says that India is the fourth most dangerous place in the world for women to live in. Women belonging to any class, caste, creed or religion can be victims of this cruel form of violence and disfigurement, a premeditated crime intended to kill or maim permanently and act as a lesson to put a woman in her place. In India, acid attacks on women who dared to refuse a man's proposal of marriage or asked for a divorce are a form of revenge. Acid is cheap, easily available and the quickest way to destroy a woman's life. The numbers of acid attacks have been rising (NCRB 2012). Acid attacks are common in Cambodia, Afghanistan, India, Bangladesh and Pakistan. Globally, 1,500 people in 20 countries annually are victims of acid attacks.

Sexual Harassment

Of the total number of crime against women reported in 1990, half related to molestation and harassment in the workplace. In 1997, in the landmark judgment in the Vishakha Case, the Supreme Court of India took a strong stand against sexual harassment of women in the workplace. The court also laid down detailed guidelines for prevention and redressal of grievances. The National Commission for Women subsequently elaborated these guidelines into a Code of Conduct for employers.

Dowry

Dowry, however, is one of the core causes of male-child preference. The practice of demanding and giving dowries has been spreading to communities where it was hitherto unknown. Dissatisfaction and avarice have combined to create social conditions where more than 6,000 girls lose their lives annually in dowry-related deaths according to the NCRB (2012). Strict laws do not seem to deter families from demanding nor from feeling like their prestige is attached to giving.

In 1961, the Government of India passed the Dowry Prohibition Act, making dowry demands in wedding arrangements illegal. However, many cases of dowry-related domestic violence, suicides and murders have been reported. In the 1980s, numerous such cases were reported. A 1980 report claimed 400 bride burning (kitchen fires) cases. Within a span of 10 years, it rose to 5,800 in 1990. Among the urban educated, such dowry abuse has reduced considerably (Kumar 2006).

Child Marriage

Child marriage was traditionally widely prevalent in India, and the practice still continues in some parts of rural India. Historically, child brides would live with their parents until they reached puberty. The practice led to many social evils. In the past, child widows were condemned to a life of great agony, shaved heads, living in isolation and being shunned by society. Although child marriage was outlawed in 1860, it is still not totally eradicated as a practice. According to UNICEF's 'State of the World's Children—2009' report, 47 per cent of India's women aged 20–24 were married before the legal age of 18, rising to 56 per cent in rural areas. The report also showed that 40 per cent of the world's child marriages occur in India (UNICEF 2009).

Trafficking

The Immoral Traffic (Prevention) Act was passed in 1956. However, many cases of trafficking of young girls and women have been reported. These women are either forced into prostitution, or as domestic work or as child labour.

Eve Teasing

Eve teasing is a euphemism used in India and sometimes in Pakistan, Bangladesh and Nepal for public sexual harassment, street harassment or molestation of women by men. Many Indian activists blame the rising incidents of such sexual harassment against women on the influence of 'Western culture'. In 1987, The Indecent Representation of Women (Prohibition) Act was passed to prohibit indecent representation of women through advertisements or in publications, writing, painting, or in any other manner.

CREATING A VIOLENCE FREE WORLD FOR WOMEN: THE ROLE OF CIVIL SOCIETY

In India, even in the twenty-first century, women cannot step out of their houses at any time of the day feeling assured of their physical and sexual safety. The fear of violence and teasing restricts a woman's anatomy, curtails her mobility and her ability to work and participate in social activities. Even today in India, women can't travel at night in secluded places, and sometimes even in daytime at crowded places. Numerous incidents of physical/sexual abuse and culturally justified violence happen every day to women in this country.

CASE STUDY: THE NIRBHAYA RAPE CASE

The 2012 Delhi Gang Rape Case involves a rape and murder that occurred on 16 December 2012, in Munirka, a neighbourhood located in the southern part of New Delhi, when a 23-year-old female physiotherapy intern was beaten and gang raped in a bus in which she was travelling with her male companion. There were only five others in the bus, including the driver, all of whom raped the woman. The woman died from her injuries 13 days later while undergoing emergency treatment in Singapore.

The incident generated widespread national and international coverage and was condemned by various women groups, both in India and abroad. Subsequently, public protests against the Government of India and the Government of Delhi for not providing adequate security for women took place in New Delhi, where thousands of protesters clashed with security forces. Similar protests took place in major cities throughout the country.

Public Protests After the Rape

Public protests took place in New Delhi on 21 December 2012 at India Gate, the Parliament of India, and at Rashtrapati Bhavan. Similar protests occurred throughout the country. The protests have also been explained as expressions of middle-class angst arising out of a collapse of a social contract between them and the liberal state. Protestors cited the sex crime rate statistics in Delhi as the highest among Indian cities. Police figures show a rape reported on average every 18 hours; reported rape cases rose by nearly 17 per cent between 2007 and 2011 (NCRB 2012). Calling the case a 'Wake-up call', the regional programme director for U.N. Women South Asia said, 'There are rape cases in almost all cities and rural areas, where the victim dies immediately because of the brutality of the crime' (UN Women 2013).

After the Death

After the victim's death on 29 December 2012 protests were staged all over India. Many of the mourners carried candles and wore black dress. The New Year's celebrations were scaled down to a large extent, with the Indian armed forces and some clubs and hotels in Delhi cancelling their New Year parties. Since her death, the unprecedented protests against rape have continued across India and have motivated the media and police to focus on the rising incidents of rape and sexual harassment in the country. Sexual assaults have made headline news almost daily. After a woman from the Indian state of Punjab was raped under similar circumstances, a senior police spokesman said, 'the increased media reporting and the protests have created an awakening among women, and they are now coming forward like never before to report rape and want to fight for justice. This has also made our police force more sensitive to these cases.

International Reactions

The American embassy released a statement on 29 December, offering their condolences to the woman's family and stating 'we also recommit ourselves to changing attitudes and ending all forms of gender-based violence, which plagues every country in the world' (US Embassy 2012). The United States Government has granted the victim, *Nirbhaya*, the 2013 International Women of Courage Award. In Paris, people participated in a march to the Indian Embassy where a petition was handed over asking for action to make India safer for women. UN Secretary General Ban Ki-moon issued this statement: 'Violence against women must never be accepted, never excused, never tolerated. Every girl and woman has the right to be respected, valued and protected' (Ban Ki-moon 2013).

The United Nations Entity for Gender Equality and the Empowerment of Women called on the Government of India and the Government of Delhi 'to do everything in their power to take up radical reforms, ensure justice and reach out with robust public services to make women's lives more safe and secure'. Demonstrations were also been held in Bangladesh, Pakistan, Nepal and Sri Lanka. The protests there have taken not only inspiration from the Indian protests, but are also focusing on local issues about rape and domestic violence.

THE JUSTICE VERMA COMMITTEE AND CHANGES IN INDIAN LAW

In immediate response to the Civil Society outrage and demands for harsher laws for rapists, The Criminal Law (Amendment) Ordinance, 2013, was promulgated by the President of India on 3 February 2013, which provided for amendment of the Indian Penal Code, Indian Evidence Act and Code of Criminal Procedure, 1973, on laws related to sexual offences. The ordinance provided for death penalty in case of rape (TOI 2013). Subsequently, Indian Parliament legislated to ensure that Indian Law provides for stringent punishments to rapists.

Women want to live in a violence-free world, which is a worthy goal. Efforts to achieve it, at the very least, put us further along the path of progress. We have increased opportunities to shine the spotlight on violence, examining its twisted roots in a new light and consider the ways in which each one of us is implicated. That is certainly something to pay attention to.

The remarks of Executive Director of UN Women, Michelle Bachelet on 8 March 2013 at the International Women's Day commemoration at the United Nations in New York indicate the urgency and the relevance with which the issue needs to be tackled. She made a rallying call to the international community to move forward on gender equality and women's rights. Ms. Bachelet highlighted the progress that has been made in the last century but called for more robust actions and commitment to ensure the protection of the rights of women and girls to live in dignity, free of violence and discrimination (Bachelet 2013).

> We have moved forward with the 1979 Convention on the Elimination of All Forms of Discrimination against Women, CEDAW, the 1994 Programme of Action of the International Conference on Population and Development and the ICPD+5 Key Actions for further implementation. We have moved forward with the Platform for Action of the 1995 Fourth World Conference on Women in Beijing, the Security Council's landmark resolution 1325 on women, peace and security, its subsequent resolutions and all international human rights conventions. My message today is: We cannot move backwards, we must keep moving forward. It is what we owe to millions of women fighting for their rights around the world … . There can be no peace, no progress, no equality without women's full and equal rights and participation. And there can be no gender equality without women's realization. Women's realization of their full reproductive rights, their right to sexual and reproductive health are essential to the empowerment of women and to gender equality.

REFERENCES

Bachelet, Michelle (2013). Remarks of United Nations Under-Secretary-General and Executive Director of UN Women at the International Women's Day Commemorative Event at the United Nations. 8 March 2013.

Ban Ki-moon (2013). At http://www.un.org/apps/news/story.asp

Chattopadhyay, K.D. (1983). *Indian Women Battle for Freedom*. New Delhi: Abhinav Publications.

Constitution of India (1950). Articles 39(a) and Article 42.

Encyclopaedia of Indian Women (2005). 11 Volumes, New Delhi: Eastern Book Corporation.

Ghosh, S.K. (1999). *Indian Panorama: Triumphs and Tragedies*. Vol. III, New Delhi: APH Publishing Corporation, p. 1187.

GOI (2006). *Sample Registration System, Maternal Mortality in India: 1997–2003: Trends, Causes and Risk Factors*. New Delhi: Registrar General of India. Available at http://ideas.repec.org/p/ess/wpaper/id753.html.

Kalyani, M.S. and Shiva Kumar, A.K. (2001). *Women in India: How Free? How Equal?* New York: UNDP.

Kumar, A. (2006). *Indian Women: Status and Contemporary Social Issues*. New Delhi: Anmol Publications, p. 325.

The Hindu (2012). India Loses 3 Million Girls in Infanticide. New Delhi, 9 October 2012.

TOI (2013). Justice J.S. Verma Committee Submits Report on Rape Laws. New Delhi, *Times of India*, 23 January 2013.

UNDP (1997). *Human Development Report*. New York: Oxford University Press.

UPI (1997). Kitchen Fires Kill Indian Brides with Inadequate Dowry. New Delhi, 23 July 1997.

UNICEF (2012). Child Marriage in India. An Analysis of Available Data (2012). New Delhi: UNICEF.

—- (2009). *State of the World's Children Report*. New York: UNICEF.

US Embassy, New Delhi, India (2012). Statement on the Death of New Delhi Assault Victim. 29 December 2012.

Venkatachalau, R. and Srinivas, V. (1993). *Female Infanticide*. New Delhi: Har-Anand, p. 50.

New York Times (2012). At http://www.nytimes.com/2012/06/15/world/asia/in-mumbai-a-campaign-against-restroom-injustice.html?pagewanted=all.

UN Women (2013). At http://womensdevelopment.wordpress.com/crimes-against-women.

CHAPTER 12

Gender, Governance of Commons and Livelihood Security

A study of the North Bengal Tea Region of India

Padam Nepal and Lalit P. Tirkey

Most of the academic deliberations in the global south constitute the enabling as well as the disabling aspects of the methods and the pedagogies invented, styled and tailored in the West.[1] Ambivalent as it is the postcolonial world exhibits a society that needs to be studied anew with methods homespun and more accommodating to the lived realities of the same. The global south is faced with multi-level dilemmas. At one level is the problem of adopting, inventing/birthing and acceptable methodologies and at another level is the problem of shedding the methodologies and pedagogies implanted through the colonial encounter.[2]

The first level of the problem reflects the contested nature of the voices in the global south and the plurality of the society. The second level of the problem refers more to the contestation of the dominant methodologies in more or less incoherent unison by the global south.[3] Amidst the mélange of theoretical, methodological, pedagogical contest in the south, there exists a rather strong discomfort of the south to the dominance of the north and also the contentious engagement of the south within itself when it comes to 'gender studies'. Gender studies in India has conveniently been understood to mean 'women's studies' overlooking the definitional encapsulations within the ambit of 'gender'. Gender studies in other words exclude the other sexual or bodily located identities.[4] Acknowledging the limitations of the gender studies so construed, but yet reinforcing the current trends of treating gender studies synonymous with women's studies, the present chapter would again be exclusivist in its nature, taking 'women' as a 'gendered' category for the present study.

Being an analytical exploratory and descriptive study based on an emergent approach, we have used a *mixed* method of study, a sort of a hybrid methodology, synthesizing the merits of both qualitative and quantitative methodologies. The study has made an extensive analysis of the documents, reports, newspaper clippings, newsletters and fliers on the subject under investigation. We have also conducted field surveys for the collection of primary data, using tools such as in-depth interviews (semi-structured and structured), nonparticipant observation and informal discussions with primacy.

THE STUDY AREA AND CONTEXT

Geographically, the study area covers most parts of hills and plains of the Darjeeling District, and Northern part of the Jalpaiguri District, what was once called as *Western Dooars*. Specifically, the three regions or 'tea districts' situated in the eastern Himalaya and Himalayan foothills of West Bengal, lying between 26E0′16 and 27E0′00 N parallels of latitude and between 88E00′4 and 89E0′53 E longitudes on the northern most part of the state, comprising the Hills and Terai of the Darjeeling District and Doors of the Jalpaiguri District, constitute 'the North Bengal tea region'.

The Indian Tea Industry, since its inception, has contributed significantly to the national and provincial economy, including the initial development and economic growth of North Bengal[5] (Ghosh 1987; Munsi 1980) tea region. It has played a pivotal role in the regional economy of North Bengal by providing livelihoods to thousands of households for more than a hundred year (Sarkar and Lama 1998). As a matter of fact, even in the twenty-first century, this industry is providing livelihoods to thousands of households by indirect employment and sustenance through ancillary jobs to many more households (Ghosh 1987; Sarkar and Lama 1998). However, in recent decades, particularly from late 1990s to early 2000s, the Indian Tea Industry has undergone serious crises due to various reasons.

According to some analysts, the rising production and labour cost, falling tea prices due to oversupply of tea and decline of demand in the global market, combined with stiff competition from many tea producing countries and other factors have caused a huge slump in the profit, leading to the crises in the India's tea industry (Goddard 2004). It is understood that even in the worst scenario, the larger tea producers or tea-owning companies are capable of switching to alternative industries for their profit-making or income generation. But what happens to the tea workers whose livelihood almost exclusively depends on tea garden work for survival? More than a million tea workers in India face threats to their livelihood security in the face of uncertainty surrounding the Indian Tea Industry in the form of 'sick tea gardens',[6] temporary or indefinite lockouts and ultimate closure of many tea gardens.

Studies show that in recent years a large number of workers are threatened by further tea garden closure while in plantations that remain open, workers suffer wage cuts, tougher picking demands, increased short-term insecure contracts and appalling living and working conditions (Goddard 2004; Thapa 2012). North Bengal is one of the most badly affected tea regions in India by the brewing crises. During the normal operation of tea gardens, the workers' livelihoods remain merely at the subsistence level; on the other hand, the livelihood insecurity of tea workers and their households gets accentuated whenever gardens get closed or abandoned. One of the foremost factors contributing to the livelihood insecurity of the North Bengal tea garden workers is the low wage structure, which is one of the lowest among the tea producing regions in India (see Table 1).

Table 1 *Wage (₹/day) differential in tea gardens of different tea growing Indian states*

State	*2005*	*2006*	*2007*	*2008*	*2009*	*2010 Onwards*
North Bengal*	48.40	50.90	53.40	56.40	57.40	67.70
Assam*	51.10	53.40	56.10	59.00	62.70	69.00
Karnataka	71.00	73.00	75.00	77.00	81.44	85.00
Tamil Nadu	73.00	75.00	77.00	79.00	84.44	89.00
Kerala	78.36	80.36	82.36	84.36	88.80	94.00

Sources: Computed from Report of CEC (2003).

* The wages in North Bengal and Assam exclude ration (3.26 Kg and 2.44 kg wheat per week) the workers and their dependents receive.

To add to their woes, wage cuts, irregular or delay in wage payments, increasing job reduction leading to more unemployment, and above all, malnutrition and starvation deaths in some tea gardens have negatively affected the psyche of tea workers in this region (Biswas et al. 2005; Talwar et al. 2003). But what actually accentuates the livelihood insecurity of workers is their sole dependence or over-reliance on the low paying tea garden work, which constitutes the central livelihood activity of a large number of tea garden households. Besides, the management and government apathy have aggravated the situation, but the combination of various factors has accentuated the livelihood threats of most tea workers in the region.

Alternative livelihood options or multiple livelihood choices are necessary not only as safety nets during crises in tea gardens but also as source of income diversification. Generally, the viable alternative livelihood opportunities are conspicuous by their absence in or around the tea gardens of North

Bengal; some odd jobs available are not enough to absorb large number of unemployed workers (Bhadra 1992). Moreover, the tea workers, despite living in tea gardens of North Bengal (as elsewhere), have no rights over other natural resources. This deprivation makes the workers' households difficult to cope during garden lockouts, thereby accentuating livelihood insecurity and making workers' community more vulnerable to stress and shocks. Access to CPRs as sources of alternative livelihood is essential not just for the economic development, but also for the enhancement of livelihoods security, which, however, is not accessible to them. Therefore, the non-availability of alternative livelihoods options have contributed to the continuing poverty and backwardness of tea workers in the North Bengal tea region constituted mainly of ST and SC population (See Table 2).

Table 2 *Distribution of SC/ST population in the three North Bengal districts of West Bengal*

District	*Percentage of SC Population*			*Percentage of ST Population*		
	1981	*1991*	*2001*	*1981*	*1991*	*2001*
Cooch Behar	47.03	49.84	51.76	0.61	0.57	0.60
Darjeeling	12.58	14.25	16.15	10.60	14.75	13.78
Jalpaiguri	34.02	34.61	36.99	19.35	22.20	21.04
N. Bengal	27.69	29.91	29.10	11.21	11.29	16.29
W. Bengal	25.22	21.98	23.62	5.72	6.63	5.59

Source: India Census (2001).

Thus, the scheduled tribes (STs) and scheduled castes (SCs) are perhaps the most seriously affected communities by the brewing crises and uncertain future facing the North Bengal tea industry, particularly due to the financial crunch and lockouts of many tea gardens. The largest labour force in the tea plantations of Assam and West Bengal, the two major tea-producing India states, comprise chiefly of scheduled groups, namely, the tribal and lower caste communities, who were brought as indentured migrant workers from the central provinces of India more than a century ago (Bhadra 1992; Bhowmik et al. 1996; Karotemprel and Roy 1990). The districts of Darjeeling and Jalpaiguri, the two major tea-producing districts, are characterized by a sizable proportion of ST population (21% and 13.8%, respectively) as compared to the state average of 5.6 per cent while SCs too are in sizable number in other districts of the region (North Bengal Report 2002) (see Table 3).

Table 3 *Gender and educational status*

Gender		*Education Category*					*Total*
		Illiterate	*Cl. 1–5*	*Cl. 6–9*	*Cl. 10–12*	*College*	
Male	Count	73	102	80	41	1	297
	%	15.2%	21.3%	16.7%	8.5%	.2%	61.9%
Female	Count	99	46	34	4	0	183
	%	20.6%	9.6%	7.1%	.8%	.0%	38.1%
Total	Count	172	148	114	45	1	480
	%	35.8%	30.8%	23.8%	9.4%	.2%	100.0%

The starvation cases in the Dooars region of North Bengal are the indicator that tea workers, particularly from the ST and SC sections, have become the most vulnerable and non-resilient to shocks and stresses that was manifested in the form of 'sickness', closure or abandonment of many tea gardens. According to the studies done by Talwar et al. (2003) and Biswas et al. (2005) from 2003 to 2008 during and after the closure or abandonment of about 18 tea gardens in this region, majority of children, women and aged who had succumbed to starvation death due to sickness following malnutrition and other factors belonged to the scheduled groups. There are many other challenges for securing of livelihoods in the closed tea gardens of North Bengal that exacerbate the vulnerability of tea workers, especially from the ST/SC communities. However, one of the major factors contributing to this accentuated livelihood insecurity is the pattern of governance of the commons in the tea region, which constitutes the central concern of the present chapter.

TEA COMMONS: THE EXISTING GOVERNANCE PATTERN AND ACCENTUATED LIVELIHOOD INSECURITIES

Common Pool Resource (CPR) refers to the natural resources that have common ownership or is considered resources for common use with or without having open access. In India, CPRs include village pastures and grazing grounds, village forests and wood lots, protected and un-classed government forest, wasteland, common threshing ground, water drainage, ponds and tanks, rivers, rivulets, water reservoirs, canals and irrigation channels (Beck 2000; Jodha 1986). Thus, there are many resources that could be pooled commonly by poor people and utilized for enhancing their livelihood. CPRs play important role in the life and economy of rural folks by providing economic sustenance (Jodha 1986). The available commons in the North Bengal tea region context include water, vested land, forest cover, pastures and grazing grounds, sand and gravel in the riverbeds in the vicinity of the gardens.

The North Bengal tea region that forms part of the Himalayan and sub-Himalayan region is endowed with diverse resource base. However, since the British planters started establishing, and subsequently expanding tea cultivable land, the forested area, even marshy landscape were transformed into commercial tea. In some tea garden premises, components of common property land resources can be found in the form of community pastures and grazing ground, apart from some woodlots, but they are fast disappearing. One of the main reasons for the disappearance of these CPRs from the tea garden lands is the continuing expansion of tea cultivation as mono crop land use pattern covering expansive landscape while in most tea gardens only the remnant of forest covers are found in some corners (Nepal and Tirkey 2012; Tirkey 2005). In the rural areas, 'the major problems faced by the CPRs are related to the decline of land resources through physical loss due to submersion under changing river courses and also due to allocation of CPR lands for agricultural and non-agricultural uses, including allocation for public purposes like roads, buildings, and of late to the so-called Special Economic Zones'.

GENDER, GOVERNANCE OF COMMONS AND LIVELIHOOD INSECURITIES: THE EXISTING SCENARIO

Governance of the commons has become a contested terrain today. Having moved beyond Hardin's (1968) 'Tragedy of the Commons' narrative, commons scholars have examined governance arrangements in diverse resource systems with multiple user groups at local, regional and global scales (Dietz et al. 2003; Ostrom et al. 2002). The emphasis on rules of access, exclusion and subtractability, and the identification of design principles or enabling conditions for the management of common pool resources are major contributions (Agrawal 2002; Baland and Platteau 1996; Ostrom 1990). However, in the Indian context, much of the policy formulations appear to have been caught up with Hardinian dilemma as evident from the existing nature of the commons governing regimes, with the stringent policies constantly constraining the access to commons by the rural folks.

The situations in tea regions are all the more complex with the shift from 'governance' to the 'control' of the commons by vested interests in connivance with the management. This has complicated the access to commons and accentuated the livelihood insecurity of the garden workers, the worst victim of the situation being the women workers. It is the womenfolk of the garden who are most affected because of the denial of the right to access the commons in the tea garden situations. This is because women are still the custodians of the household activities, beyond their normal daily wage labour they sell. The womenfolk are responsible for collecting drinking water, firewood for cooking, procure green vegetables and save assets for future use. However, the existing pattern of the governance of the commons in the tea garden premises coupled with the poor educational status of the women in the tea regions, the women have miserably failed to secure the everyday livelihood requirements for their households.

This is due to several factors. Women in the tea region are worse off in terms of literacy and education. One of the most important assets within the human capital is 'education' for the individuals and households needed to ensure multi-faceted empowerment (Ellis 2000). Education serves as a powerful tool for moving nations, communities and households towards a more sustainable future (The Education Charter 1999). Basic education is essential for improving the workforce and public participation in any civil society while also playing crucial role for more sustainable future (The Education Charter 1999). Like in other sectors, even in the tea sector, women workers are found to be at the margins. It has been generally found in almost all the tea-producing countries that women, despite constituting the largest work force in tea plantations, have more disadvantages with low education and skill development (Gain 2009). The case in North Bengal tea gardens is no different. The social restrictions even in the tea garden households prevent them from attending elementary schooling or household compulsions lead them to discontinue education for the sake of their male siblings.

The finding presents some significant statistics. Among the older generation of tea workers, a very high percentage of female workers (55%) had 'no education' as compared to 25 per cent male workers having 'no education'. Again, while there was significant difference in the educational level of male vis-à-vis female in elementary/primary education (approximately, 35% vs. 25%) and junior high school education (approximately, 28% vs. 18%), there was a wide gap when it came to high school and higher secondary education (Cl. 10–12 level). Approximately, 13 per cent male workers had attained high school or higher secondary school education as compared with only 3 per cent female workers. The lack of education among the female workers is reflected in their being engaged in unskilled tea plucking work. Finding corroborated by field visits shows hardly any female worker in clerical post in the surveyed gardens or securing white-collar job outside the tea garden premises.

Ownership of resources, particularly land, water and forest, provides livelihood security and aids the intervention against economic crises, besides providing regular subsistence income for improving the livelihoods. In the government leased plantation land, tea workers do not have rights over the land they occupy. Only 22.55 per cent households own some plots of land (1–3 Bigha), whereas an overwhelming majority (77.45%) is landless. Besides land, other natural resources, particularly the Common Property/Pool Resources (CPR), are beyond the access of tea garden workers. However, in North Bengal, even the vacant and unutilized land in most tea gardens is not made available for workers. The argument for the denial of land rights is that tea cultivation fields are government lands given in lease to the tea planters for a fixed number of years (Sharma 1999), and hence, it cannot be given to the landless tea workers. Of course, being part of an organized sector such as tea industry, tea garden workers have never been considered poor or brought under BPL category. Many tea gardens are endowed with rich vegetation, water bodies and other natural resources; they are also endowed with common resources such as water, vested land, forest cover, sand and gravel. Yet, the tea garden workers cannot claim rights over them; in extreme cases, some tea workers from closed/abandoned tea gardens have been witnessed to collect minor forest produce or dig out pebbles from the river bed to be sold for food.

The combined powerful forces of planters and contractors have also ensured that the marginal tea garden communities do not have right over the 'commons' in and around tea gardens, such as forest resources and vested land or open access to sand, gravel or water from the rivers/streams. However, the tea workers cannot claim rights over them. Normally, what the village-community can rightfully claim having common property rights in rural India (Berkes 1998) is denied to the tea garden workers because they come under industrial workers category. The deprivation and denial from accessing these common resources have led to the reactionary measures taken by some workers of Gandrapara, New Glencoe and Dooteriah by encroaching forested land and recklessly quarrying rivers flowing through the garden areas. Paradoxically, the past history shows that colonial rulers, including tea planters, ruthlessly exploited natural resources of the region, and timber, jute, tobacco and other plants were taken out as raw material without reinvestment. Today, different tea garden managements in the name of tea cultivation drive continue to marginalize the CPR land in the tea garden premises, thereby denying the tea workers even community pasture and grazing ground.

Furthermore, the loss of forest cover in the tea garden vicinities has accentuated the livelihood insecurities of the tea garden women. The constructions of gender and gendered practices have been influenced by culture, political environment, legal and governance structures, markets and religion. But across all cultures women have played the reproductive role and have handled household chores, whereas men have been handlers of productive activities such as earning (Pandolfelli et al. 2007). It is in this gendered role that forests come to play an important role in the lives of rural women, as they depend on forests to meet the needs of the household. Consequently, their dependence on forests is more than men.

A large-scale deforestation took place in the nineteenth century when many trees were cleared to begin tea cultivation in the Darjeeling Hills as well as plains of Terai and Dooars (Grunning 1911; O'Malley 1907). Researches by Ives and Messerli (1989), Sarkar and Lama (1986) and Schickhoff (1995) provide evidence of problems caused by deforestation following tea cultivation and its expansion. These were manifested in the form of loss of biodiversity and wildlife, gradual drying up of springs/channels and problems of landslides/soil erosion in the Himalayan and sub-Himalayan regions. In the subsequent years, as the population multiplied, competition for food, fuel and other resources intensified, causing local people to turn to destructive practices (Kaniyal 2003; Schickhoff 1995). This effect is felt even in tea garden regions, although cleared forests were replaced by tea bushes, which, at least, continued to have some degree of soil stabilizing influence.

Findings show that some tea gardens of all three regions witnessed two phases of deforestation: first in the mid-nineteenth century, when forested areas were extensively cleared during the creation of tea plantations. Second, during the first half of the twentieth century, to meet the requirements of First and Second World Wars, plenty of forest trees were cut down, although the intensity of deforestation was higher at the time of the Second World War (Sarkar and Lama 1986). Third, episodes of deforestation in tea gardens of all three tea regions followed by the temporary closure (notable being the Gorkhaland Agitation led to frequent garden lockouts without any pay) beginning at fag end of the twentieth century, which still persist during political agitations in the hills and the plains. During such situations, the out-of-work labourers are compelled to fell forest trees for selling timber and making charcoal to generate income and secure their livelihoods (Tirkey 2005).

The cumulative effect of these past and recent activities resulted in the loss of biodiversity, wildlife and gradual decline of water table (Sarkar and Lama 1986). The combination of tree logging and altering of land to suit tea cultivation has had negative effect on the shear strength and shear stress of the soil, causing imbalance of the land. In fact, the observations show that even in recent years, successive garden managements tend to convert the vacant and unutilized land, including forested and stream area, into tea cultivation land. Every expansive measure for tea industry has led to the disappearance of tree cover and denudation of the area in the plantations.

The loss of forest cover has had adverse effect on many resources, especially land and water that would provide alternative livelihood to the tea garden workers. Loss of forest meant loss of fodder and other products that were being used for livestock besides additional food stuffs for the local population. Loss of forest meant loss of medicinal plants and shrubs and other herbs due to denudation of fertile land that had worked as a source of local medicine as well as source of food. Loss of forest also meant that in the time of crises, tea garden residents could not depend on forest to extract timber for sale and exchange them for food and money for managing households.

Deforestation also resulted in gradual drying up of springs and streams that would have otherwise helped in crop cultivation and spawning of different fish species as source of food and income. Finally, the loss of forest cover also accentuated land sliding and soil erosion, thereby degrading the land. As a result, the possibility of household land being used for kitchen gardening to generate livelihood resources too got jeopardized, and the situation is continuously getting aggravated, thereby rendering it more difficult for the tea garden womenfolk to cope up with stresses and shock emanating from livelihood failures.

CONCLUSION

Interrogating the Possibilities/Complexities of Reform for Gender-Friendly Governance of the Commons

What is evident from the above discussion is that the womenfolk in the North Bengal tea region have practically no access to the available commons in the garden premises. But on the other hand, they being the custodians of household livelihood securities confront complex contours of insecurity to meet the daily requirements of their households. Their woes are compounded by the lack of education and capacity building and the consequent 'ignorance' in the *enclave economy* of the tea gardens. This is revealed from the fact that education, which is one of the prime components of human capital that is essential to provide capabilities to individuals and households for securing better livelihood opportunities, is relatively not accessed by the garden women. Without education or for lack of good education, human capabilities become stunted. Hence, the tea workers in general and the tea women in particular are most vulnerable to shocks and stresses such as malnutrition, hunger and diseases after the abandonment or closure of tea plantations on which their sole livelihood depends. This owes primarily to the lack of education, training and skill development for the garden population in general and womenfolk in the garden in particular, to be able to secure alternative livelihoods. This calls for a necessity to reform the governance of tea commons.

The decision making over natural resource allocation and management is the privilege of the state, although policies on areas such as Joint Forest

Management stress on community-based management system justified on the grounds of local livelihoods, economic opportunity and environmental sustainability. Yet, improving governance of commons requires much more than getting policies adopted and framing right regulations. It depends critically on the effective functioning of state agencies, alongside the private sector and civil society, to help translate policy goals into practice.

Hence, effective and gender-friendly government reforms for governance of commons require inclusive *representation* of affected groups, particularly the poor and vulnerable, in policy formulation and development planning at all levels; robust mechanisms of *accountability* to ensure that individuals and groups granted decision-making authority are held responsible for the public consequences of their choices and do not abuse their authority; and institutional *capacity* to enable public, private and civil society actors to fulfil their roles effectively; to adapt to changing circumstances and to negotiate implementation challenges as they emerge. Navigating the challenges of governance for common-pool resources requires action at several levels. It requires improvements in the more systemic attributes of governance – stakeholder representation, mechanisms of accountability and institutional capacity – that influence the prospects for successful community-based resource management. Strengthening institutions to manage the commons is not simply a matter of removing state interference and letting local communities get by as they see fit. Progress in governance does, however, require a willingness to look beyond written policy, law and regulation, to critically examine how power is exercised in practice and how such exercise of power impinges on access to commons or otherwise. Such reform of the governance of the commons throws-up possibilities of increased access to commons by the rural populace, including, as in the present context, the tea workers in general and the women in tea gardens in particular. However, it is quite unlikely that the reforms will take place without pressing for such reforms by the affected community.

The capacity to assert the right to access and to demand for a reform of the process of governance of commons is conditioned by the awareness and capacity of the affected community. Capacity and awareness, on the other hand, are conditioned by access to education and the possibility of formation of social capital[7] and cultural capital.[8] The majority of workers in the tea gardens of North Bengal, particularly in the *Terai-Dooars* regions belong to the ST and SC communities who are already considered economically backward and socially marginalized in the society. These communities, during the focus group discussions, have revealed that there are different socio-cultural organizations, and majority of workers and their households are affiliated to one or the other local organizations. Socio-cultural organizations such as *Majdoor Kalyan* and *Samaj Sewa Samitee*[9] bring about better bonding among the tea workers of homogenous as well as heterogeneous ethnic groups. As one trade union leader from Belgachi tea garden affirmed, *'Tea garden community is a very harmonious community; despite coming from different ethnic and linguistic groups, we never have inter-social group fights or conflicts. Here all the workers live like brothers and sisters, participating in one another's celebrations and funerals' (Personal Interview, January, 2010, Belgachi Tea Garden).*

Nevertheless, the tea garden households lack strong socio-cultural capital, something that would enhance their livelihood prospects. These social organizations bring the workers together for social and cultural functions but do not have the wherewithal to enhance their social status or provide better livelihood security; these organizations are limited in their influence that they exert on the higher institutions.[10] Therefore, though there is a good social bonding among workers and other garden residents within same garden, similar bonding and social affiliations do not exist among the inter-tea garden residents. Thus, due to lack of community and social bonding across gardens, 'workers do not find a potent platform for addressing various grievances and Also, for lack of vertical (patron/client) connections and groups, the tea workers lack collective bargaining power and access to wider political and civic institutions.

In other words, socio-cultural organizations, despite having large memberships, do not enjoy bargaining power in the wider institution. Lack of strong social networking and affiliation means they have remained voiceless sufferers since the inception of tea industry in the region. The lack of strong social capital has had its historical background. In the typical Indian tea gardens, with 'island' kind of social networks that always insulated the garden residents from other rural social groups, tea workers and their household members were compelled to have membership or social affiliation only among themselves (Bhadra 1992). The tea workers, constituting chiefly of socially marginal and economically backward scheduled groups, have been socially excluded by the mainstream society. One inherent social factor that has implicitly hindered in the extraction of benefits for their socio-economic betterment and livelihood promotion is the social exclusion that the scheduled groups have suffered besides their history of being descendent of indentured labourers.

Lack of strong socio-cultural capital among the tea garden workers can also be explained from the fact that the workers, especially of the scheduled groups, have been excluded from being part of the decision-making processes in the tea plantation system, and thus, they have remained at the mercy of other dominant groups. Thus, lack of or weak social capital has impeded access to and/or the sanctioned use of a number of other resources such as healthcare, access to credit/insurance market and accessibility of land and CPRs. It is an acknowledged fact that smoothly functioning commons go hand in hand with substantial reserves of social capital, but the ultimate test of that social capital is whether it can serve the community in a time of crisis. Studies among the village communities of Uttaranchal and Himachal Pradesh have shown that by strengthening their social capital in the form of community-based management of commons, they were able to access the use of forest and land that they were once deprived.

Likewise, if the socio-cultural organizations of the tea workers become powerful, they will be able to demand access to vested land, sand, gravel from riverbeds and other resources of open access and utilize them through community-based resource management. This has not been able to take place now and these CPRs in the vicinity of the tea gardens (especially sand and gravel from riverbed) have been controlled and appropriated by contractor guilds, and the tea garden people have no right whatsoever over these resources.

This failure to build strong socio-cultural and political capital owes to the enclave nature of the tea industry wherein there is a deliberate attempt on the part of the management to keep the workers at bay through active creation of ignorance. This can be evidenced from the absence of corporate social responsibility on the part of the industry, coupled with the reinforcement of the social evil of drinking to establish that tea garden families are addicted to liquor and do not think of future. To elucidate a little further, Shanon Sullivan and Nancy Tuana (2007) have discussed at length the concept of ignorance and its socio-cultural, political and epistemological implications. Ignorance, in a common parlance, is often thought of a gap in knowledge. It is viewed as an epistemic oversight, seemingly accidental, or a consequence of the absence or scarcity of time and resources at the disposal of the human beings to investigate and comprehend their world. Although, Sullivan and Tuana (2007) agree that such ignorance may exist, they point out the possibility of other varieties of ignorance: actively produced lack of knowledge or an unlearning for purposes of domination and exploitation. Such forms of ignorance may take different forms, namely, the centre refusing to allow the margins to know, or, centre's ignorance deliberate constructions of its own ignorance of injustice, cruelty and suffering meted out to the margins.

In the case of the North Bengal tea workers, the enclave economy actively constructs ignorance – both refusing to allow the margins (the tea workers in general and the tea garden women in particular) to know (as evidenced from the absence of education and consequent absence of awareness among the workers) and the deliberate unknowing on the part of the industry of the pain and suffering of its workers (an attitude of indifference on the part of the management even at the hunger and starvation deaths of the workers).

However, drawing from Foucauldian discourse theory's[11] curiosity as to how experience enters into or is barred from entering into what counts as knowledge, while at the same time drawing upon other relevant competing and complementary perspectives for its frame of analysis, the study reveals that, the deprivation meted out to the workers in general and womenfolk in particular in North Bengal tea region, coupled with the simultaneously enabling and disabling culturally embedded processes[12] in the region have resulted in search for alternative roots of knowing (e.g. interrogating the enclosure and commoditization of commons as an issue of protest by Adivasis Vikas Parishad [AVP]) via strengthening political capital[13] and through the micro politics of protest towards reconstructing the history that represents the oppressed, wherein the epistemology of the oppressed has attempted to reframe both analytical power and domination in knowledge process as a transcending domain of praxis. Thus, the North Bengal tea region is witnessing a series of struggles emanating as micropolitics of the marginal communities, both in the hills of Darjeeling and plains of Terai and Dooars tea gardens, directed primarily towards the fulfilment of the livelihood security needs amidst the emergent brewing crisis.

NOTES

1. *Cf.* C. Alvares (2011), cited in Anup Shekhar Chakraborty, *Detoxification, Alteration, Mutation, Hybridisation: Queering Social Science Research in the South*. Paper Presented at the Forum on Contemporary Theory, XIV International Conference Theme 'Transcending Disciplinary Decadence: Exploring Challenges of Teaching, Scholarship, and Research in the Humanities and the Social Sciences', 18–21 December 2011.
2. *Cf.* Introduction: The contemporary reconfiguration of social theory. In Steven Seidman (1997). *Difference Troubles: Queering Social Theory and Sexual Politics*. Cambridge, UK: Cambridge University Press, pp. 1–20.
3. *Cf.* G.K. Varghese (2011); Pulapre Balakrishnan (2011). A house for social sciences. Government Review of ICSSR, *Economic and Political Weekly XLVI* (33), pp. 29–31.
4. In this process of identifying the locational as well as positional sources of sexual or bodily related identities, the human body becomes the site for defining and determining sexual orientations (through things such as the

search for the gay gene or assertions that gay men have larger fingers, etc.). The body thus becomes the ready-reckoner for information generation, data analysis and interpretation in order to arrive at the sexuality(ies) of individuals and then categorize them accordingly, often, to oppress the studied. *Cf.* Bryan S. Turner (1997). *The Body and Society*. Beverly Hills, CA: Sage; Judith Butler (1993). *Bodies That Matter: On the Discursive Limits of 'Sex'*. New York: Routledge.

5. In the initial stage, immediately after the great partition of 1947, the term 'North Bengal' was a vague one. From that time, this term took the shape of a verbal geographical area that had no official recognition. But its socio-political and cultural character remained something different, which did not come to be highlighted. Though North Bengal is a particular geographical area in the northern part of West Bengal comprising five districts (presently six districts) of the northern part of West Bengal, still its remarkable socio-cultural feature and identity cannot be denied. During recent times, so many scholars of different fields are trying their best to explore and highlight the issues of North Bengal. Even some measures have already been taken from the part of administration (government) considering its importance. But the roots of this issue and problem are yet to be investigated and emphasis should be given properly on the particular points that are related with socio-cultural practices and identity question
6. The state of financial crunch or bankruptcy that leads to limping of a tea garden. For industries, according to Companies (Second Amendment) Act, 2002, 'Sick Industrial Company' means an industrial company which has (i) The Accumulated losses in any financial year equal to 50 per cent or more of its average net worth during four years immediately preceding such financial year; or (ii) Failed to repay its *debts* within any three consecutive quarters on demand made in writing for its repayment by a *creditor* or creditors of such company. The notion of 'sick' gardens is also derived from the same source and applies similarly in the case of tea industry. Such 'sickness' is caused by both internal and external factors such as mismanagement, diversion of funds, wrong dividend policy, deliberate 'milking' of the unit by the owners, labour disputes and so on. For further details, *cf.* Government of India (2002). *The Companies (Second Amendment) Act 2002*, Ministry of Commerce; Government of India (1991). *Tea Companies (Acquisition and Transfer of Sick Tea Units) Amendment Bill* (the Bill to amend the Tea Companies [Acquisition and Transfer of Sick Tea Units] Act, 1985) placed to the Parliament of India.
7. This capital refers to the social network, group membership and social affiliation among members of a society and cultural group that help in accessing higher institutions and enhancing their livelihood and social security. Unlike other capitals, socio-cultural capital is rather intangible and a

value-oriented asset that many individuals and households utilize as a safety net for coping with adversities (Deb 2009).

8. Culture is a highly ambiguous concept that is difficult to define (Schech and Haggis 2000). An inadequate consideration of the cultural perspective oversimplifies not only people, but also their resourcefulness and capacities and, thus, the complexity and diversity of resource entitlement and livelihood opportunities. Undertaking scholars have emphasized the significance of a cultural perspective throughout livelihood analysis, and established cultural capital as a new concept 'within' livelihood context, where 'cultural-traditions' can be explicitly treated as a useful resource in strengthening livelihood sustainability among rural communities (Daskon 2009; Daskon and Binns 2009). French Sociologist Pierre Bourdieu (1999) first introduced the concept of cultural capital, and later on Throsby (1999, 2000) discussed this concept in detail by referring to economic analysis. However in this analysis, *cultural capital* expands beyond Bourdieu's suggestions and provides a cohesive framework for social inclusion, equality and social security enabling different forms of action and resistance, which are empowering local communities. It is important to be aware that rural livelihoods comprise numerous capabilities and assets that are defined by the local cultural and historical contexts of a particular community.

   In case of the North Bengal tea workers, it is seen that during times of crisis, many male workers have taken recourse to traditional crafts making such as bamboo baskets and other handicraft items saleable in the market using whatever available Non-timber Forest Products (NTFPs) at their disposal to earn the household livelihood. Thus, tea workers' communities are knowledgeable and capable of self-reliant organization that displays a thriving livelihood resilience based on ingenuities and intangible values that have been present with them for generations.

   Hence, cultural traditions are not 'always' an impediment and are rigid structures that fail to negotiate risks and often retard effective social relations reciprocity and, more importantly, the livelihood choices of people. Factors causing livelihood insecurity are not only confined to economic reasons in the garden, far-fetched it may appear, but the loss of forest cover also has had consequences leading to insecurity of tea garden residents. The loss of forest cover with time made the raw materials for making cultural artifacts for market inaccessible. Thus, the traditional and cultural knowledge that could have contributed to livelihood resilience came to a standstill, rendering cultural resource insignificant. Yet, paradoxically, cultural traditions have not always been effective in strengthening livelihood strategies and household resistance. In some instances, people's traditions have weakened their adaptability during difficult times. Some uncontrollable situations can force people to abandon their inherited industries or move to another source of income. In case of the tea workers under investigation, it was seen that only a few had inherited their cultural habits of crafts making and most had not. This owed, as revealed from interviews with some elderly people in the gardens, to the locational displacement from their traditional land for a profession in tea garden's enclave economy, far off from their traditional cultural habitations.

9. Every tea garden in North Bengal has social organizations that keep the bonding among the tea garden households and also by taking care of their welfare and socio-cultural functions such as wedding and funeral.
10. Focus groups and informal discussions revealed that while there are many social organizations catering to specific social, religious and cultural groups among the tea workers, they do not provide them with true dignity outside the tea garden premises. The main reason being that these socio-cultural organizations, having horizontal affiliation only among the tea garden residents, are also confined merely to their own tea gardens. Even though some socio-cultural organizations have similar aims and objectives across the tea gardens, hardly any organization has cross-sectional or horizontal network that binds the workers across the gardens for some common cause, aimed at enhancing their livelihood.
11. Social science researches have begun to fruitfully use the work of Michel Foucault to analyse and problematize many practices and structures of the production of knowledge. For Foucault, resistance was inherent within relations of power, and resistance was itself predicated on the existence of a free subject. Resistance was not an isolated, quixotic event; rather, Foucault saw it as a means of self-transformation through the minimization of states of domination. As Ortner (1995) notes, resistance at one time was a fairly unambiguous concept, connoting an oppositional response to the exercise of domination, which itself was seen as non-problematic, as a fixed and institutionalized form of power. Foucauldian interpretations of less formalized, more pervasive and everyday forms of power and James Scott's work (1985, 1990) on equally 'everyday forms of resistance' have complicated the delineation of what is or is not resistance (Scott 1985, 1990). In the present study, since we are involved in discussing the resistance against the dominant notions of development pursued by the Indian developmental state, the Foucauldian framework may be fruitfully employed in the analysis of the present kind.
12. In recent years, livelihood scholars have drawn extensively upon notions of 'cultural embeddedness' to explore how spatially variable sets of cultural conventions, norms, values and beliefs shape a community's innovative performance in dynamic livelihood contexts. Brumbaugh (2002) proposes that what one knows about a culture in terms of beliefs, values, behaviours and norms comes as a result of living in that culture. Members of a

sub-culture, then, have access both to the majority culture, which pervades mainstream life and media, and to their own minority culture, which may be learned primarily at home or in a small community. Cultural embeddedness refers to the overall cultural 'feel' of a situation/context, and such context's/situation's embeddedness lies somewhere on a continuum between the lived experience of one's own sub-culture and the influence of the majority culture that forms the immediate environment of the sub-culture of a community. In the context of livelihood studies, *embeddedness* may be broadly defined as the set of social relationships between economic and non-economic actors (individuals as well as aggregate groups of individuals, that is, organizations), which in turn create distinctive patterns of constraints and incentives for economic action and behaviour (Hess 2004; Jessop 2001). Thus, cultural embeddedness has quickly established as a conceptual lynchpin of the livelihood studies literature, our understanding of the causal mechanisms and everyday practices through which spatially variable sets of socio-cultural conventions, norms, attitudes, values and beliefs shape and condition livelihood contexts and mechanisms. Since embeddedness is a product of the dialectical interaction of a culture and its environment, overall, therefore, cultural embeddedness is not pre-given, inherited or static, but continually remade via these various causal mechanisms and practices which might usefully be grouped together in terms of their effects on three *general* sets of 'relations of embeddedness', namely: (a) those between individuals and individuals of a given sub-culture; (ii) those between individuals and the cultural community; and (iii) those between the cultural community and its wider environment wherein a majority culture is situated. In this way, the cultural values, attitudes, expectations and behaviour of people in a given cultural context are informed by those of its *lead* civic, educational, political and labour institutions. These spill over to the people of a sub-culture through the course of time, in effect setting the social rules and defining the norms of behaviour across local and regional cultural contexts. This has been used in the study as a culturally embedded process. In the case of the present study, it is seen that the livelihood contexts are influenced and situated in such processes wherein the sub-culture of the tea workers encounters the majority culture outside the tea garden's enclave economy. The cultural differences between the majority culture and the sub-culture has led to the production of politics of exclusions of the tea workers by the majority culture, with both empowering and disempowering effects on the workers' community in terms of addressing the issues of livelihood. Whereas at times the politics of exclusions meted out to the tea workers jeopardizes their attempts to combat livelihood insecurities because of their failure to interact meaningfully with the dominant culture, and hence disempowering to respond to livelihood insecurity issues, yet on the other hand, such politics of exclusions sets room for introspection and construction of the 'difference' of the cultural community (tea workers) with the majority cultural group culturally, socially, economically and politically. Such introspection and construction of difference facilitates a recourse of culture and cultural resources for reassertion of their identity (e.g. the case of Gorkhas in Darjeeling Hills and the assertion of identity by the AVP in the Terai and the Dooars region in the plains), which in turn contributes to the formation of stronger social and cultural capital as a means to address the problem of livelihood insecurity.

13. Advocated by Baumann and Subbir (2001), this asset refers to the ability of individuals and households to use power in support of political or economic position that enhances livelihood. After years of struggle, the tea workers in all the three tea regions have realized the potential of forming their own political organization. In the Darjeeling Hills, even in the past, people were politically more conscious and the political parties, such as the Gorkha League, Gorkha National Liberation Front (GNLF) and even the Congress and Communist Parties were dominated by the local Gorkha leaders. Yet, the interest of the political leaders laid more on their own political ambitions and to a lesser degree on the aspirations of the hill people but seldom on the grievances of tea garden workers. Even the trade unions themselves were affiliated to parties for the promotion of personal interest rather than the welfare of the tea workers. That is why, perhaps, the Gorkhaland Movement of mid-1980s did not really empower the tea garden workers politically to enhance their livelihood status. In contrast, the second half of the last decade has provided them with the impetus of bargaining for their livelihoods under the new political power called the *Gorkha Jana Mukti Morcha* (GJMM). In fact, the GJMM-backed workers' union has for the first time enhanced tea workers livelihood – by forcing the Darjeeling Planters Association (DPA) to raise the daily wages from ` 67 to ` 90 since March 2012. The Terai and Dooars tea regions have traversed different political paths.

    Despite producing some MPs and MLAs from CPI, CPI(M), Congress, RSP, Forward Block and independent parties in the 'reserved constituency' for ST candidates, the Adivasis of Terai-Dooars never benefited, neither could they make themselves powerful political bargaining power. In the backdrop of this, the recent emergence of a political force in the region in the form of AVP has become very significant. AVP has taken up the causes of the scheduled groups, especially those belonging to the tea gardens. Although, it is early to speculate its real impact on peoples' livelihoods, this emerging political force has already empowered the workers under its affiliate Progressive Tea Workers Union (PTWU) and succeeded in raising the wage to ` 85/day (since October 2012) from ` 67, besides also pressurizing the recruitment of SC/ST candidates as local staff in the government offices and schools.

REFERENCES

Agrawal, A. (2002). Indigenous Knowledge and the Politics of Classification. *International Social Science Journal*, *54*(173), September, pp. 287–297.

Alvares, C. (2011). A Critique of Eurocentric Social Science and the Question of Alternatives. *Economic and Political Weekly XLVI*(24).

Baland, J.M. and Platteau, J.P. (1996). *Halting Degradation of Natural Resources: Is There a Role for Rural Communities*? Rome: FAO.

Baumann, P. and Subbir, S. (2001). Linking Development with Democratic Processes in India: Political Capital and Sustainable Livelihoods Analysis. ODI Natural Resources Perspectives Paper No. 68, London: ODI.

Beck, U. (2000). *Brave New World of Work*. Cambridge: Cambridge University Press.

Berkes, F. (1998). Indigenous Knowledge and Resource Management Systems in the Canadian Sub-Arctic. In F. Berkes and C. Folke (Eds), *Linking Social and Ecological Systems: Management Practices and Social Mechanism for Building Resilience*. Cambridge: Cambridge University Press.

Bhadra, M. (1992). *Women Workers of Tea Plantations in India*. Delhi: Heritage Publishers.

Bhowmik, S.K., Xaxa, V. and Kalam, M.A. (1996). *Tea Plantation Labour in India*. New Delhi: Friedrich Ebert Stiftung.

Biswas, S., Chakraborty, D., Berman, S. and Berman, J. (2005). Nutritional Survey of Tea Workers on Closed, Re-Opened and Open Tea Plantations of the Dooars Region, West Bengal, India. In *Final Report: Malnutrition of Tea Workers*. Calcutta: W.B. Agricultural Workers Associations.

Bourdieu, P. (1999). The Forms of Capital. In J.G. Richardson (Ed.), *Handbook of Theory and Research for Sociology of Education*. New York: Sage.

Brumbaugh, A.M. (2002). Source and Non-Source Cues in Advertising and Their Effects on the Activation of Cultural and Sub-Cultural Knowledge on the Route to Persuasion. *Journal of Consumer Research*, 29 September 2002.

Butler, J. (1993). *Bodies That Matter: On the Discursive Limits of 'Sex'*. New York: Routledge.

Centre for Education and Communication (2003). *Crisis in Indian Tea Industry: A Report*. New Delhi: S.M. Graphics.

Daskon, C. (2009). *Culture, Traditions and Sustainable Rural Livelihoods: A Case Study from the Kandyan Villages, Central Sri Lanka*. Ph.D. Thesis, Department of Geography, University of Otago, Dunedin, New Zealand.

Daskon, C. and Binns, T. (2009). Culture, Tradition and Sustainable Rural Livelihoods: Exploring the Culture-Development Interface in Kandy, Sri Lanka. *Community Development Journal 45*(4), pp. 494–517.

Deb, A.K. (2009). *Voices of the Fishantry: Learning on the Livelihood Dynamics from Bangladesh*. Ph.D. Thesis, Department of Natural Resource Institute, University of Manitoba, Winnipeg, Canada.

Dietz, T., Ostrom, E. and Stern, P. (2003). The Struggle to Govern the Commons. In Ostrom et al. (Eds), *The Drama of the Commons*. Washington, DC: National Academy Press.

Ellis, F. (2000). *Rural Livelihoods and Diversity in Developing Countries*. London: Oxford University Press.

Gain, P. (2009). The Story of Tea Workers. *Forum 3*(6).

Ghosh, T.K. (1987). *Tea Gardens of West Bengal: A Critical Study of Land Management*. Delhi: B.R. Publishing.

Goddard, S. (2004). Tea Break: A Crisis is Brewing in India. *Action Aid*, International Tea Committee Annual Bulletin, UK.

Grunning, J.F. (1911). *Eastern Bengal and Assam District Gazetteers.* Jalpaiguri/Siliguri: N.L. Publishers.

Hardin, G. (1968). The Tragedy of the Commons. *Science 162*, pp. 1243–1248.

Hess, M. (2004). Spatial Relationships? Towards a Reconceptualization of Embeddedness. *Progress in Human Geography*, *28*(2).

Ives, J.D. and Messerli, B. (1989). *The Himalayan Dilemma: Reconciling Development and Conservation*. London and New York: Routledge.

Jessop, R. (2001). Regulationist and Autopoieticist Reflections on Polanyi's Account of Market Economies and the Market Society. *New Political Economy 6* (2), pp. 213–232.

Jodha, N.S. (1986). Common Property Resources of the Rural Poor in Dry Regions of India. *Economic and Political Weekly 30*(27), pp. 1169–1181.

Kaniyal, J.S. (2003). Regional Imbalances and Sustainable Crop Farming in the Himachal Himalaya, India. *Ecological Economics 48*, pp. 419–435.

Karotemprel, S. and Roy, B.D. (1990). *Tea Garden Labourers of North East India*. Shillong: Vendrame Institute Publications.

Munsi, S. (1980). An Enquiry into the Nature of Frontier Settlement: Case Study of Hill Darjeeling. Occasional Paper No. 34, Calcutta: Centre for Studies in Social Sciences.

Nepal, P. and Tirkey, L.P. (2012). Livelihood Insecurity of North Bengal Tea Workers: Contours, Complexities, Challenges and Opportunities. In H. Sinha and A. Kumar (Eds), *Governance of Commons and Livelihood Security*. Ranchi: XISS.

North Bengal Report (2002). Report on Comparative Backwardness of North Bengal Region. Study Sponsored by Planning Commission, Government of India, New Delhi: Institute of Applied Manpower Research.

O'Malley, L.S.S. (1907). *Darjeeling, Bengal District Gazetteer*. New Delhi: Logos Press.

Ortner, S.B. (1995). Resistance and the Problem of Ethnographic Refusal. *Comparative Studies in Society and History 37*(1), pp. 173–193.

Ostrom, E. (1990). *Governing the Commons: The Evolution of Institutions for Collective Action.* Cambridge: Cambridge University Press.

Ostrom, E. et al. (1999). Revisiting the Commons: Local Lessons, Global Challenges. *Science 284*, pp. 278–282.

Ostrom, E. et al. (Eds) (2002). *The Drama of the Commons*. Washington, DC: National Academy Press.

Pandolfelli, L., Dohrn, S. and Meinzen-Dick, R. (2007). Gender and Collective Action: Policy Implications from Recent Research. Policy Brief 5, CAPRI.

Sarkar, F.L. and Lama, M.P. (1998). *Tea Plantation Workers in the Eastern Himalayas: A Study on Wages, Employment and Living Standards*. New Delhi and Lucknow: Atma Ram & Sons.

Schech, S. and Haggis, J. (2000). *Culture and Development: A Critical Introduction*. Oxford, UK: Blackwell Publishers.

Schickhoff, U. (1995). Himalayan Forest-Cover Changes in Historical Perspective: A Case Study in the Kachan Valley, Northern Pakistan. *Mountain Research and Development 15*, pp. 3–18.

Scott, J. (1985). *Weapons of the Weak: Everyday Forms of Peasant Resistance*. New Haven: Yale University Press.

—- (1990). *Domination and the Arts of Resistance: Hidden Transcripts*. New Haven: Yale University Press.

—- (1998). *Seeing Like a State: How Certain Schemes to Improve the Human Condition Have Failed*. New Haven: Yale University Press.

Sharma, K.K. (1999). *Tea Industries in India: An Introduction*. Delhi: Arora Offset Press.

Sullivan, S. and Tuana, N. (Eds) (2007). *Race and Epistemologies of Ignorance*. Albany: State University of New York Press.

Talwar, A., Chakraborty, D. and Biswas, S. (2003). Study on Closed and Re-Opened Tea Gardens in North Bengal. A Report Prepared by Paschim Bengal Khet Majdoor Samiti and International Union of Food (IUF), Agriculture, Plantation and Allied Workers Association. Available at http://www.sanhati.com/wp-content/uploads/2008/01/teagardebstudy.pdf.

Thapa, N. (2012). Employment Status and Human Development of Tea Plantation Workers in West Bengal. NRPPD Discussion Paper 11.

The Education Charter (1999). *A Global Consensus Statement of Values and Ethics for Building Sustainable Better Livelihood for Education Youth of 21st Century*.

Throsby, D. (1999). Cultural Capital. *Journal of Cultural Economics 23*, pp. 3–12.

—- (2000). *Economics and Culture*. Cambridge: Cambridge University Press.

Tirkey, L.P. (2005). *Geo-Ecological and Socio-Economic Implications of Closure of Tea Plantations in the Darjeeling Hills*. Master's Thesis, University of Manitoba, Canada.

Turner, B.S. (1997). *The Body and Society*. Beverly Hills, CA: Sage.

Varghese, G.K. (2011). Rethinking Social Sciences and the Humanities in the Contemporary World. *Economic and Political Weekly XLVI* (31), pp. 91–98.

CHAPTER 13

Lucknow to Nagaland via Delhi

Journey of an 'Adventurous Indian Woman' – Narrating Experiences from the Field

Rashi Bhargava

The month of May was my first week in the field, and I had just finished an in-depth interview with one of my respondents. As I was about to take leave, I was bid farewell with the most unexpected statement, a comment or a compliment, still an unresolved mystery for me. But I must confess, on that particular day, I was more enthralled by that statement than the data I had managed to collect – I was the 'adventurous Indian woman' who had taken up the daunting task of coming as far as Nagaland – a conflict-ridden zone to conduct 'research'. After all, who really does that? Absorbed in the admiration (I really thought it to be so), I recorded the incident in my field diary and almost forgot about it until two weeks later.

It happened during the third week of my stay in Kohima. I was in the midst of conducting an interview when my respondent received a phone call. Excusing himself, he answered the call and told the person that he will return the call a little later as he is in the middle of a conversation with an 'Indian woman' who has come to research on the Naga Nation. I simply smiled and continued our conversation. At the end of the day, when I was reflecting on the day's happening, unlike the last incident, I could not brush the incident aside without pondering over it. However, that deliberation was short-lived as I was more anxious about establishing rapport in the field and collecting data.

But the next incident which took place, some six weeks into my fieldwork, compelled me to reflect upon the past incidents as well. During a casual conversation, the person I was interacting with commented, 'So what have you been eating for the past one and a half month? You must be a strict vegetarian?' Looking at my bewildered expression, he added, 'aren't you a Brahmin from North India? You people must be strict vegetarians. You must not be into drinking as well? Though Nagaland is a dry state but then people here love to drink'. After this incident, I could not help but reflect upon the various incidents that directly or indirectly made me an 'object' of my subjects.

As I reflected upon these three incidents (there were many others, but these three, I thought, were the major ones), it dawned upon me that these were no casual remarks. Rather they had something concrete to offer. They were subtle hints at my social, economic, cultural and also political (unconscious for me) position. I was not just a researcher, but a 'North-Indian woman' researcher who is also a citizen of the Indian nation-state. It would be a fallacy to state that I was not conscious of my position; however, what astounded me was the swiftness with which my respondents brought it up in the conversations.

This chapter, therefore, begins with an investigation of the stereotypical constructions of a 'caste-Hindu woman' hailing from India and the methodological concerns and challenges that accompanied it in researching a society that has a history of conflict with the Indian nation-state. It further seeks to explore the vitality of these constructions embedded in the larger context of the socio-political and historical past of the Naga society, in not only conducting empirical investigation but also providing a space in which the researcher negotiated and re-negotiated with her understanding of the 'self' and the status of the 'other', she was constantly conferred upon.

This chapter is borne out of the various events I encountered during fieldwork for my doctoral research, which aims to look at the changing character and role of 'civil society' in the state of Nagaland in contemporary times. More than often, the civil society in Nagaland is understood with respect to its role in impending six decades long armed conflict between the Naga people and the Indian State. It would not be a fallacy to assume that the existence of prolonged armed conflict in the region renders the dynamics of civil society in Nagaland extremely complex, and makes its theorization tremendously difficult. However, in the contemporary times, the history of Naga society cannot be articulated exclusively around Naga people's dissent and resistance, first to the colonial administration and then to the Indian State. Rather, one can locate an arena that not only exhibits structured dissent and organized resistance in the form of Naga national movement but also houses everyday forms of survival and resilience of the people making space for newer and varied issues, which are often side-lined in the scholarship.

My research, thus, aims to engage with 'multiple meanings' that are conferred upon the contemporary civil society in Nagaland and the various contradictions that occur within it and, render intelligible in sociological terms, the structure and functioning of the civil society in Nagaland as understood within its specific cultural settings. Since, the problem under study demanded a closer look into various social and political processes that have a bearing on the idea of civil society in Nagaland, the empirical phase of the research design used the fieldwork method. The fieldwork for this research followed the French/German tradition of several successions of short fieldwork, termed as 'extensive' fieldwork (Srivastava 2011), in the state of Nagaland.

Adopting the semi-structured and unstructured interview method, many former members and erstwhile leaders from among the Naga public domain, senior and many educated members of the community were interviewed on various issues, especially those concerning the Naga political issue, the growing rift between eastern tribes and the western tribes, the role of civil society, people's understanding of the civil society in Nagaland and so on. Informal discussions and long conversations were also held with many individuals from different walks of life including academicians, journalists, activists and youths to receive their responses on some pertinent issues relating to Naga history, culture and the role of church in the socio-cultural and political domain of the society.

SITUATING THE FIELD: A GLIMPSE OF THE SOCIO-CULTURAL AND POLITICAL HISTORY

The state of Nagaland is located in the North East of India, bounded by Myanmar in the east, Assam in the west and Arunachal Pradesh and a part of Assam in the north with Manipur in the south. It lies between the parallels of 98-degree and 96-degree east longitude and 26.6-degree and 27.4-degree latitude north of the equator. The state capital is Kohima, and the largest city is Dimapur. The state of Nagaland has an area of 16,579 sq. km with a population of 1,980,602 as per the recent census conducted in the year 2011. The state consists of 11 administrative districts, inhabited by 16 major tribes along with other sub-tribes.

The state of Nagaland was formally inaugurated on 1 December 1963 as the 16th state within the Union of India. It was formed after 15 years of continuous Indo-Naga conflict, which seemingly reached a negotiation with the 16-point agreement between the Indian State and the Naga National Workers under the aegis of Naga National Council. The state is inhabited by the people of Indo-Mongoloid race called the *Nagas* who are ethnically, culturally and historically distinct from the people of the Indo-Aryan and Indo-Dravidian stock residing in the other parts of the country. However, it is important to mention that the term 'Nagas' is generic and is perceived to have originated as part of the colonial rhetoric (Nag 2002). Nagas is a conglomeration of diverse tribes having certain differences within themselves. In addition to Nagaland, they also inhabit hilly regions of the states of Assam, Manipur and Arunachal Pradesh.

However, creation of the state of Nagaland did not mark an end to the Indo-Naga conflict but provided an impetus to the beginning of just another phase – one that continues till date. The Naga demand for sovereignty forms the core demand of this conflict with the Indian State refusing to give into that demand. The demand for a separate Naga Nation is based on the claim that the Nagas are physically, culturally, socially and ethnically a distinct group who have never been conquered by anyone. Consequently, once the British retreated from the Indian subcontinent, the Nagas presumed that they should be free to choose their own fate. Notwithstanding the Naga demand, after the British left India, the Naga inhabited areas were incorporated within the Indian and the Burmese territory. The Naga demand for sovereignty goes back as far as the Simon Commission in 1929 and continues till date, creating intense antagonism between the Naga Nation and the Indian nation-state. However, much has changed in the process. The most significant being the emergence of a vibrant civil society in the region, which became the focal point of my research.

HISTORY OF RESEARCH ON NAGA SOCIETY

The Naga society and the various tribes that constitute the larger group called the Nagas have been exposed to various anthropological and sociological researches since the advent of Christianity and the establishment of British administrative rule in the area. Consequently, I did not anticipate arousing much astonishment with my presence in the field as a 'researcher' assuming that the Naga society had been familiar with the entire process of research. However, contrary to my belief, my entry into the field was (and is still, I have just finished my third leg of fieldwork) eyed with amazement rousing feelings ranging from appreciation to scepticism. As I tried to decipher the cause of such reactions, I located it in that very history of research which I thought would be conducive to my work.

While looking at the history of research studies conducted on and in the Naga society, one can outline four phases. Though these can in no way be seen as insulated from each other, for the purpose of our analysis, it becomes imperative that we arrange them in a chronological order. The first phase consists of the works (mostly travelogues and detailed monographs) undertaken by the British administrators, historians and anthropologists and their spouses mainly produced during the colonial period in the Indian subcontinent. In addition to the above, there were accounts produced by numerous American and British missionaries. The common thread that connected these accounts was the tendency to 'exoticize' the societies of the east and look at them from the prism of the Western societies. Consequently, emerged the obligation of the white man to 'civilize' the hitherto, savage, barbarous and uncivilized people. This according to Srinivas can be summed up as a phase 'when not only the basic theoretical framework but even ethnographic information about the third world countries came very largely from Western Anthropologists' (Srivastava 2011).

Following this was the period after Second World War, which in India corresponded to the period of post-independence. It is in this phase as noted by Srinivas 'the information about the social and cultural phenomena and their analysis and interpretation, at least in a few third world countries' most likely came from the 'indigenes' (Srivastava 2011). However, in case of Nagaland, this second set of works needs to be contextualized within the 'nation-building' project of the newly established Indian government. Thus, one needs to distinguish the works at two levels: first, though the information was collected and analysed by the indigenes, they came from the scholars who were not embedded in the socio-cultural and historical context of the Nagas. Second, many of these scholars appropriated the Western theoretical frameworks as drawn by Western scholars before them. Thus, one can infer that this phase was mostly dominated by the writings of what I would call the 'native-outsiders' – the 'native' scholars from the 'Indian mainstream' who though were producing accounts of communities within the Indian territory were still researching the 'other' in the periphery vis-à-vis the caste Indian. However, the works produced during this time period were not insulated from the literature that was produced in the colonial period. Rather, the administrators and the policy makers depended heavily on the colonial accounts, thereby re-affirming the 'exoticized' and 'essentialized' writings on the region. The sociologists and the anthropologists from mainland India, who were looking at creating indigenous accounts, too could not keep their biases at bay. It is not very difficult to locate the reason that lay in the 'distinct' social, cultural and political history of the region. There was a certain neglect of the history and culture of the region creating a 'crisis of representation' (Marcus and Fischer 1986, cited in Srivastava 2011).

In response to this crisis that received further push from the introduction of education and exposure, emerged the indigenous intelligentsia of Nagaland that voiced its disappointment with the 'mis-representation' of the Nagas and their society. Consequently, it paved way for the emergence of the insiders' accounts or what is often called 'native anthropology' (Srivastava 2011) to offer to the world a 'correct' insight into the Naga life-world and its corresponding worldview. The attempt was to move away from 'exoticism' and produce 'reflexive accounts' (Srivastava 2011) on the Naga Society. This process, however, cannot be distanced from the macro-politics that had taken roots in the region. Thus, the emergence of indigenous literature and reflexive accounts of the Nagas cannot be divorced from the larger political agenda of the Naga intelligentsia – the demand for a sovereign Naga Nation. This was also the period when research by 'outsiders' had become a rarity more so because of the tendency to discourage researchers from outside to conduct any study on the Nagas. The rationale given for such a move was to avoid such situations where in there is any possibility of mis-representation of the Nagas and their social realities. However, it is often difficult to judge whether these micro histories have really succeeded in freeing themselves from the trap of Western models to explain local/regional histories. This would need a matrix of 'plural concepts' and 'alternative models' of theory (Alatas 2006) to explain the empirical phenomenon of the region, which is often missing in these histories.

The last phase, though, is not as clearly marked out as the other three; it does follow the larger trend of political practices in the region. This is the phase in research that I see as the most recent one and also the most ambivalent. It can be characterized by the re-entry of (if I may still use the term) outsiders who are faced with the double task of first to get accepted within the scholarly community of the region, which is mostly dominated by the native scholars, and second to exercise caution while producing an account on the Nagas lest she/he falls into the trap of mis-representation. However, this phase also presents the situational advantage, which in my opinion is the existence of alternative sets of the literature outlining myriad works on the region. In contemporary times, the researchers have access to alternative sets of works produced from different vantage points, which offer a possibility of a more comprehensive analysis.

PLACING MYSELF IN THE FIELD

Consequently, it is quite apparent that I moved into my field with a combination of advantages and disadvantages. Since, my work is mainly concentrating on the organized civic networks in the State, it touches upon the issue of Naga national movement and the Indo-Naga conflict as well. More importantly, a number of my respondents have a very strong notion of the difference between the Nagas and the 'mainland' Indians corresponding to the difference between the Naga Nation and the Indian nation. During my fieldwork I noticed that since I belonged to the latter, people felt an urgent need to impart the 'correct' information to me so that I develop the 'right' view of the Naga society. I was constantly reminded that the Naga society is an alien entity for me and consequently demanded immediate and right familiarization with the same. Furthermore, many of my respondents asked me to exercise caution so as to not fall into the trap of mis-representing the Nagas, their culture, society and history, like many before me have done.

While I tried to negotiate between the correct information and the information, I realized that this tussle was also an implication of my topic of research, which is quite 'sensitive' (I have been told that 'n' number of times). And my political location as the citizen of India and a denizen of New Delhi – the Indian political centre, I had to constantly negotiate with the scepticism that came my way. However, it was extremely interesting to note how there were varying notions of correct that can be placed on a continuum with one extreme being occupied by those who are strictly for the Naga sovereignty, and therefore stressed more on the correct and the right discourse and cautioned against mis-representation of the Naga society. While the other extreme featured such people who have come to accept the present situation of the Nagas and were in the process of getting acclimatized to it. This group was a little less anxious about the kind of information that they shared with me. However, what connected the two groups was their approval for a researcher who had come from Indian mainland to study the Naga society and thus has the right to know the 'truth'. Even though, at times, this approval came with statutory warnings.

Such experiences made me recall the dynamics of fieldwork as noted by Srivastava, 'fieldwork is a didactic experience for the investigator as well as his/her respondents' (Srivastava 2011) wherein the fieldworker is not the only one calling the shots but the respondents control the situation as well so much so that at times they chart out the process of data collection for the researcher ranging from suggestions for whom to interview to what questions to ask to how to interpret that information. And in a situation like mine where the power dynamics was played out at every stage, I was hardly ever in control of the situation. It is in this process that my identity as an Indian coupled with that of a 'woman' further affected by my topic of research posed different questions and challenges in my work.

Thus, my physical features, my socio-cultural background and my personal history became objects of inquiry for my subjects. Because of my physical features, the closest anybody could place me was Assam and it would shock them to the core, the moment I would disclose that I come from Uttar Pradesh but have been in Delhi since my graduation days. Like most states in India, Uttar Pradesh too has certain stereotypical notions around it, which are in complete contrast to that of Nagaland. Unlike Nagaland, which is predominantly a tribal state with almost 95 per cent population as Christian, Uttar Pradesh is often seen wrought with caste and communal politics and gender inequality. With such a background, my presence in Nagaland raised many eyebrows and kindled shock among the inhabitants of the state.

However, after the initial shock, I was still addressed with caution as I was the 'other' – the upper caste-Hindu woman who would definitely be a vegetarian as my religion would demand, would resent liquor, would need assistance at every step and would be uncomfortable in the company of men. As a result, I had landed into a situation where the observer became the object of observation and surveillance instead of the other way round. There were not just cultural underpinnings to it, but it was also politically motivated making a clear distinction between the member of the Indian nation and that of the Naga Nation. Thus in my case, the 'othering' that I was constantly being subjected to was at three distinct levels: one at the level of a researcher who is an outsider and needs help; two at the level of the caste-Hindu woman coming from a state located in mainstream India wherein my social, cultural and political identities were merged and third at the level of the suppressed Hindu woman who was positioned vis-à-vis the liberated and emancipated Naga women.

Of the three levels mentioned above, the one that I found most difficult to negotiate with was the constant positioning of the Naga women as freer than their counterparts in the rest of India. This presumption was embedded in the larger discourse in and on the Naga culture and traditions, which prides itself in 'giving' equal space to its women.

One can locate an example of the constant reiteration of this pride in the contemporary times, especially due to the emerging clashes between the sphere of men and that of women owing to the recent demand for 33 per cent reservation for women in the municipal elections. However, my discomfort emerges from the contention that increased visibility is not synonymous with empowerment that is to say that locating more women in the public space does not necessarily mean that the women in Nagaland are more empowered. I had to constantly negotiate with my own beliefs and those of my respondents and at times it caused me immense frustration and pain to just sit and listen to the opinions and perceptions of the people regarding gender sensitivity and equality, the lack of which was evident in simple statements such as 'we give our women full freedom'. I could not help but wonder that if gender equality is embedded within the Naga society and culture, then where the question of the men granting freedom to their women arises. Shouldn't their freedom be theirs without the men making an 'effort' to grant it to them?

Just to give a fair chance to their argument, it is important to mention that there do exist some very overt differences between my situation in a place, such as Uttar Pradesh or Bihar and that in Nagaland. Being a woman was apparently not an obstacle to my process of research, especially with regard to my mobility. Safety of women in the public domain is not as serious an issue in Nagaland as it is in other parts of the country, say for instance, Delhi. Unlike my experiences in places such as Haryana, Bihar and Madhya Pradesh, where using public transport was a matter of grave concern, in Nagaland I did not have to bother about getting sexually harassed in public transports. My dressing too never became a point of concern for me. I did not have to think much about what to wear for the fear of being gazed at. And most importantly, what struck me the most was the indifference that people showed to my marital status. Unlike my fieldwork experiences in northern India where before anybody would ask my name, they would ask about my marital status, and then follow it up with statements such as, 'Oh! You are still not married, then 'how do your parents allow you to move around on your own?' In Nagaland, inquiries about my marital status were negligible. This is not to say that marriage as an institution does not hold much significance for the people in Nagaland. Rather what I really wanted to bring to the fore are the stark cultural differences that existed between the two societies – one that I came from and the one that I was researching.

It was during my casual conversations that I came to know that in Naga society, women do not marry very early as is the case in places such as Haryana and Rajasthan and also it is very common for women in Nagaland to remain unmarried. It is not in culture of the Nagas especially the ones in the towns to ask women about their marital status. It was a welcome change as I was not judged by my marital status, or my visibility in the public domain. However, such manifestations though being of much comfort in the beginning became the very reason for me to delve deeper into the issue.

After spending time in the field, I could not help but notice the disjuncture between the theoretical and the empirical as manifested in the rift between the so-called men organizations and the women's organizations. There were many incidents that indicated towards the existence of gender inequality in the Naga society, but for the benefit of this chapter I will narrate only a few of them. Since my universe of study includes people in authority in the organized state-level networks in Nagaland, I could not help but notice that the apex bodies have been divided between the core organizations and the women's organizations. In the core organizations, the higher ranks were occupied by men while women's participation in the higher echelons of the organizations is limited to such organizations that are categorized as 'women organizations'. Some of the women organizations are even seen as the frontal organizations of the apex civil society bodies and are not considered being of equal importance as the male-dominated organizations.

What startled me was the context in which such a situation was prevalent. Because of the Indo-Naga conflict, there is huge evidence regarding the greater political participation by Naga women as compared to their counterparts in the other parts of the country. Thus, as per the statistics that I gathered during my data collection, none of the apex bodies (barring the women organizations) despite their history of 40–50 years can boast of having had equal participation from the women. One of the oldest civil society organizations in Nagaland has had only one woman general secretary in more than 60 years. And upon asking specifically about women participation at the higher echelons of the organization, I was informed that earlier there was a post reserved for the women. It was the post of the personal secretary/assistant to the president! However, in the present scenario, that post too has been scrapped out. The other one that is also considered as an example of women's participation in the organization is that of the secretary for women affairs, which too largely remains unoccupied. At the level of districts and villages, it is not the case, as the above-mentioned post, more than often, does manage to find an occupant. This trend can be found at different levels of the structure of the civil society domain in Nagaland and that of the organizations.

Similar lack of marked gender differences can also be seen in the general awareness and cognitive ability levels of the people in Nagaland. For instance, about the 33 per cent reservation issue, there have been varying opinions, but the one that caused much discomfort to me was by one of the girls in her 20s who said 'for me it is nothing but an attempt to be able to get a share from the cookie jar' and by the 'cookie jar' she did not mean 'power' but 'corruption' – the possibility of hoarding black money that many feel the Naga political sphere offers in present times.

Thus, I realized that being in the field takes a toll not just on one's physical being but also on one's psychological being. I had to constantly deal with my positioning as a woman who must have suffered a lot being part of a rigid patriarchal set-up, unlike the women of the society I was researching on as they were 'free', 'empowered' and occupied 'equal' position as the men.

TURNING THE TIDE IN MY FAVOUR

The above-mentioned events unsettled me in the beginning, only to get the better of me, later. Thus, unlike initial phase of my fieldwork wherein I would try to justify my position from the word 'go', in the later phases, I stopped explicating the underpinnings of my social, cultural, political and academic location. I rather went ahead with a ready acceptance of my position and started to focus on the process of securing data from my field as well. Thus, another aspect that started to assume significance for my work was the process of narration, the categories used by my subjects and the terms in which they described their everyday world to an outsider. And these concepts and categorization have historical, social, cultural and political underpinnings – something that I was trying to locate from the information that was imparted to me.

My reflexivity helped me to shift that location from hard-core information to the entire process of collecting data and conducting fieldwork, the topic for which the fieldwork was conducted and the person undergoing that process. Thus, I also incorporated the story-narration technique in my methods of data collection. It was thus for me a process of not just presenting myself to my field but also how I was being shaped within that performance. It was an important learning that helped me in my latest phase of fieldwork. In contrast to the usual pattern where the relation between the researcher and the researched is marked by hierarchy, with the researcher occupying the dominant position and the researched the passive object, the researched in my field in Nagaland was active participants who transformed me and my work in due course.

It also set me thinking that despite the constant 'othering', what aided me in getting accepted in my field. In hindsight, I feel that one of the major reasons that facilitated my research was my academic institutional placement. Coming from Jawaharlal Nehru University (JNU), where many of these have either studied or have sent their children or aspire to send them, I was assigned a much prestigious position. This aspiration, as I inferred, is closely related to the present situation whereby the only opportunity to secure employment in the state is in the form of the government jobs. Private jobs are a rarity and entrepreneurship is difficult to achieve given the political environment in the region (heavy taxation from the undergrounds). In addition, my topic of research also found many takers. In the contemporary times, civil society in Nagaland has much to offer in terms of constructing discourse, creating public opinion and thereby influencing the public, addressing developmental, social, economic, cultural issues and even mediating in conflict situations as has been witnessed in more than six decades of armed conflict between the Naga people and the Indian State. It assumes much significance and any research conducted on the topic is received well. After all, the Naga society is still at a crossroad wherein they are trying to balance between their cultural and historical roots, with their political and economic goals with a growing alienation among the youngsters.

CONCLUSION

Since, the beginning of fieldwork tradition, there has never been an iota of doubt that it transforms everyone, albeit differently, who is party to it. During the course of my fieldwork, much had changed on account of the conditions and the situations I was wedged in. The transformations came gradually through my constant negotiations and re-negotiations with the 'empirical' and the 'theoretical' and my 'self' and the 'other' that I was in Nagaland. These helped me to learn and unlearn during the process. These transformations, which were a conscious effort on my part, were not only a survival strategy but also became a methodological necessity as my work progressed. The realization that I was constantly an object of their observation, and analysis, helped me reach another stage in my research. Consequently, my research, which in the beginning was embedded within a larger framework of structural analysis with attempts to grasp the local constructions of the concept of civil society, was shifted to the domain of interpretive sociology and critical analysis. Following which, I became interested not only in the issue of the process of data collection but also in the process in which that data was imparted to me, affected by the way I presented myself in the field. The catch here is that in that presentation, I was constantly (earlier unconsciously and later consciously) engaged in the production of my 'self' amidst my encounter with the status of the 'other' that I was constantly conferred upon. Thus, the young Indian woman tracing her journey from Lucknow to Nagaland via Delhi became a researcher engaging not just in observing her subjects, but also in reconstructing herself in the process based on her relations to others in the field that became essential to the production and presentation of 'her'.

REFERENCES

Alatas, S.F. (2006). *Alternative Discourses in Asian Social Science: Responses to Eurocentrism*. New Delhi: Sage.

Nag, S. (2002). *Contesting Marginality: Ethnicity, Insurgency and Sub-Nationalism in North-East India*. New Delhi: Manohar Publishers and Distributors.

Srinivas, M.N. (2011). The Insider versus the Outsider in the Study of Cultures. In V.K. Srivastava (Ed.), *Methodology and Fieldwork*. 3rd impression, New Delhi: Oxford University Press, pp. 413–420.

Srivastava, V.K. (2011). Introduction. In V.K. Srivastava (Ed.), *Methodology and Fieldwork*. 3rd impression, New Delhi: Oxford University Press, pp. 1–50..

Part III

Empirical Evidence of the Equity Scenario

CHAPTER 14

Women and Water

The Impact of Natural Resource Depletion in the Central Himalayan Region of Uttarakhand

Reetesh Sah

Uttarakhand is located between 28° 43'–31° 27' N latitudes and 77° 34'–81° 02' E longitudes. The River Tons separates the state from the state of Himachal Pradesh in the northwest, whereas the River Kali separates it from Nepal in the east. The Greater Himalaya is the northern boundary of the state and is also the international border with China (Tibet). Foothills in the south are bound by Uttar Pradesh (Government of Uttarakhand 2011). Starting from the foothills in the south, the state extends up to the snow-clad peaks of the Upper Himalayas making the Indo-Tibetan boundary. The region, being situated centrally in the long sweep of the Himalaya, forms a transitional zone between the per-humid eastern and the dry to sub-humid western Himalaya. Uttarakhand became the 27th state of the Republic of India on 9 November 2000.

This chapter attempts to describe and analyse the complex relationship between women and local ecology in marginalized mountain areas of the Central Himalaya. Scarcity of vital eco-services and depletion of traditional resource management systems have adversely impacted gender equity. The scarcity of water due to poor water management and its impact on lives of Himalayan women is studied in this chapter.

The average annual rainfall of the state, as recorded, is 1,547 mm. With an altitudinal variation ranging from 200 m to more than 8,000 m above mean sea level (msl). The climate of the state is quite harsh particularly in winter when temperature goes occasionally below freezing point in many of the subdivisions of the state. The state of Uttarakhand, embodying the Kumaon and Garhwal Himalayas with a geographical area of about 53,485 sq. km supports a human population of 10,116752 persons as per the 2011 Indian Census Reports (Census of India 2011). The state also comprises two administrative divisions – Garhwal and the Kumaon, consists of 13 districts –

Dehradun, Uttarkashi, Chamoli, Pauri Garhwal, Tehri Garhwal, Rudraprayag, Haridwar (in Garhwal division), Almora, Pithoragarh, Nainital, Bageshwar, Champawat and Udham Singh Nagar (in Kumaon division). It is further divided into 46 Tehsils, 73 Towns and 95 Development Blocks, 7,541 Gram Sabhas, 671 Nyaya Panchayats and 16,826 inhabited villages. The population constitutes 0.83 per cent and 21.4 per cent of the total population of Indian Republic and Indian Himalayan Region (IHR), respectively. Within an altitudinal variation ranging from 200 m to more than 8,000 m above mean sea level the state comprises five lithotectonically and physiographically distinct subdivisions; namely, the Outer Himalaya comprising the Terai and Bhabhar, Sub-Himalayan belt of the Siwalik, the Lesser Himalaya, the Great Himalaya and the Trans-Himalaya or Tethys. Human habitation is found up to an altitude of 3,500 m above msl; however, the zone between 1,200 and 2,000 m, largely falling in the Lesser Himalaya (1,500–2,500 m above msl), is densely populated.

The decennial growth rate of the population of the state for the decade 2001–2011 was 19.01. In this region, the human population is continually increasing and the region is experiencing major difficulties in sustaining its growing population on its squeezing environmental resources – land availability, forests and grasslands, water resource and so on. Much of the environmental resource degradation is governed by mountain specificities, namely, inaccessibility, fragility, marginality, diversity (heterogeneity), niche (natural suitability) and adaptability (human adaptation) apart from the growing population. They result in limited external linkages and replication of external experiences, slow pace of development, intraregional imbalances and underutilization of regional potential (Uttarakhand State Perspective and Strategic Plan 2009–2027).

The Central Himalayan region of India constitutes the states of Himachal Pradesh and Uttarakhand which came into being in 2000, when the mountain areas of Uttar Pradesh were administratively separated recognizing the fact that socially, ecologically and economically the region's management and development needs differed. The state is interspersed with rivers, deep valleys, high peaks, gorges, uplands, glaciers and snows (Chauhan 2010). A total of 75 per cent of population is approximately in rural regions.

The Himalaya is a vast mountain system, spread across eight countries in Asia. In India, though it covers only 18 per cent of the geographical area, it accounts for more than 50 per cent of the country's forest cover, a 40 per cent of its endemic species. In the Indian Himalaya, agriculture is a minor land use, with only about 10 per cent of the area as net sown area, located in patches across the forest landscape. Nevertheless, this area is ecologically, socially and economically exceptionally important. Traditional crop-livestock mixed farming continues to be the basis for livelihoods of local communities and is the backbone of the rural economy (Rao and Saxena 1996).

The Himalayan mountain system is dotted with 12 rivers, out of 18 major rivers of the country. Hundreds of small rivulets and thousands of streams make the Himalayas as 'Water Bank of Asia'. This constitutes 42 per cent of the total of the country. It is ironical that these rivers have not been of any use to the local resident, except for the minor utilities in the form of watermill, occasional irrigation, not exceeding 2 per cent of the total potential use (National Commission for Women [NCW] 2005).

The Himalayan watersheds are under constant threat of mass wasting and erosion caused by depletion of forest cover, unscientific agronomic practices and hydrologic imbalances. The ever increasing population, the need to provide a better quality of life to the people and the pressure on natural resources are further compounding the problem. Out of the total of 7.66 lakh hectare of cultivated area in the state, 4.21 lakh hectare area is rain-fed. An insight into the rain-fed regions reveals a grim picture of poverty, water scarcity and fragile ecosystem. Land degradation due to soil erosion by low rainwater use efficiency, high population pressure, acute fodder shortage, poor livestock productivity, under investment in water use efficiency, lack of assured and remunerative marketing opportunities and poor infrastructure are important concerns of enabling policies. The challenge in rain-fed areas, therefore, is to improve rural livelihoods through participatory watershed development with focus on integrated farming system for enhancing income, productivity and livelihood security in a sustainable manner (Government of Uttarakhand 2011).

CLIMATE

The annual rainfall in Uttarakhand is 1,700 mm, however the total number of rainy days is about 100; and most (95%) of the precipitation that falls in the catchment area as surface water is lost due to steep slopes and mountainous terrain. The total annual requirement of the human population, animal population, agriculture and industry is estimated to be around 3 per cent of the annual precipitation received. The state has about 0.55 million hectare of unirrigated land and the majority of it falls in the hilly areas of the state, which is also home to the poorer sections of the populace. A total of 47.42 per cent of persons in the state are below poverty line, and the most vulnerable sections are living in the hilly areas of the state (Uttarakhand State Perspective and Strategic Plan 2009–2027).

In the *Terai* and *Bhabhar* tracts adjoining the plains of western Uttar Pradesh, a typically tropical climate prevails. Sub-tropical climatic conditions are experienced in the Siwalik hills, the Doon valleys and up to an elevation of about 800 m in the lower Himalaya.

The temperate climate prevails between 800 and 2,400 m, and alpine conditions occur above 2,400 m. Therefore, across the state temperatures may vary from tropical to icy cold on the same day (Chauhan 2010).

THE WATER REGIME

The predominantly hilly state of Uttarakhand has a varied hydrogeological set-up and can be divided broadly into two distinct hydrogeological regimes, namely, the Gangetic alluvial plain and the Himalayan mountain belt. The former is covered with a vast expanse of alluvium and unconsolidated sedimentary material of varying size fractions (ranging from boulder to clay) and is a promising zone for ground water development. The latter zone, being predominantly hilly, offers much less potential for large-scale development of ground water. Ground water in the hilly region occurs mostly in fissures/fractures and emerges as springs. The springs are amenable to small scale development of ground water resources in the State (Uttarakhand State Perspective and Strategic Plan 2009–2027).

When drought-like conditions prevail, most of the remotely located springs in the hills start drying up or the discharge is reduced to such a level that they are unable to fulfil the basic requirement of the residents. There is also a drastic reduction in the flow of major rivers in the state. In the Himalayan region, *naula* (12 m deep well, mostly lined to get water from seepage), *dhara* (spout springs) and hand pumps (at few places) are the main sources of water for irrigation and household consumption, because rural water supply (if it is available) is either irregular or unwholesome. Except the spout spring, which delivers water at the ground surface naturally, *naula* and hand pump are artificial methods to extract water from the sloppy aquifer. Perennial or non-perennial nature of these water sources depends upon the aerial coverage of the discharging aquifer. In turn, these aquifers are recharged by rain or by snow-melt water, which gets infiltrated through the land surface and percolates to join the aquifers. The natural rate of groundwater recharge is reckoned to be 31 per cent of the total annual rainfall. Therefore, soil characteristics and land use play a major role in recharging sloppy aquifers. Deforestation, grazing and trampling by livestock, erosion of top fertile soil, forest fires and development activities (e.g. road-widening, mining and building construction) cause reduction in the infiltration rate and sponge action of the land and thus the failure of the watershed, which results in unchecked flow of water during the monsoon to cause a sudden swelling of streams and rivers, so that there are floods in the foothills and even in the plains, and droughts in the villages located on the slope of the mountains. Regarding nature's role, there is about 30–40 per cent decline in average rainfall over the past 50 years. Under such circumstances, rainwater harvesting and its storage is the only option left with us (Uttarakhand State Perspective and Strategic Plan 2009–2027).

Hierologically, Uttarakhand is a typical mountainous system. Precipitation takes the form of rain, sleet and hail in the valleys and lower reaches, while it falls as snow in the higher reaches. Glaciers in the Himalayan ranges give rise to large rivers such as the Ganga, Yamuna and Kali. Rainfed seasonal rivers (Sitla, Swarna, Tons, Nun, Bindal, Kans, Rau, Asan, etc.) drain the lower Himalayan and Shivalik ranges. Most rivers are known for their flash floods, which cause high levels of erosion, and damage crop and villages mainly in the districts of Haridwar and Udham Singh Nagar. Non-glacial rivers originating from springs and ground water sources (the Khoh, Ramganga, Kosi, Gola and Nandhaur) are also common in the Lesser Himalaya (Chauhan 2010).

Glaciers melt naturally during the summer and under stable climatic conditions. Ice lost through melting is replenished by winter precipitation in the form of snow. However, in many of the higher arid and semi-arid areas, people are dependent not only on the amount of glacier melt water but also on the timing of the water flow. The water has to be available at critical times for irrigation. Snow-pack and glaciers provide a buffer between when the precipitation falls as snow and is released as water. The melt season is often the warmest, driest time of the year, providing large volumes of runoff for irrigation when it is most needed. However, snowfall is gradually decreasing and the warmer summer temperatures are causing the glaciers to retreat (Chauhan 2010).

TRADITIONAL WATER MANAGEMENT SYSTEMS

The use of water resources in a multifarious context gives rise to different management systems, which are peculiar to conditions through which they emerge. The main sources of water in Uttarakhand are rainwater, glaciers, rivers, lakes, streams (of all sizes) and springs. Uttarakhand lies in the monsoon belt and thee communities in this region learned to collect rainwater, store it and use it for a variety of purposes throughout the year. Thus, a unique water harvesting civilization took shape in this region. In the pre-colonial period although the state was not responsible for providing water to its citizen, it had no intervention in the various uses of water by its people. There was community management of water for irrigation and drinking as per the need of the people. Traditional water management took birth from this system. The local communities had the right of ownership over the use of local natural resources and the state recognized this right (Rawat and Sah 2009).

Water was revered and regarded as sacred. Since, the water bodies were considered to be sacred, they were well maintained. It was so sanctified that river or Pani Dhara marriage, which was publicly performed in a sacred place in a river or spring, was given due recognition by the society (Lal 1920). Both the river or Pani Dhara and the Kumbh Vivah were given legal recognition. In the former, the nuptial ceremony was solemnized in the presence of a water body. According to Kumbh Vivah, when the bridegroom was inevitably absent, the bride was formally married to a pitcher of water representing him. Traditionally in Kumaon, the main systems of water harvesting are *guls*, *naulas*, *dharas*, lakes, *kund*, *khal*, *simar* or *gazar* and water mills. Many of these technologies are still in use and provide a significant proportion of the water requirements of the people (Rawat and Sah 2009).

The traditional systems are being detailed below:

(i) In Uttarakhand, cultivation is done largely on terraced fields, and since ancient times, the problem of irrigating the fields was resolved by diverting water from nearby streams or rivers through channels called *guls*. They are the best example of water resource management in the hills and are usually dug along the contours of the slope. Apart from irrigation, guls were used for drinking water and for running *gharats* or water mills.

(ii) *Naulas* are designed to collect water from subterranean springs. The flow of these springs is very sensitive and can be disturbed by seismic activity and human disturbance.

(iii) A *dhara* is a common source of drinking water and can be compared with a drinking water fountain.

(iv) *Simar* are also known as gajar. Gajar is a marshy tract of land in an agricultural field and is created by the ground water.

(v) *Chuptaula* are basically water holes for animals and are found mostly in high altitudes for use of graziers. They are not permanent in nature, and water is collected in them from springs or from points where water oozes out from the ground.

(vi) *Khals* are large depressions in mountainous areas used for rainwater harvesting. Mostly they are on top of ridges in the saddle between two crests. At times, small ponds are also dug for collecting rainwater. During the lean period, water accumulated in *khals* is used for irrigation purposes.

(vii) *Dhaan* is a structure in which water collected from small and big streams gives the shape of a lake. The accumulated water is used for bathing of domestic animals and irrigation (Rawat and Sah 2009).

(viii) In the higher reaches, there are many gads and *gadheras* (mountain streams), which earlier used to flaunt an abundance of water throughout the year. As a consequence, a variety of water harvesting structures arose within different socio-ecological settings, mainly for domestic use. Often well-to-do land owners would build the physical structure and the source was then managed by the community. Water for household use was, and continues to be, obtained from springs, flowing mountain streams or built rainwater harvesting structures.

(ix) Open water bodies, such as ponds, masonry tanks, *chappris*, *chaals* or *talaais*, provide water. For domestic consumption, people prefer to harvest below-ground seepages (*naulas*) or tap springs (*dharas*) (Chauhan 2010).

Traditionally, water management at the household level has been a woman's task. Sources in the mountains usually lie at considerable distance from habitations and women spend 2–4 hours a day collecting and carrying water to and fro. In many villages, they spend up to 8 hours a day. Estimates show that on an average, a hill woman walks over 3,000 km in a year. Apart from the labour and time spent, the carrying of heavy loads over long rough and difficult terrain cause numerous physical and health issues, which plague women in the mountains (Chauhan 2010). Women believe that traditional methods of water harvesting were the best. By their own efforts, where government has failed, villagers are making at hilltops to charge spring, an age-old practice (NCW 2005).

CHANGING WATER SCENARIO AND WOMEN

Hydrological studies over the last decade have presented abundant evidence that the water resources in this region are deteriorating. Uttarakhand state is today is experiencing a severe water shortage. This crisis has been caused by several factors such as deforestation, soil erosion, source depletion and population explosion. It has also been caused by unplanned and wrong development, poor management by government and people, ignorance and lack of awareness and, especially, by all-pervading corruption. The custom of community management has got drastically reduced. Rural areas are facing an acute water shortage, so that the state women need to travel long distances to fetch potable water. They are facing many problems because of water shortage. In summer not only family members but domestic animals are also suffering because of the scarcity of water. The water shortage problem is so severe in several villages in the rural Uttarakhand. Women fear the worst during the summer season as the water crisis is at the top during this time. Since India's independence in 1947, various interventions of the government to provide water to remote villages have led to a decline in the creation and management of traditional water harvesting structures, impacting huge areas adversely.

At the same time, ground water abstraction has increased, though often badly placed hand pumps quickly become seasonal. Deep water aquifers are tapped only in the plains below the foothills. Lakes, wetlands and marshy areas rarely provide water for irrigation, though almost all such areas are used for livestock grazing and for collecting a variety of natural produce such as fodder and thatch. At present, 11 of the 13 districts in Uttarakhand face regular water shortage, particularly of drinking water. The other two districts in the foothills have ample groundwater sources. Though numerous water supply schemes have been created in the mountains many stop functioning within a few years of construction, falling into disuse and disrepair (Chauhan 2010).

In spite of the fact that the Yamuna and Ganga, the two major rivers of the country, have their origin in the state, there is an increasing shortage of drinking water. Springs and streams are drying up, and the hydrological patterns in Himalayan mountain regions are changing. The dependence on traditional methods of water conservation is increasing. Many schemes have become defunct due to depleting water sources, coupled with population shifts. Their rehabilitation or replacement requires considerable capital investment. By government statistics, in 2006 there were 17,948 habitations (villages and hamlets) including those in the not covered and partially covered (NC/PC) categories that had to be provided with water supply (Chauhan 2010).

The fact is that the fodder crisis is part of the larger land and water crisis of rural areas. Better agricultural productivity on private lands is a sure-shot source of additional fodder. But, this productivity is limited by the non-availability of water to irrigate crops. That is why the villagers need to take their animals to graze in forestlands. Part of the problem is there is no water to grow crops, and so no agricultural residues for animals to eat. Water then becomes the first enabling tool. It is, therefore, imperative that we link fodder security to water security – building water recharge structures for irrigation (Uttarakhand State Perspective and Strategic Plan 2009–2027).

It is widely acknowledged that women are the key managers of water and energy in the household. In mountainous regions, where rural is often synonymous with remote, collecting water and fossil fuel are time-consuming tasks, which are performed mostly by the women folk. They have a direct stake in the management of natural resources, and their active involvement enhances the sustainability of any initiative. Conventional development interventions in energy and water have largely overlooked activities that women can take charge of themselves (TERI 2011). Women are the water providers in India. In villages, they walk long miles and in many semi-urban and urban areas they wait long hours to bring water for the drinking and cleaning needs of their families. The water crisis translates into an increasing burden for women as water providers. And with increasing water scarcity and water pollution, water-related diseases increase. Women as care givers also carry a disproportionate burden of water-borne diseases (NCW 2005).

The government scheme of water supply has largely failed due to its appropriate nature, poor maintenance and distribution. This has plunged Himalayan villages in a severe water shortage. In Uttarakhand, out of the total 16,000 villages, 8,800 villages have been marked as water scarce villages. The districts such as Almora, Pauri, Tehri, Pithoragarh and Chamoli are facing drinking water crises, where 72 per cent women and 14 per cent children have to bear the responsibility of carrying potable water. The average 60 per cent women have to walk ½ km while 10 per cent of them walk 4 km for fetching water. The villagers are not satisfied with the government schemes (NCW 2005).

Women are suffering a lot in every Himalayan village where the water problem is severe. Natural water sources are drying up, which adds the kilometres walked by women every day to quench the thirst of their family as well as animals. Women are the major workforce in the whole Garhwal Himalaya region. They work from early morning to late evening to serve the family. They do all household work from cooking to cleaning and washing clothes and soiled utensils, as well as looking after their children and animals. Women also collect the water required for cooking, cleaning, washing, bathing and drinking both for human beings and animals (NCW 2005).

In rural Uttarakhand, women are contributing up to 90 per cent of the total workforce in agriculture and animal care. The participation rate of women in the economy of the state is much higher than several other states and also the national average. The work participation rate of women has been constantly increasing at a higher rate than that of men in the state over the past few years. These women play a crucial role in agricultural development and allied fields, including crop production, livestock, horticulture, post-harvest operations, and fisheries. It has been generally recognized that the work burden among women in the state was very high and that they have to participate in all domestic and non-domestic activity, including social and religious functions, in the absence of male family members. But the financial and other matters related to decision making, on an aspect, were more or less handled by male family members. 'Women participate in almost all the agriculture operations while the participation of male family members is confined to a limited number of operations' (Tribune News Service 9 January 2012).

In the study of Report of National Commission for Women (NCW), it is established that in the village Kandakholi, in District Tehri, which is situated above 1,800 m msl, that there is pipeline from government, but water is supplied weekly or sometimes fortnightly, only for one hour. There is no natural source nearby. The government water supply is through a pumping system, lifted from Bhilangna River a tributary to Bhagirathi River which is at about 700 m msl. Now, they have reduced the number of animals reared only because of increasing water crisis. The only water source close to the village is about 1.5 km. The discharge rate is only 1.0 litre per minute. A woman has to wait for minimum of 1 hour to fill 20 litre of water. They get up early in the morning to queue for water and go to bed late around 11.30 after storing enough water for next day's work (NCW 2005).

In a study of the National commission for Women, India (NCW), women reveal that they take a bath, one by one, and only once in a week because of the water problem. Or, they go very early or very late to the spring to take a bath or wash the clothes. The water table level is falling every year. So, they are afraid of the drying up of the only existing natural water source. Similar stories were told by the women in other villages also. It was observed that a glass of water is much more precious than kerosene oil in the villages where people have to travel more than 8 km for one brass pot (*gagri*) of water, or have to pay to more than ₹ 50 for one 15 litre of tin. Most women walk on an average of 5–10 km per day just to fetch the water. In some villages the condition is worse, where women walk between 20 and 24 km per day spending 5–9 hours per day just for water. Villagers also blamed the government for the failure of the hand pump scheme everywhere. According to them, natural water sources are drying wherever there are hand pumps (NCW 2005).

A Survey by NCW in Jaunsar area of District Tehri Garhwal, villages Nagthat, Duena, Vishoi, Gadol, Jandoh, Chitar, Chichrad and Gangoa, reveals that water in the region is mostly acidic in nature. Water problem in Chitar and Gangoa villages is very severe, where men and women carry water on mules for 8–10 Km far from the village. Because of the poor water quality, most of the villagers in the regions are suffering from many diseases related to skin and teeth. Natural resources of water in the area are very few, and they are also disappearing very fast. During the survey by NCW it was observed that they are not getting enough water for their animals, so they have to take their animals to a spring about 2–3 km away (NCW 2005).

Women are not able to do their routine household work due to the time spent on fetching water. Most of the women in water-scarce villages suffer from joint and back pain. Education of the girl child also gets affected in such villages because the girls join mothers in bringing water. Boys also spent their time on water collection, as well as on taking the animals to the water sources, which adversely affects their studies. Water mills in most of the villages are either closed or are seasonal, because of the reduction in water in the streams (NCW 2005).

The Himalayan state of Uttarakhand is landlocked and relatively remote. Among its 9 million inhabitants, more than 60 per cent live in rural areas, and their per-person income falls more than 20 per cent short of the country's average. In 2006, only half of Uttarakhand's rural population had access to clean and safe drinking water. For that reason, Uttarakhand's women often wake up early and walk for several hours to fetch the day's water from distant springs. Then they return home, carrying heavy loads on their heads over steep hillsides. What is more, many catchment areas are degrading and springs drying up. As a result, their task is becoming increasingly onerous, particularly during summertime. Previous efforts to bring water to these communities have not been sustainable or financially viable (IDA – India 2000).

CONCLUSION AND POLICY RECOMMENDATIONS

It is important to understand that water is an economic commodity with multiple uses. Protection of fresh water resources is the need of the hour for water managers. It should be used judiciously, and policies must be formulated to address the needs of women and to work towards their empowerment. The focus on water management system requires a holistic approach aided by modern knowledge and technology but in consonance with traditional knowledge system and the actual local needs. It is essential to redeem the people's interest in environment, and instead of de-empowering them, they should be made partners in the whole process of planning, implementation and the real beneficiaries of the endeavour. Well-developed information systems for the purpose and a strong political will are the prime requisites.

Water and forests are intertwined, at ground level they cannot be understood separately. Large parts of the forests in Uttarakhand are situated in the sensitive catchments areas of the rivers. These catchments are not only rich in biodiversity, but they are also tied with our long-range ecological security and perpetuity of our rivers and glacier systems. The treatment of forest ecologies for maintaining the water supply in rivers and springs should be initiated in the sub-watersheds, and the smallest unit, the micro-watershed, should be prioritized. They should be adopted as the smallest unit of development. The function of this micro-management would be to implement development and management plans at the river basin level and to empower and involve the watershed communities in planning and development.

It is also suggested that appropriate water conservation measures should be used. People as stakeholders should be made aware and trained on the techniques of water conservation. Restoration of the traditional methods of water conservation, the traditional water management system which holds traditional wisdom, should be encouraged and must be included in the government policies. Conservation of water in the fields as *chals* and *khals* (large depressions in mountainous areas used for rainwater harvesting) should be made compulsory at every village. Natural water sources should be restored without any change in their ecological surroundings.

In this region, irrigated agriculture was practiced since ancient times. It may be assumed that the local water mill technology (*gharats*) has an ancient past. *Gharats* should be developed because they can also run on a lesser amount of water.

Rainwater harvesting must be introduced at every village and town level. Various systems of water harvesting, depending upon the source of water supply, may be implemented such as *in situ* rain water harvesting can be done through *bunding* and terracing, contour farming and mulching, rain water or direct surface run off harvesting through roof top collection, dug out ponds, storage tank, diversion and channel. Stream flow or run off harvesting through *nala bunding*, water harvesting dam, percolation tank, ponds and sub-surface flow harvesting. Proper water conservation measures should be used.

People should be made aware and trained in the modern as well as traditional techniques of water conservation. Women should be trained as water managers for the better utilization of water. The role of Panchayati Raj Institutions and NGOs in the management of rural water supply must be encouraged and government schemes should be implemented properly. The government should implement a comprehensive collection of household energy and water provisions. Future proposals should be designed, keeping in view of population and specially the women as they are dealing with the water.

These changes at the state and national level would impact positively on the community specially the women. Water availability would be certainly improved and crop yields could increase. The result will be food security in the long run and better health, education and empowerment for the women of the region.

REFERENCES

Census of India (2011). The Office of the Registrar General and Census Commissioner, New Delhi: Government of India.

Chauhan, Malavika (2010). A Perspective on Watershed Development in the Central Himalayan State of Uttarakhand, India. *International Journal of Ecology and Environmental Sciences 36*(4), pp. 253–269.

Government of Uttarakhand (2011). Integrated Watershed Management Programme Preliminary Project Report for State of Uttarakhand, 2011–2012. Dehradun: Watershed Management Directorate, Uttarakhand.

IDA India (2000). Water on Tap Improves Rural Quality of Life. Available at http://www.worldbank.org/projects

Lal, Panna (1920). *Kumaon: Local Customs*. Allahabad: Superintendent, Government Printing Press, United Provinces, p. 7.

National Commission for Women (NCW) (2005). Report on Women and Water Research Foundation for Science, Technology and Ecology. New Delhi: National Commission for Women.

Rao, K.S. and Saxena, K.G. (1996). Minor Forest Products Management: Problems and Prospects in High Altitude Villages of Central Himalaya. *International Journal of Sustainable Development and World Ecology 3*, pp. 60–70.

Rawat, A.S. and Sah, R. (2009). Traditional Knowledge of Water Management in Kumaon Himalaya. *Indian Journal of Traditional Knowledge*, *8*(2), pp. 249–254.

The Energy and Resources Institute (2011). *Creating Innovative Solutions for a Sustainable Future: Women Pave the Way for Conservation*. New Delhi: TERI.

Tribune News Service, Nainital, 9 January 2012. Available at http://www.tribuneindia.com/ (retrieved on 12 February 2013).

Uttarakhand State Perspective and Strategic Plan (2009–2027). Watershed Management Directorate, Dehradun, Uttarakhand.

CHAPTER 15

Assessment of Nutritional Status of Girls in Government Primary Schools in India

Chhavi Arya and Lata Pande

Children are the supreme asset of any nation, and their well-being is the basic concern of every nation. Their health is not only an indicator of the socio-economic standard of living of the country but also reflects the values and belief of the society. The school age is a dynamic period for growth and development as children undergo physical, mental, emotional and social changes (Khader 1996). The age of 10–12 years is a period of steady growth. Elementary school years (10–12 years) are nutritionally significant because this is the prime time to build up stores of nutrients and to prepare for rapid growth of adolescence (Bakhetia 1994). The way pre-teen children eat influences their health during childhood, during teen years and for the rest of their lives.

It is estimated that 75 million malnourished children exist in India and out of that 75 per cent are girls. Good nutrition during this period is basic for survival and good health. Malnutrition in this phase leads to physical and mental growth retardation, poor school participation and reduced work capacity. Improvement in health and nutrition status of children improves their school participation, attention capacity and results in better academic performance (Lahiri et al. 1990). Malnutrition and related diseases are common and widespread in India. The female child belonging to low socio-economic status is most vulnerable to prevailing circumstances of deprivation, discrimination, poverty, hunger and malnutrition.

Gender-based discrimination against female children is pervasive across the world. It is seen in all strata of the society and manifests in various forms but this situation is particularly true in India. In India, the female child is treated inferior to male child. Here the discrimination against a female child starts even before her birth. A skewed sex ratio of 914 females per 1,000 males gives some insight of the problem. Iron deficiency anaemia is highly prevalent among school girls and seriously affects their growth. Young girls are to be future mothers, and an undernourished mother cannot give birth to a healthy baby. The female child in India does not have equal access to proper nourishment and health care. Food intake pattern of children are significantly determined by existing social custom, beliefs, superstitions, religion and socio-economic strata (Swaminathan 1993). Many studies have been conducted on infancy and adolescence, considerably less attention is paid to school age and more data on nutrition assessment of these children is needed to access the scale of problem. Considering the above-stated facts, the present study was conducted with the objective to evaluate the socio-economic and nutritional status of female children (10–12 years).

MATERIAL AND METHODS

The present study was conducted in Government School No. 5, College Road Ludhiana, Punjab. Most of the girls studying in this particular school belonged to low socio-economic status. The school staff and parents of children were willing to co-operate in the study. A sample of 30 girls aged 10–12 years was randomly selected for the study. The date of birth of girls was taken from school records. Interview schedule was developed to collect general background information of the respondents. This interview schedule was pretested on 10 children (other than those selected for the study) to ensure validity.

Assessment of Nutritional Status

The methods used to evaluate the nutritional status were dietary survey, anthropometric measurement and clinical examination. Dietary survey was conducted through 24-hour recall cum weighing method for three consecutive days. Daily nutrient intake of each respondent was calculated using MSU Nutriguide computer programme developed by scholars (Song et al. 1992). In case of anthropometric measurements, height, weight, mid-upper arm circumference (MUAC) and triceps skin fold thickness were recorded according to standard methods by Jelliffe (1966). Information on various clinical symptoms was collected (Jelliffe 1966) to identify symptoms of deficiencies. The help of a doctor was also taken. Appropriate statistical tests such as percentages, mean and standard error were used to analyse collected data.

RESULTS AND DISCUSSION

Assessment of Socio-economic Status of Respondents

All respondents came from low socio-economic status with total monthly income below ₹ 4,000. Majority of respondents dwelled in overcrowded unhygienic settlements and slums. It was observed that 76.7 per cent respondents lived in nuclear families with majority (66.7%) having three to six members. Twenty-three per cent respondents lived in joint families having six to nine family members. Majority of the girls, that is, 56.7 per cent were first born among siblings in the family. Illiteracy among parents of the respondents was found to be 23.3 per cent for father and 30 per cent for mother. However, majority of the parents were literate. Majority (66.7%) of the fathers worked as labourers, rest were self-employed and very few were in service sector. Almost 50 per cent mothers were also engaged in income-generating activities.

Dietary Habits of the Respondents

Dietary habits of the respondents showed that 43.3 per cent respondents were vegetarians, 26.7 per cent were ova-vegetarian and 30 per cent were non-vegetarian. Majority of the respondents showed preference for junk foods and snacks. However, many girls showed dislike for healthy foods such as milk, green leafy vegetables and non-vegetarian food stuffs. As high as 66.6 per cent of the respondents skipped meals and majority of them (65%) skipped breakfast.

Intake of Various Food Groups by the Respondents

The average daily intake of various food groups of the subjects has been presented in Table 1. The average daily consumption of cereals by the respondents ranged from 122 to 238 g with a mean intake of 198 g. The mean cereal intake was much below the value suggested by ICMR, that is, 320 g. An intake at such a level was low and could meet only 61.2 per cent of the intake suggested for this age group. Wheat and rice were the main cereals consumed by the respondents. Inadequate intake of cereals has also been reported by Chandna and Sehgal (1995) among school children in Haryana. The intake of pulses of the respondents ranged from 25 to 51 g. However, the mean intake of pulses was 38 g. On comparison with ICMR standards, pulse intake had 54 per cent adequacy level. Similar findings have been reported by Bapat and Aspatwar (1993).

The average daily consumption of green leafy vegetable ranged from 6 to 24 g with an average intake of 22 g. The average daily intake of green leafy vegetables was much below the intakes suggested by ICMR with an adequacy of only 22 per cent. The respondents did not show preference for green leafy vegetables. It was also observed that the intake of green leafy vegetables decreased further in summer season due to non-availability of green leafy vegetables. The average daily consumption of roots tubers and other vegetables was 112 g. These vegetables contributed to a major portion of the diet of the respondents. The per cent adequacy of these vegetables was almost 1½ times than the suggested intakes of ICMR.

The per cent adequacy of milk and milk products was 24 per cent. Low intake of milk and milk products could be because of low purchasing power of low socio-economic group. The average daily consumption of fats and oils ranged from 15 to 40 g with a mean intake of 24 g. The per cent adequacy of fats and oils was 68.6 per cent. The average daily consumption of sugar and jiggery was 15 g. The per cent adequacy of sugar and *jaggery* was 30 per cent. Overall it was observed that the average daily intakes of most food groups was below the suggested values, however the intakes of important foods such as pulses, green leafy vegetables, milk and milk products were exceptionally low.

Nutrient Intake of Respondents

The average daily intake of various nutrients by the respondents has been presented in Table 2.

Table 1 *Average daily food intake of the respondents*

Food groups (g)	*Intake of respondents (g)*	*Suggested intake (g)*	*Per cent adequacy*
Cereals	198 ± 12.56	320	61.2
Pulses	38 ± 5.21	70	54.0
Green leafy vegetables	22 ± 9.18	100	22.0
Roots tubers and other vegetables	112 ± 8.24	75	149.3
Fruits	36 ± 13.01	50	72
Milk and milk products	60 ± 5.98	250	24
Fats and oils	24 ± 2.43	35	68.6
Sugar and jaggery	15 ± 1.97	50	30.0

Source: Suggested intakes by ICMR (1987).

Table 2 *Average daily nutrient intake of respondents*

Nutrient	*Intake of respondents*	*RDA*	*Per cent adequacy*
Energy (kcal)	1,246 ± 111.30	1,970	63.2
Protein (g)	35.06 ± 4.16	57	61.5
Total fat (g)	31.36 ± 3.86	55	57
Calcium (mg)	211.56 ± 25.86	600	35.3
Iron (mg)	11.2 ±2.94	19	58.9
β-carotene (Fg)	1,286 ± 418.17	2,400	53.6
Thiamine (mg)	1.0 ±0.32	1.0	100
Riboflavin (mg)	0.52 ± 0.09	1.2	43.3
Niacin (mg)	9.36 ± 1.78	13	72.0
Ascorbic acid (mg)	30.13 ± 8.16	40	75.3

Source: RDA (ICMR 1990).

The average daily energy intake of respondents was 1,246 kcal as against the recommended dietary allowance (RDA) of 1,970 kcal. The existing dietary intake could meet only 63.2 per cent of the RDA in terms of energy. In case of protein and fat, the average daily intakes were 35.06 g and 31.36 g, respectively, which could meet 61.5 and 57 per cent of the RDA. It was observed that nutrient intakes of energy protein and fat were insufficient and were below the RDA. On an average, the respondents were receiving 211.56 mg of calcium and 11.2 mg of iron per day. The intake of these minerals could match as little as 35.3 and 58.9 per cent of the RDA. The nutrient intake of vitamins such as β-carotene (1,268 Fg), riboflavin (0.52 mg), niacin (9.36 mg) and ascorbic acid (30.13 mg was below the RDA and could respectively meet 53.6 per cent, 43.3 per cent, 72.0 per cent and 75.3 per cent of the RDA.

Anthropometric Profile of Respondents

Anthropometric measurements serve as good indicators of past and present nutritional status of individual. Pattern of growth and physical state of body though genetically determined are profoundly influenced by nutrition. Hence, anthropometric measurements serve as useful criteria for assessing nutritional status. The anthropometric profile of respondents with respect to height and weight has been presented in Table 3.

The mean height of respondents was 135.8 cm and mean weight was 25.7 kg respectively. In terms of height the respondents 94.2 per cent of were below the NCHS standards and 93.7 per cent of the respondents were below the ICMR standards. Here it must be considered that this 'is a pre-pubertal growth phase for girls. In terms of weight, the respondents could attain only up to 67.8 per cent of the ICMR standards.

Table 3 *Anthropometric profile of respondents*

Parameters	*Averages attained*	*NCHS standard*	*ICMR standard*
Height (cm)	135.8 ± 10.45	144.2	144.963
Weight (kg)	25.7±4.81	35.6	37.9

Further in terms of anthropometric parameters, MUAC and triceps skin fold thickness were also measured. The results on these parameters have been presented in Table 4. Measurement of MUAC proves to be a useful and practical means of assessing protein calorie deficiency. Triceps skin fold thickness is used as an estimate of arm muscle size (Swaminathan 1993). In case of MUAC and TSF, Jelliffe standards were used for comparison. The mean MUAC of respondents was 16.07 cm as against Jelliffe standards of 20.7 cm. The respondents could match up to 80.3 per cent of Jelliffe standards in terms of MUAC. The mean TSF of respondents was 7.12 cm as against Jelliffe standards of 10.36 cm. The respondents could match up to 68.72 per cent of Jelliffe standards in terms of TSF. Results showed that on an average the respondents measured lower for MUAC and TSF in comparison to Jelliffe standards.

Table 4 *Mid-upper arm circumference and triceps skin fold thickness of respondents*

Parameters	*Averages attained*	*Jelliffe standard*	*Per cent of standard attained*
MUAC (cm)	16.64	20.7	80.3
Triceps skin fold thickness (cm)	7.12	10.36	68.72

Table 5 *Prevalence of clinical symptoms among respondents*

Clinical sign	*Per cent respondent showing clinical symptom of deficiency*
Eyes	
Pale conjunctiva	43.3
Lips	
Angular stomatitis	3.3
Cheilosis	10
Gums	
Spongy	6.7
Bleeding	20
Teeth	
Mottled enamel	6.7
Dental caries	40
Skin	
Pale skin	50

Prevalence of clinical signs of nutrient deficiencies has been presented in Table 5. Clinical examination is an important practical method for assessing the nutritional status of a community. It is based on examination of changes believed to be related to inadequate nutrition that can be seen or felt in superficial epithelial tissue (Jelliffe 1966). The deficiency signs commonly observed were pale conjunctiva and paleness of skin due to iron deficiency, angular stomatitis and cheilosis due to deficiency of B complex and spongy bleeding gums due to deficiency of vitamin C. Dental caries were also commonly observed due to poor oral hygiene.

CONCLUSION

From the findings of the present study, it can be concluded that the studied sample of girls belonged to families with meagre family incomes and with less purchasing power. The living conditions of respondents were unhygienic and overcrowded. Dietary habits of the respondents revealed that a majority of the respondents skipped meals, which further contributed to malnutrition. The average daily intakes of most food groups were below the suggested values. The intakes of important foods such as pulses, Green Leafy Vegetables (GLVs), milk and milk products were exceptionally low.

In tune with the low dietary intakes, the respondents could not meet RDAs for vital nutrients such as energy, protein, fat, calcium iron and β-carotene. Representing a malnourished state, the respondents had a low score on all of the assessed anthropometric parameters in comparison with established standards. Clinical examination revealed that the majority of the respondents suffered from anaemia. Provision of ample measures to address the issue of malnutrition is suggested. The need for a comprehensive strategy focusing on nutrition counselling and nutrition intervention is implicated.

REFERENCES

Bakhetia, P. (1994). *Nutritional Status and Its Impact on Physical Performance of School Girls*. Unpublished M.Sc. Thesis, Punjab Agricultural University, Ludhiana, India.

Bapat, M.M. and Aspatwar, A.P. (1993). Nutritional Status of Pre-School and School Children in Slums of Bombay Suburbs. *Ind J Nutr Dietet 30*, pp. 127–133.

Chandna, S. and Sehgal, S. (1995). Comparative Nutritional Status of School Going Boys and Girls (9–12 years) of Panipat City. *Journal of Dairying, Food and Home Science 14*, pp. 221–228.

ICMR (1987). *Nutritive Value of Indian Foods*. Hyderabad: National Institute of Nutrition.

—- (1990). *Nutrient Requirement and Recommended Dietary Allowance of Indian*. A Report of the Expert Group of the Indian Council of Medical Research, Hyderabad: National Institute of Nutrition.

Jelliffe, D.B. (1966). *The Assessment of Nutritional Status of the Community*. Geneva: World Health Organization.

Khader, Vijay (1996). Anthropometric Measurements of Primary School Children (6–10 years) in Vallabah Vidyanagar, Gujarat. *Ind J Nutr Dietet 34*, pp. 15–19.

Lahiri, S.K. et al. (1994). Study of Impact of Epidemiological Factors on Intelligence of Rural Children Belonging to Low Socio-Economic Status. *Ind J Public Health 38*, pp. 133–142.

Song, W.D. et al. (1992). *Nutriguide: Asian Indian Foods Nutritional Analysis Computer Program*. Michigan: Michigan State University.

Swaminathan, M. (1993). *Essentials of Food and Nutrition Fundamental Aspect*. Vol. I, Bangalore: The Bangalore Printing and Publishing Co. Ltd., pp. 557–558.

CHAPTER 16

Gender Equality and Health

Case Study of a Central Himalayan Village

Ila Bisht and Jyoti Joshi

All of written and oral history presents clear evidence of discrimination in different forms against women on the basis of their gender in all societies of the world. Even in countries such as United States and United Kingdom, till the beginning of nineteenth century the women did not have voting rights. The violence against women, inequalities in social structure, exclusion of women in decision-making processes, preference for baby boy, prenatal tests for sex determination of the foetus, deprivation in education, nutrition and health concerns, inequalities in the sharing of power and decision making at all levels, a lack of respect for and inadequate promotion and protection of the human rights of women and inequalities in managing natural resources and safeguarding the environment are some examples of gender bias present in the society. Biological sex differences are very few and are unimportant in terms of determining gender inequality because gender inequalities are socially determined and can be changed with change in attitudes, privileges and practices prevailing in the society.

Gender includes both women and men and obviously affects both adversely, but in the current situation gender inequality has affected women more adversely. This is why in the last few decades; attention at national- and international-level forums has been drawn to issues such as gender sensitization, gender equality, gender budgeting and gender justice. Global literature also reflects this fact in its various manifestations. India is a country with more than 70 per cent of its population residing in rural areas, it is therefore important to examine the condition of women in our villages. Women are considered to be the agents of change but a large number of rural women live in abject poverty and are subjected to various forms of exploitation both inside and outside the home. Amartya Sen has elaborated that 'Burden of hardship falls disproportionately on women' due to seven types of inequality, which are mortality – gender bias in health care and nutrition, selective abortion and female infanticide, basic facility – lack of education and skill development, special opportunity – inaccessibility to higher education and professional training, employment, absence of job/in-service promotion and lack of ownership of house, land and property.

The 1995 Beijing Platform provides 'an agenda for women's empowerment' signed by all governments that is seen as 'a necessary and fundamental pre-requisite for equality, development and peace'. The *Millennium Development Goal (3)* envisages that gender equality is both a goal in itself and a condition for the achievement of the other goals. The Task Force on Education and Gender Equality has also elaborated on the implications of MGD-3 for all the other goals. According to the World Bank, improving health care for women offers the biggest return on health care spending for any demographic group of adults along with other multiple payoffs such as well-being and productivity of women, significant benefits for families, communities and national economies (www.worldbank.org) (Iyer et al. 2011).

The principle of gender equality is enshrined in the Indian Constitution in its preamble, fundamental rights, fundamental duties and directive principles. The Constitution not only grants equality to women, but also empowers the state to adopt measures of positive discrimination in favour of women. In recent years, the empowerment of women has been recognized as the central issue in determining the status of women. The National Commission for Women was set up by an act of Parliament in 1990 to safeguard the rights and legal entitlements of women. The 73rd and 74th Amendments (1993) to the Constitution of India have provided for reservation of seats in the local bodies of panchayats and municipalities for women, laying a strong foundation for their participation in decision making at the local levels Uttarakhand has provided for 50 per cent reservation for women in all elected bodies of three-tier Panchayati Raj Institutions (PRIs). The last elections in the year 2008 have taken place after the above amendments by the government and as such more than 50 per cent elected women representatives are occupying positions in PRIs at all three levels. Reservation for women in PRIs has been viewed as one of the vital steps towards the women's empowerment.

The Eleventh Five Year Plan (2007–2012) focused on inclusive growth to reduce the social disparities. It has given clear priority to gender equity and recognizes women as agents of sustained socio-economic growth and change. The Twelfth Five Year Plan (2012–2017) focuses on improved delivery of Reproductive and Child Health and Nutrition services, involvement of private sector and strengthening public-private partnerships, improved performance of the disease control programmes and their integration with other schemes, improved access to drugs and diagnostics and population stabilization with gender balance. The present chapter attempts to carry out a scientific and systematic social research to gain knowledge of the issues related to the health indicators for Central Himalayan women, taking the case of women in a village of district Almora for intensive study. An attempt has also been made to assess the health awareness level of rural women through a case study of village Dadholi of Sult Block, which is about 150 km from district head quarter of Almora.

STUDY DESIGN

The present chapter is part of the research work on 'Health Programmes and Empowerment of Rural Women: An Evaluation', which has been undertaken on the basis of field study conducted in three randomly selected development blocks of district Almora. This chapter focuses on the gender equity and health indicators for District Almora with a case study of women's health awareness in village Dadholi of Sult Block in the district.

Area of Study and Method

The area for the case study chosen is the revenue village Dadholi of development block Sult in District Almora. The village is one of the six villages chosen randomly for the research work following an exploratory cum descriptive research design. The socio-economic profile of the village is given in Table 1.

Table 1 *Village profile of Dhadoli, District Almora*

Total Population (2001)	*General*	*SC*	*OBC*
429	252	128	49

Both primary and secondary data were collected and used for the research study. Interview schedule and PRA tools were used to collect primary data from the village. Secondary data were taken from the published documents and records such as census figures, AHS data and Parivar Register.

Sampling and Sample Size

Stratified random sampling was used to select the development block. From within each block, two villages have been selected randomly using random number table. Dadholi is one of such randomly selected villages in Sult Block. Fifty married women with age above 18 years were randomly selected and interviewed using interview schedules.

GENDER EQUITY AND HEALTH INDICATORS FOR DISTRICT ALMORA

Gender roles are those behaviours, task and responsibilities that a society considers appropriate for men, women, boys and girls. Gender equity means fairness and impartiality in the treatment of women and men in terms of rights, benefits, obligations and opportunities. By creating social relations in which neither of the sexes suffers discrimination, gender equity aims at improving gender relations and gender roles, and achieving gender equality. Treatment may be equal or different, but should always be considered equivalent in terms of rights, obligations and opportunities. Gender balance is the equal and active participation of women and men in all areas of decision making, and in access to and control over resources and services. United Nations considers gender balance fundamental to the achievement of equality, development and peace. Gender mainstreaming is globally recognized as a strategy for achieving gender equity. A key strategy for gender equity lies in women's empowerment, which is achievable through gender mainstreaming by the process of assessing the implications for women and men of any planned action in all areas and at all levels. Important parameters for gender equity include sex ratio, literacy level and health indicators such as crude birth rate, crude death rate and infant mortality.

The population of Almora district according to the 2011 census stands at 621,927 with 290,414 males and 331,513 females, making it the sixth most populated district in the state in spite of registering a negative growth between 2001 and 2011. For Almora district, negative growth of 1.73 per cent was recorded between 2001 and 2011. Sharpest decline has been observed in Sult and Bhikiyasain blocks.

Sex ratio (number of female per 1,000 male) is an important indicator of women's status in the society. For Uttarakhand, overall sex ratio has improved by only one point to become 963 in 2011 as compared to 962 in 2001 but child sex ratio (0–6 years) has declined from 908 in 2001 to 886 in 2011 for the state. Sex ratio for district Almora is much above the national and state average and stands at 1,142 in 2011 and is slightly less than 1,145 in 2001.

FINDINGS AND DISCUSSION

A case study of the village Dadholi of Sult block in district Almora was undertaken to ascertain the level of health awareness among the village women of reproductive age. The findings of the study are summarized below:

(i) The study has revealed that 78 per cent women perceive health as absence of illness, and only 10 per cent consider health to be mental, social and physical well-being. About the frequency of health check-up, it was found that 80 per cent women get their health examined only when they fall ill and only 10 per cent women get their health checked up twice a year.

(ii) As far as treatment of illness is concerned, it was revealed that 36 per cent women start taking treatment in the initial stage of their illness, whereas 40 per cent women start taking treatment only when they fall seriously ill. During study, it was evident that the ANM/ASHA usually focuses only on the lactating mother and child health care, whereas other persons in need of health care often do not receive proper attention. There is need to develop holistic approach in this regard. Due to lack of awareness, there is absence of appropriate level of ownership of government health schemes among the community members.

(iii) Quite often hygiene and health care needs of people vary from village to village and within the same village. It is therefore imperative to follow bottom-up approach to identify specific health care needs of the people and suitably tweak the programmes. This is possible only when there is inbuilt flexibility in the government health schemes, and implementing staff has desired attitude so that the problems can be addressed accordingly.

(iv) About 66 per cent women are always eager, curious and interested to know and discuss health-related issues but are not always able to do so due to lack of accessibility to the services of knowledgeable persons. Around 8 per cent were not eager to discuss health-related issues.

(v) On the issue of actual discussions with ANM/ASHA, it was found that about 48 per cent women discuss health-related problems with ANMs on every possible opportunity and 4 per cent women never discuss the same.

(vi) Most women (62%) get some information on health services from health department/government System, followed by the medium of TV/radio and newspapers, which covers about 24 per cent village women.

(vii) Rural women (66%) think that female doctor is necessary for consultation/treatment of health-related issues for women, whereas 26 per cent feel this could be done by any qualified doctor.

(viii) Women (80%) had no awareness about the flagship scheme of health and family welfare department namely *Janani Shishu Suraksha Karyakram* (JSSK).

(ix) Only about 12 per cent women got their health checked up thrice before the delivery, and about 60 per cent women got prenatal check-up only once.

(x) On the issue of delivery care, it was found that only 32 per cent deliveries were institutional deliveries, and about 40 per cent women deliver their child at home with the support of skilled health personnel such as ANM.

(xi) Only 72 per cent women had *Jachcha-Bachcha* cards, and out of these about 85 per cent availed most of the services on time.

(xii) On the issue of mother-child care, it was found that only 56 per cent women get postnatal check-ups and about 44 per cent women did not get postnatal check-ups.

DISCUSSION

The above findings need to be interpreted and discussed in light of the socio-economic and cultural values and practices.

Preference for Male Child

One reason for the adverse juvenile sex ratio is the increasing reluctance to have female children. During the field study, it was revealed that there still exists a very strong preference for male child among both parents across different social groups. This attitudinal problem was rampant in the whole area and was not found to be affected by higher education level or better economic condition of the family. In one case (village Balna), a woman had given birth to 11 girl children with 10 of them surviving, and had not yet adopted any family planning measure to stop further pregnancy. Similarly, a woman with four children, including one male child, wanted one more male child as she believed that it better to have at least two sons to ensure against unforeseen death of a male child in future. Census 2011 data has revealed that there is net drop in sex ratio (female per 1,000 males) from 908 in 2001 to 886 in 2011. During 2011, child (0–6 years) sex ratio in Uttarakhand is 894 in rural areas as against 864 in urban areas.

Prenatal Sex Determination

The PNDT Act 1994 has very strong provisions that prenatal test for sex determination is an offence. The offence under the act is cognizable, non-bailable and non-compoundable, but its weak implementation has been a major area of concern. There are three committees at national, state and district level to monitor/implement the act. Some major shortcomings in the effective implementation of the act include lack of regular meetings, no submission of report in Form-F by the diagnostic centres. In the absence of regular reports in Form-F, no meaningful and effective monitoring and resulting action is possible. The effective implementation of this act along with attitudinal changes in the society has the potential to stabilize the population growth with gender balance.

The impact of preference for male child in society includes declining sex ratio, deterioration and decline in women's health because of forcible pregnancy/conception and abortions. According to annual health survey 2010–2011 conducted by the Government of India, crude birth rate (CBR) and crude death rate (CDR) for Almora were 16.3 and 6.1, respectively, which are lower than the respective state average of 18.6 and 6.6 (Figure 1).

For Almora district, the CBR in rural areas is higher by 4.6 than urban areas, whereas female CDR was significantly less than the male CDR in the

Figure 1 *Crude birth rate and death rate in the study area*

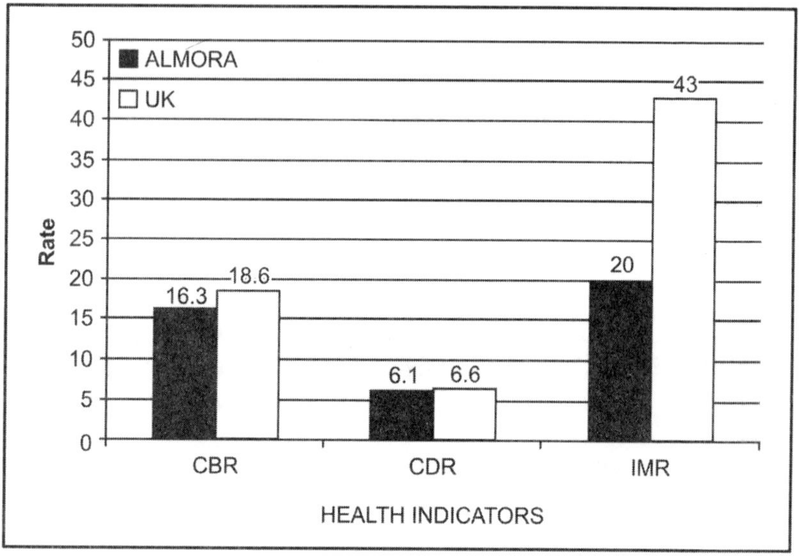

district by 4 and 2.9 points, respectively, for rural and urban areas. Female IMR was significantly higher than the male IMR by 2 points (11%) for rural areas of the district. Under-5 mortality rate for district Almora was 25, which is significantly lower than the state average of 53 with almost equal rate for male and female. District Almora and Pauri have registered negative growth in population in the decade.

Overall sex ratio has marginally improved in the state but child sex ratio (0–6 years) has declined in hill districts also. Champawat, Almora, Bageshwar, Pauri and Pithoragarh are such hill districts where child sex ratio has declined as compared to 2001.

Table 2 *The comparative literacy rate for India, Uttarakhand State and District Almora*

Literacy rate (2011)	*Persons*	*Male*	*Female*
India	74.04	82.14	65.46
Uttarakhand	79.63	88.33	70.70
Almora	81.06	93.57	70.44

Source: Census of India 2011.

The rate at which literacy has improved over the decade (2001–2011) is 5.5 per cent more for women than men. (Table 2) Closer study of the data has revealed that literacy level among rural women is less than that among urban women in the same period. The disparity between male and female literacy as well as among the rural and urban women is quite large and significant and warrants for attitudinal changes and resource mobilization. There is vast gap between the literacy levels of men and women. One positive development in the field of education and literacy in the past two decades has been the definite change in the attitude of the hill society of Uttarakhand as a whole, whereby each family is now sending all their children to schools at least at primary level. During the field study in the entire sample villages, it was found that almost all children above 6 years of age have been enrolled in nearby schools, though in most cases wherever affordability permitted bias to send the male children to nearby private English-medium schools was evident. The dropout rate in 6–17 years age group for girls and boys in rural areas of Almora district was 3.3 and 1.8, respectively.

Land Ownership

Under the Hindu Succession Act, 1956, females are granted ownership of all property acquired either before or after the signing of the act, abolishing their 'limited owner' status. However, it was not until the 2005 Amendment that daughters were allowed equal receipt of property as with sons. This invariably grants females property rights. Under Uttarakhand Zamindari Abolition and Land Reforms Act, the widow also has share in the agriculture land along with his sons. It was also observed that in cases of new purchase of land, particularly in urban areas now some males are buying lands in the name of their spouse, mainly to avail lower stamp duty benefits and partially due to gradual change in their attitude towards the women.

CONCLUSION AND POLICY RECOMMENDATIONS

On the basis of the study, the following conclusions are made regarding measures to improve awareness regarding health among the rural women and thus, to improve the health indicators. There is need for adopting a bottom-up approach to identify the specific health-related issues of rural women and fine tune existing programmes accordingly.

There is an urgent need to increase awareness among the rural women about the government health schemes and their benefits available to them through more and more decentralized camps in the rural areas after wide publicity through appropriate means. Awareness programmes should also be in local dialect to increase the participation of the local community. Education level of women needs further impetus to empower them to move towards gender equity. This should include vocational trainings so that their income level also gets improved to feel empowered.

The professional health workers usually focus only on the lactating mother and child health care, whereas there is felt need to focus on entire women health issues of the women of varying age profile. Greater sense of ownership needs to be developed in the community about the government health schemes by more frequent and effective interaction between the health workers and the women. This is expected to improve the understanding and confidence of the women to have better access to the facilities provided by the government. Sensitization of both men and women to develop positive attitude towards the girl child and to stop discrimination between son and daughter is necessary.

REFERENCES

Government of India (2011). Annual Health Survey, Uttarakhand (2010–2011). New Delhi: Office of the Registrar General and Census Commissioner.

Iyer, Uma, Elayath, Nitya and Akolkar, Arti (2011). Magnitude and Determinants of Overweight and Obesity in 6–12 Year Old School Children of Vadodara City. *Curr Pediatr Res 15*(2), pp. 105–109.

CHAPTER 17

Contemporary Health Policies in India

Examining the Status of Women's Health in India

Priyanka Neeraj Ruwali

Achieving gender equity in health implies eliminating unnecessary, avoidable and unjust health inequities, which exist as a result of the social construction of gender. It means that women and men have the same opportunity to enjoy living conditions and services that enable them to be in good health, without becoming ill, disable or dying by causes that are unjust and avoidable. The gender perspective in health involves linking the division of power and labour between women and men to their epidemiological profiles. By so doing, we can help to explain how and why men's and women's health profiles differ. Women and men are different with regard to their biology, the roles and responsibilities that society assigns to them and their position in the family and community. These factors have a great influence on causes, consequences and management of disease in ill health and on the efficacy of health promotion policies and programmes. During planning and implementing health promotion and disease prevention strategies, gender is an issue that is often neglected.

Gender inequities in health are concentrated in three types of imbalance, which are as follows:

(1) Between health risks and opportunities to enjoy health (health status and determinants) – women face a greater number of unavoidable health risks, in part because of their reproductive role. However, other factors such as less access to nutrition, education, employment and income mean that women also possess less opportunity to enjoy good health.

(2) Between health needs and access to resources again largely because of their reproductive role, women have more and different health needs than men, yet they have less opportunity to access health resources, from nutrition and education to health services.

(3) Between responsibilities and power in health work women make up the majority of both paid and unpaid health workers. Yet, because they are

concentrated at the lower end of the health labour force, they have less ability to influence health policy and decision making.

This chapter examines the cotemporary policies regarding women's health in India and seeks to link the efficacy of these with the status of women's health. It is vital to study and analyse whether governmental policies regarding women's health are responsive to ground realities especially in rural India.

Women in India suffer from various sorts of diseases including pregnancy-related complications, unsafe deliveries, improper prenatal and postnatal care and miscarriage. Mental health problems associated with puberty, identity crises and role transitions also constitute a large proportion of the burden for adolescent girls. Occupational hazards due to physical labour and domestic work (especially in agricultural areas) can be particularly damaging for the underdeveloped and undernourished adolescent girls. Women are afflicted with a considerable hidden burden of disease, which is often not accounted for in morbidity figures. Evidence indicates that there is a trend towards the growing burden of non-communicable diseases, in India and the world (ARROW 2005; Taylor 2010). In a review of Indian studies, Davar found that women are twice as likely to suffer from common mental disorders as men, which is supported by global prevalence rates (Davar 1999). Violence against women remains high in India and a study by INCLEN reported that 40.3 per cent of the women sampled reported at least one instance of physically abusive behaviour in their lifetime (INCLEN 2000). A report by WHO-SEARO discusses how suicide, an extreme manifestation of these hidden burdens, is now a leading cause of death among young women in India and China (WHO 2008).

Today, there is a growing recognition, among health professionals, researchers and policy makers, of the widespread and profound implications of gender-based inequities in health. There is also emerging evidence that integrating gender considerations into interventions has a positive effect on health outcomes across various domains (Boerder et al. 2004). Even though knowledge of gender differences in health is increasingly available, it does not always translate easily into realities of health planning and programme implementation.

The field of health promotion is no exception: the lack of translation of knowledge about gender inequities in health into health promotion interventions leads to misallocated resources and weakened potential for success. For example, violence against women, arguably the most extreme phenomenon of gender inequality, affects millions of women. Until recently, the magnitude and health consequences of domestic violence against women have been neglected in both research and policy (Garcia-Moreno 2002). We have now clear evidence (ARROW 2005) that gender-based violence (GBV) causes physical and psychological harm. In addition, it undermines the social, economic, spiritual and emotional well-being of the survivor, the perpetrator and society as a whole, but it also compromises the trust relationship between men and women. The social, economic, psychological, physical and emotional relationship harm to individuals from GBV constitutes a major health concern that requires creative and imaginative responses from the plethora of policy makers and intervention agencies dealing with health promotion and prevention of violence. In particular, lack of attention to the hidden emotional outcome of GBV, loss of trust, loss of dignity and a deeply compromised self-esteem need to be addressed alongside housing, economic support, social welfare and legal issues as part of an integrated health promotion strategy (Eckermann 2001). Following is an analysis of some of the national health programmes:

NATIONAL HEALTH PROGRAMMES

(i) Revised National Tuberculosis Control Programme (RNTCP) DOTS Strategy

(ii) National Cancer Control Programme

(iii) National Aids Control Programme

(iv) National Iodine Deficiency Disorders Control Programme

(v) National Mental Health Programme

(vi) Nutritional Programmes

(vii) National Programme for Control of Blindness

The RNTCP adopted Directly Observed Treatment (DOTS) to diagnose, cure and reverse the epidemic. The National Health Profile (2007) provides the data related to tuberculosis, which is restricted to numerical figures such as the number of cases, deaths, prevalence rates for both the sexes and case fatality rates. The data reveal that the tuberculosis incidence rates are higher for males at all ages except in childhood when they are higher in females (National Health Profile 2007). Studies have reported that sex differentials in prevalence rates begin to appear between 10 and 16 years of age and remain higher for males than females thereafter. Though the reasons for the higher male prevalence and incidence are poorly understood, the differences in tuberculosis notification rates between men and women may reflect biological differences (i.e. sex difference) in the epidemiology of tuberculosis, differences in the societal roles of men and women (gender differences) that influence the risk of exposure and/or gender difference in access to care (WHO 2008). The

National Health Profile (2007) shows that men are more exposed to the risk of pulmonary tuberculosis than women. Some studies report an increased delay for males in the time lapse between the onset of symptoms and the patient's first contact with a health care provider.

A study in India found that males were less likely to be notified than females, which suggests that the under notification of male TB cases could be because of employed men find it difficult to take leave from work to attend health centres that are open only during the day (WHO 2008). Further, the genital TB, which is often difficult to diagnose in both men and women, is relatively rare in men. These findings have important implications for the programme planners. Mainstreaming gender in the Revised National Tuberculosis Control Programme should address issues such as difference in risk of exposure to infection, in health seeking behaviour and health systems response, economic consequences and stigma associated with being known as a tuberculosis patient between males and females. Similarly, keeping the programme objectives in focus, undertaking research to find the impact of gender on factors such as smoking initiation, types of tobacco used, depth and frequency of inhalation, differential response to diagnosis and health-seeking behaviour as manifested in men and women would be critical sources to identify the treatment strategy including counselling for various groups accordingly.

There is also a need for regular data collection on tobacco use disaggregated by sex and age, which will clearly allow identification of trends and health effects on males and females of all the ages. This coverage could also include comorbidities such as depression, drug addiction and added risk of HIV/AIDS. Applying a gender perspective to each component could enhance the implementation further, but this will require sound multidisciplinary research to produce appropriate recommendations for the most effective directions (WHO 2008). The programme must take into account the interventions that may be initiated in the community, school-based discussion of the health impacts, gender expectations for both males and females to foster greater self-awareness and, thus, resistance to gender-based advertising and harmful social norms against TB. It implies weaving financial components required to address these issues and evaluation as to whether this fund has been utilized as per the planned intervention in the national programme.

According to the National Health Profile (2008), the estimated prevalence of blindness in India in 2004 is 10.2 per 1,000 in males and 12.2 per 1,000 in females, whereas the estimated incidences of blindness in India in 2004 are 1,002,063 per year among males and 1,129,985 among females (WHO 2008). Females are more vulnerable when it comes to prevalence as well as estimated incidence rates of blindness, with a possibility that some women may be left unnoticed. One of the possible reasons could be found in the barriers to use eye care services, which vary considerably for women and men (Ministry of Health and Family Welfare 2005).

Some of the barriers that prevent women and men from receiving eye surgery are cost of surgery, inability to travel to a surgical facility, difference in the perceived value of surgery, lack of access to information and resources and fear of poor outcome. It is important to address the sex differentials and gender inequities while planning for the programme activities in the use of eye care services such as (i) at the local level, it is important to identify the barriers that prevent women from receiving eye care services and to design gender-sensitive programmes to reduce these. (ii) Counselling services especially for women should be organized, focusing on the benefits and removing the fears. (iii) Peer motivators (women to women) are likely to be more effective than health workers in promoting the use of eye care services including surgery. (iv) Blindness programmes should monitor cataract surgical coverage rates by sex as well as monitor the outcome of surgery by sex. (v) Special incentives may be charted out for women, for example, concession in rates of surgery. Further, an analysis of the important differences between women and men in the underlying mechanisms of HIV/AIDS infection reveals that the social and economic consequences of HIV/AIDS stem from factors related to physiology, sexual behaviour and socially constructed 'gender-related expectations' and other factors. There are factors associated with roles and responsibilities, access to resources and decision-making power related to sexual patterns in any society.

A number of studies have examined the role of gender inequalities on women's risk and vulnerability to HIV/AIDS. As per the WHO Fact Sheet 5, women are more susceptible than men to get infection of HIV in any given heterosexual encounter, due to the greater area of mucous membrane exposed during sex in women than in men. Gender norms influence women's vulnerability to HIV. Violence (physical, sexual and emotional), which many women experience at some point in their lives, increases their HIV/AIDS vulnerability. Women assume the major share of care taking in the family including for those living with and affected by HIV. Much of the care taking is unremunerated and is based on the assumption that this is a role that women 'naturally' have to undertake adds to their burden. The entire project staff should be given awareness as to how women are more vulnerable to HIV, and the ways and means of addressing these issues within the socio-cultural norms of any community. Gender should constitute one of the key reference points during appraisal, monitoring and evaluation of individual sexual health projects.

As far as HIV/AIDS is concerned, it is important to discuss the sexually transmitted infections (STIs) as many of these can be treated. NACO has been making special efforts to promote early diagnosis and treatment of STIs as part of its family health awareness campaign. NFHS-III studied the prevalence rate of STIs, by adding variables such as abnormal genital or bad smelling discharges and genital sores or ulcers in 12 months prior to the survey. It found that 11 per cent of the women and 5 per cent of the men who ever had sex, had an STI or STI symptom. Women are more susceptible and prone to these due to their physiology. Therefore, public awareness and education about these infections and methods of preventing them to women is important.

The National Cancer Control Programme (NCCP) is another important programme and the National Health Profile (2008) reveals that 37.4 per cent of the cancer incidences are in cervix (19.1%) and breast (17.3%), which are women specific. Cancer at the oral cavity site is 10.9 per cent among males and 0.5 0 per cent among females. The first goal of the NCCP is primary prevention of cancer (Ministry of Health and Family Welfare 2005; National Institute of Health and Family Welfare 2002). Health education offers the greatest public health potential and the most cost-effective long-term method of cancer control. The cancer incidence may be brought down if due emphasis is given on 'early detection' of cancer in women.

There is a need for initiating interventions for the programme to be gender sensitive as well as site specific. For example, the national programme needs to build in specific health education and counselling strategies for both men and women, keeping the higher prevalence rates for different types of cancers. Dinshaw et al. pointed out that periodic examination by Pap smear and mammography is the accepted standard for early detection of cervix and breast cancers. In an Indian scenario, the health workers may be trained to tackle early detection as a routine public health, and women should be advised to undergo this as a routine investigation at least once a year (Dinshaw 2004, 2005). The evaluation of implementation status of the National Iodine Deficiency Disorders Control Programme in India (2006) does not contain any disaggregated data regarding the number of men and women surveyed. (National Institute of Health and Family Welfare 2002). This type of information is an important component not only from the point of view of cooking as the responsibility of women but also from the point of view of maintaining the nutritional status of children and the family.

Hence, the programme components need to build and reflect how gender could be used to curb the disease through health education, communication and information strategies. Analysing the life cycle of women, one observes that the older women are more vulnerable to manage and get treatment as they age. To effectively reach older people, interventions have to take into account the above-mentioned gender realities. The restrictions on women's power and autonomy detailed above also imply that the older women do have difficulty than older men in accessing public services such as healthcare. For certain conditions such as mental health problems, the gender norms may make it more difficult for women than men to come forward. The ways in which gender affects the ageing people, their capacities and health seeking behaviour needs to be examined and addressed if interventions are to be truly effective. Data in the National Health Profile on mental health are not disaggregated on the basis of gender but on the basis of major and minor mental disorders. In the case of mental disorders, the role of family is irreplaceable by any other agency or institution. It is imperative to campaign for constant support of the family as women may be dependent upon the family for all purposes.

Another area of omission as a concern of the health sector is the absence of GBV. GBV is a pervasive public health and human rights problem. It can take the form of physical, sexual, economic and psychological/emotional violence within the family; child sexual abuse; dowry-related violence; rape and sexual abuse; marital rape; sexual harassment in workplaces and educational institutions; forced prostitution; trafficking of girls and women and child marriage – an issue related to health as much as human rights (WHO 2008). Around the world, at least one woman in every three has been beaten, coerced into sex or otherwise abused. Physical and sexual violence causes women and men to a lesser degree to suffer substantial morbidity and mortality, a major cause of disability, death and having dire consequences on health and well-being of women. It becomes necessary to address GBV in the health sector policies and programmes.

It has been a frequent complaint of policy makers that most statistics are not disaggregated by sex. In the male-dominated society, though women are the active players in the reproduction activities, they have no voice in the decision making in relation to their own childbearing. To reflect gender sensitiveness in the health programmes, each programme has to critically view the needs of the specific gender group: women and men, and address the health issues specifically according to the needs of the specific gender. The Third National Family Health Survey (NFHS-3) coordinated by the International Institute for Population Sciences (IIPS) under the aegis of the Government of India was conducted in 2005–2006. As did NFHS-1 (1992–1993) and NFHS-2 (1998–1999), NFHS-3 provides information on fertility, mortality, family planning, HIV-related knowledge and important aspects of nutrition, health and health care.

Unlike the earlier surveys, however, NFHS-3 interviewed men aged 15–54 and never married women aged 15–49, as well as ever-married women, and included questions on several emerging issues such as prenatal mortality, male involvement in maternal health care, adolescent reproductive health, higher-risk sexual behaviour, family life education, safe injections and knowledge about tuberculosis. In addition, NFHS-3 carried out blood testing for HIV to provide, for the first time in India, population-based data on HIV prevalence. NFHS-3 collected information from a nationally representative sample of 109,041 households, 124,385 women aged 15–49, and 74,369 men aged 15–54. The NFHS-3 sample covers 99 per cent of India's population living in all 29 states. From among all the women and men interviewed nationwide, 102,946 were tested for HIV. NFHS-3 provides estimates of HIV prevalence for adult women and men at the national level, for Uttar Pradesh and for five high HIV prevalence states (Andhra Pradesh, Karnataka, Maharashtra, Manipur and Tamil Nadu). Additionally, health investigators tested blood haemoglobin levels of women and men and of children aged 6–59 months to assess the prevalence of anaemia. NFHS-3 also collected information on population and health indicators for slum and non-slum populations in eight cities, namely Chennai, Delhi, Hyderabad, Indore, Kolkata, Meerut, Mumbai and Nagpur. The 2001 Indian census found a sex ratio of 927 girls per 1,000 boys for the population aged 0–6 years. Approximately five years after the census, NFHS-3 finds the sex ratio of the population aged 0–6 years (girls per 1,000 boys) to be 918 for India as a whole. The under-seven sex ratio in urban areas is the same in NFHS-3 as in the 2001 census; however, in rural areas, NFHS-3 finds a sex ratio for this population of 921, lower than the 934 found in the census.

MARRIAGE AND FERTILITY

More than half of women are married before the legal minimum age of 18. Among women aged 20–49, the median age at first marriage is 17.2 years. By contrast, men in the same age group get married six years later, at a median age of 23.4 years. Sixteen per cent of men aged 20–49 are married by aged 18, 28 per cent by aged 20 and 58 per cent by aged 25. Women today are waiting slightly longer to marry. In the late 1990s, the median age at first marriage was 16.7 years, 6 months earlier than it is now. The median age at first marriage in India is almost two years higher for women aged 20–24 than for women aged 40–49. Urban women marry more than two years later than rural women; the median age at marriage among urban women aged 20–49 is 18.8 years, compared with 16.4 years among their rural counterparts. Fertility continues to decline in India (Table 1).

The current total fertility rate (TFR) of 2.7 is down slightly from 2.9 children per woman at the time of NFHS-2, but is still well above the replacement level of just over two children per woman. In urban areas, the TFR has reached replacement levels (2.1), but in rural areas the TFR is 3.0. In Uttarakhand the TFR is 2.6. Teenage pregnancy is common. Overall, one in six women aged 15–19 has begun childbearing: 12 per cent have become mothers and 4 per cent were pregnant with their first child at the time of the survey. Among women aged 20–49, half had a birth before they were 20 years old, and more than one in four before they were 18 years old. Early childbearing is most common in rural areas and among women with no education.

Table 1 *Total fertility rate in India*

Age-specific and total fertility rates and crude birth rates from NFHS-3 and NFHS-2 by residence, India

Age	*NFHS-3*			*NFHS-2*		
	Urban	*Rural*	*Total*	*Urban*	*Rural*	*Total*
15–19	0.057	0.105	0.090	0.068	0.121	0.107
20–24	0.166	0.231	0.209	0.179	0.222	0.210
25–29	0.123	0.146	0.139	0.127	0.150	0.143
30–34	0.048	0.069	0.062	0.057	0.075	0.069
35–39	0.013	0.031	0.025	0.018	0.033	0.028
40–44	0.004	0.009	0.007	0.003	0.011	0.008
45–49	0.001	0.004	0.003	0.001	0.004	0.003
TFR 15–44	2.06	2.96	2.66	2.27	3.06	2.84
TFR 15–49	2.06	2.98	2.68	2.27	3.07	2.85
CBR	18.8	25.0	23.1	20.9	26.2	24.8

Note: TFR = Total fertility rate expressed per woman.
CBR = Crude birth rate, expressed per 1,000 population.

KNOWLEDGE AND USE OF FAMILY PLANNING

Knowledge of contraception is nearly universal: 98 per cent of women and 99 per cent of men aged 15–49 knew one or more methods of contraception. Over 94 per cent of women and men know about female sterilization. Male sterilization, by contrast, is known only by 79 per cent of women and 87 per cent of men. Ninety-three per cent of men know about condoms, compared with 74 per cent of women. More than four in five women and men know about contraceptive pills. Knowledge of contraception is widespread even among adolescents: 96 per cent of young women and 97 per cent of young men have heard of a modern method of contraception.

The contraceptive prevalence rate for currently married women in India is 56 per cent, up from 48 per cent in NFHS-2. Female sterilization, with a prevalence of 37 per cent, accounts for 66 per cent of all contraceptive use, down from 71 per cent of all contraceptive use at the time of NFHS-2. The use of female sterilization is higher for women with less education and women who are employed for cash than for most other groups of women. The highest adoption rate of female sterilization, at 67 per cent, is among women with three children who have two sons. The most common spacing methods are condoms and the rhythm method, each used by 5 per cent of currently married women. Most men in India believe that women do not alone bear the responsibility for family planning (78%) and reject the idea that women using contraception may become promiscuous (84%). Nearly two-thirds of men know that a condom protects against pregnancy most of the time. Half of men, however, incorrectly believe that women who are breastfeeding cannot become pregnant.

MATERNAL HEALTH CARE

Among women with a live birth in the five years preceding the survey, the percentage who received different types of antenatal care (ANC) during the pregnancy for their most recent live birth, India, 2005–2006 are indicated in Table 2.

Table 2 *Antenatal care in India (2005 & 2006)*

Category of ANC Care	*Percentage of respondents-2005*	*Percentage of respondents-2006*
At least one ANC visit	76.4	69.4
Three or more ANC visits	52.0	44.9
One ANC visit in the first trimester of pregnancy	43.9	43.3
Received information about specific pregnancy complications	36.0	38.2
Received two or more TT injections during the pregnancy	76.3	68.5
Received one TT injection during the pregnancy and at least one more in the three years prior to the pregnancy	1.5	1.7
Given or bought IFA	65.1	62.6
Took IFA for at least 90 days	23.1	26.4

Note: TT: Tetanus Toxoid injection
IFA: Incomplete Freund's Adjuvant injection

The World Health Organization recommends that all pregnant women should have at least four antenatal care (ANC) assessments by or under the supervision of a skilled attendant (Table 2). Although 76 per cent of women who had a live birth in the five years preceding the survey received ANC, only 44 per cent started ANC during the first trimester of pregnancy, as recommended.

Another 22 per cent had their first visit during the fourth or fifth month of pregnancy. Just over half of mothers (52%) had three or more ANC visits. Urban women were much more likely to have three or more antenatal visits than rural women. Many women do not receive high-quality ANC. Fewer than three in four had their abdomen examined, and fewer than two in three received other services, including being weighed, having blood pressure measured, and urine and blood samples checked. Only 36 per cent received information about pregnancy complications. Sixty-five per cent received (or bought) iron and folic acid (IFA) supplements for their most recent birth, and only 23 per cent took IFA for at least 90 days, as recommended. Seventy-six per cent of mothers received the two or more tetanus toxoid injections during pregnancy for their most recent birth. Only 4 per cent of women took a drug for intestinal parasites during their pregnancy.

Thirty-nine per cent of births in the five years preceding the survey took place in health facilities; more than half took place in the woman's own home; and 9 per cent took place in parents' homes. For 72 per cent of deliveries that took place at home, the mother reported that she did not feel that it was necessary to deliver in a health facility, and for more than a quarter (26%), the mother said that delivery in a health facility is too expensive.

The more ANC visits that a woman had during pregnancy, the greater the likelihood that her delivery took place in a health facility. First births are more likely to be delivered in an institution than births at higher birth orders. Urban residence, education and wealth are all strongly and positively associated with the likelihood of an institutional delivery. Only 13 per cent of births to women in the lowest wealth quintile and 18 per cent of births to both women with no education and to scheduled tribe women are delivered in an institution. Postnatal check-ups soon after delivery help safeguard the health of mother and baby, particularly for births occurring outside of health care facilities. Almost 6 in 10 women (58%) did not receive any postnatal check-up after their most recent birth. About one-quarter of women (27%) received a health check-up in the first four hours after delivery, and 37 per cent received a health check-up within the critical first two days after delivery. Although the likelihood of a timely postnatal check-up is closely associated with having an institutional delivery, it is notable that 15–24 per cent of births delivered in institutions did not receive a postnatal check-up. Among births delivered at

Table 3 *Place of delivery, and percentage delivered in a health facility*

Urban/ Rural	*Facility availed Hospital, Primary Health Centre Nursing Home, etc.*			*Home*						
	Public Sector/Government	*Private/NGO/Trust*	*Private sector*	*Own home*	*Parents' home*	*Other home*	*Others*	*Total*	*Percentage Delivered in a health facility*	*Number of births*
Urban	28.6	0.9	37.9	26.6	5.3	0.4	0.2	100.0	67.5	14,303
Rural	14.4	0.3	14.2	59.8	10.6	0.5	0.3	100.0	28.9	42,135
Total	18.0	0.4	20.2	51.3	9.2	0.5	0.3	100.0	38.7	56,438

Source: According to background characteristics, India, NHS, 2005–2006

home, only 9–12 per cent of births received a postnatal check-up within two days of delivery (Table 3 & Table 4).

Table 4 *Maternal care indicators Maternal care indicators for births during the five years preceding the Survey in India, 2005–2006*

	Percentage who received all recommended types of antenatal care	*Percentage of births delivered in a health facility*	*Percentage of deliveries assisted by health personnel 2*	*Percentage of deliveries with a postnatal check-up 3*	*Percentage of deliveries with a postnatal check-up 3*	*Percentage of deliveries with a postnatal check-up within two days of birth*
India		15.0	38.7	46.6	41.2	37.3
Uttaranchal		16.1	32.6	38.5	35.8	32.4

NUTRITIONAL STATUS

NFHS-3 collected information on the height and weight of women aged 15–49 and men aged 15–54. The height and weight measurements provide an estimate of the body mass index (BMI), a measure of nutritional status (Table 5). The BMI is defined as weight in kilograms divided by height in metres squared (kg/m^2). A cut-off point of 18.5 is used to define thinness or acute under nutrition and a BMI of 25 or above indicates overweight or obesity. More than one-third (36%) of women aged 15–49 in India have a BMI below 18.5 indicating chronic nutritional deficiency, including 16 per cent who are moderately to severely thin. The proportion of ever-married women who are thin (33%) has decreased slightly from 36 per cent in NFHS-2. Women who are undernourished themselves are also much more likely than other women to have children who are undernourished. Obesity, the other side of poor nutrition, is a substantial problem among several groups of women in India, particularly urban women. Fifteen per cent of ever-married women are overweight or obese, up from 11 per cent in NFHS-2.

Anaemia is a major health problem for adults as well as children, affecting 55 per cent of women and 24 per cent of men (Table 6). The prevalence of anaemia for ever-married women has increased from 52 per cent in NFHS-2 to 56 per cent in NFHS-3. In Uttarakhand, 55.2 per cent women are anaemic. Studies have been done to emphasize that between 50 and 90 per cent of all pregnant women in India suffer from anaemia. Severe anaemia accounts for 20 per cent of all maternal deaths in India. Severe anaemia also increases the chance of dying from a haemorrhage during labour. Pregnant women are much more likely than non-pregnant women to be moderately to severely anaemic.

Table 5 *Nutritional status of women (Percentage of women aged 15–49, below 145 cm, mean body mass index (BMI) and percentage with specific BMI levels, India, 2005–2006*

Region	*Percentage with height below 145 cm*	*Mean BMI*	*Category according to Mean BMI Body Mass Index (BMI)[1] in kg/m2*						
			Normal	*Thin*			*Overweight*		
				thin/mildly thin/severely thin			*moderately overweight/obese/over obese*		
			18.5–24.9	*<18.5*	*17.0–18.4*	*<17.0*	*= 25.0*	*25.0–29.9*	*= 30.0*
India	11.4	20.5	51.8	35.6	19. 7	15.8	12.6	9.8	2.8
Uttarakhand	7.5	20.8	57.2	30.0	18.3	11.7	12.8	10.1	2.7

[1] Excludes pregnant women and women with a birth in the preceding 2 months.

Table 6 *Anaemia among women (percentage of women and men aged 15–49 with anaemia, India, 2005–2006)*

	Women				*Men*			
	Mild/Moderate/Severe/ Any anaemia				*Mild/Moderate/Severe/ Any anaemia*			
India[1]	38.6	15.0	1.8	55.3	13.0	9.9	1.3	24.2
Uttarakhand	40.4	13.3	1.5	55.2	17.0	1.4	0.7	29.2

[1] Excludes Nagaland.

The consumption of a wide variety of nutritious foods is important for health. Women's food consumption is less balanced than that of men. Ninety per cent or more women and men consume dark green, leafy vegetables and pulses or beans weekly; however, 55 per cent of women, compared with 67 per cent of men, consume milk or curd weekly. Consumption of fruits and other foods is less common among both women and men. Only 40 per cent of women, compared with 47 per cent of men, consume fruits weekly; 32 per cent of women, compared with 41 per cent of men, consume eggs weekly and 35 per cent of women, compared with 41 per cent of men, consume fish or chicken/meat weekly. Gender differentials in the daily consumption of most of these foods are even more marked.

THE PROBLEM OF HIV/AIDS

According to a study from Thailand, although the nationwide '100 per cent condom programme' to prevent HIV infection has led to a decrease of the infection among men, young women who were engaged in commercial sex have not been protected from the infection to the same degree as men (Kilmarx et al. 1999). Although the spread of HIV/AIDS is a major concern in India, only 61 per cent of women aged 15–49 and 84 per cent of men aged 15–49 have heard of AIDS. While awareness of AIDS has increased over time among both rural and urban women, awareness still remains low among women who are not regularly exposed to media, scheduled tribe women, women with no education, women living in households with a low standard of living and rural women. Knowledge of HIV/AIDS prevention methods differs markedly between women and men aged 15–49.

Overall, approximately 4 in 10 women and 7 in 10 men know each of the three ABC methods of prevention – abstinence, being faithful and condoms. Knowledge of each prevention method rises with increasing education and wealth. Women and men with regular exposure to mass media are twice as likely to know each of the three methods of prevention as do adults without access to media. Nationwide, the HIV prevalence rate for the population aged 15–49 is 0.28 per cent. This translates into 1.7 million HIV positive persons aged 15–49 in India in April 2006, the midpoint of the NFHS-3 survey. The HIV prevalence rate is 0.22 per cent for women and 0.36 per cent for men aged 15–49.

Table 7 *Violence against women (percentage of ever-married women aged 15–49, who have experienced physical or sexual violence committed by their husbands, India, 2005–2006)*

	Physical violence	*Sexual violence*	*Physical or Sexual violence*
India	35.1	10.0	37.2
Uttaranchal	27.3	6.1	27.8

A study done by Heise has shown that violence against women is one of the causal factors related to health problems that are often ignored by authorities once they view such behaviour as beyond their jurisdiction (Heise 1994). This is reflected in findings reported in Table 7. A substantial proportion of married women reported that they experienced physical or sexual violence at some time in their lives. More than a third (35.1%) of women aged 15–49 have experienced physical violence, and 10 per cent have experienced sexual violence. In all, 37.2 per cent of women aged 15–49 in India have experienced physical or sexual violence.

In Uttarakhand, 27.8 per cent women have experienced physical or sexual violence. Thirty-seven per cent of ever-married women have experienced spousal physical or sexual violence, and 16 per cent have experienced spousal emotional violence. One per cent of ever-married women have initiated violence against their husbands. Slapping is the most common form of physical violence experienced by ever-married women at the hands of their husband. Among all ever-married women who reported ever experiencing physical or sexual violence, 36 per cent reported cuts, bruises or aches; 9 per cent reported eye injuries, sprains, dislocations or burns; 7 per cent reported deep wounds, broken bones, broken teeth or other serious injury; and 2 per cent reported severe burns.

Many factors can prevent women from getting medical treatment. The most commonly reported problem is distance to a health facility, which is one big problem reported by one-quarter of women. As one would expect, distance is a more common challenge among rural women than among urban women. One-third of rural women cite distance to be a big obstacle to obtaining medical care. Forty-four per cent of women from scheduled tribes report distance to be a big problem. For less than 11 per cent of women in any subgroup report getting permission to go for treatment is a big problem. The percentage of those who report getting permission to be a big problem decreases with increasing education and wealth quintiles. Other than distance as a big problem, three other problems are each cited by nearly as many women (23%): having to take transport, concern that there may be no provider available, and concern that there may be no drugs available. Nineteen per cent of women report concern that no female provider will be available as being a big problem.

CONCLUSION

Patterns of health and illness in women and men show marked differences. It is natural that existing health problems are rather sex specific, though many are common to both the sexes. For example, the health problems related to cancer such as cervical and breast cancers are more specific to women, whereas prostate or testicular and penile cancers are more specific to men. It may be argued that childbearing is a natural process. However, certain phenomena such as the social circumstances, environment, gender discrimination in nutrition, health care and social support are manifested in the form of biological disorders during pregnancy and later on in the life cycle of girls and women. Taking into account the social reality in India, it is not only women who need to be educated regarding the reproductive issues, it is equally important to educate and campaign among their men counterparts.

Gender equity is not about achieving equal rate of mortality or morbidity, but about ensuring that women and men have an equal opportunity to enjoy good health. It is often pointed out that women have a longer life expectancy than men. While this is true among more privileged socio-economic groups, the difference is not just in length of life, but also in chances of survival. All other factors being equal, girls are more likely to survive *in-uteri*, during childhood, during adolescence and during adulthood. Among less privileged groups, however, the gap in male and female life expectancy narrows and even disappears, highlighting the importance of other variables such as income level.

Health is about much more than life expectancy, and so we must look beyond it to male and female quality of life and their patterns of behaviour. Although women may live longer, they tend to be more affected by long-term and chronic illness, which significantly affects the quality of their lives. It is important to note that men's health status and behaviour is as much a result of the social construction of gender as women's. The expectations that come with being male have a significant effect on men's health, which the gender equity perspective must also take into account.

A number of solutions have been proposed to help researchers; policy makers and health workers address gender inequities in health. Among the most important are: gendered analyses of health situations, including data disaggregated by sex, and development, monitoring and evaluation of 'gender indicators', such as causes of female and male mortality/morbidity; infant mortality rate by sex and cause; maternal mortality rates; women's access to pre- and post-natal care and safe delivery; the proportion of women and men employed in different levels/areas of the health sector; differences in wages earned by female/male health workers; women's and men's access to food, clean water, sanitation and immunization against diseases; proportion of women's and men's, or household, incomes spent on health services; distribution of household expenditure on health services; fertility rates; and women's access to different methods of family planning. Information on gender and health should be disseminated, at the national level in order to advocate for more gender-sensitive policies and programmes. At the community and family levels, information, education and communication initiatives should be targeted appropriately and strategically, in order to reach the key audiences. Increase women's participation in defining health priorities, planning solutions, policies and programmes, and in demanding accountability.

REFERENCES

ARROW (2005). *Monitoring Ten Years of ICPD Implementation: The Way Forward to 2015.* Asian Country Reports. Kuala Lumpur: ARROW.

Boerder, C. et al. (2004). *The 'So What' Report: A Look at Whether Integrating a Gender Focus into Programs Makes a Difference to Outcomes*. Washington, DC: Interagency Gender Working Group Task Force Report (IGWG).

Davar, B. (1999). *Mental Health of Indian Women: A Feminist Agenda*. New Delhi: Sage.

Dinshaw, K.A. (2005). Cancer Control Programme in India: Challenges for the New Millennium. *Health Administrator XVII*, 1 July.

Dinshaw, K.A. et al. (2004). Community Intervention for Cancer Control and Prevention: Lessons Learnt. *Indian Journal of Medical and Paediatric Oncology 25*(2), pp. 4–8.

Eckermann, E. (2001). *Domestic Violence: A Priority Public Health Issue in the Western Pacific Region*. Manila: WHO.

Garcia-Moreno, C. (2002). Violence against Women: Consolidating a Public Health Agenda. In G. Sen, A. George and P. Östlin (Eds), *Engendering International Health: The Challenge of Equity*. Cambridge: MIT Press.

Heise, L.L., Pitanguy J. and Germain, A. (1994). *Violence Against Women: The Hidden Health Burden*, World Bank Discussion Papers No. 255. Washington D.C.: World Bank.

INCLEN (2000). *Domestic Violence in India: A Summary Report of a Multisite Household Survey*. Washington, DC: International Centre for Research on Women (ICRW).

Khanna, R. (2010). *Policy Brief on NCDs, Gender Equality and Empowerment of Women* (unpublished report). New Delhi: SAHAJ.

Kilmarx, P.H. et al. (1999). Seroprevalence of HIV among Female Sex Workers in Bangkok: Evidence of Ongoing Infection Risk after the '100 per cent Condom Program' was Implemented. *Journal of Acquired Immune Deficiency Syndromes 21*, pp. 313–316.

Ministry of Health and Family Welfare (2005). *National Cancer Control Programme Guideline.* New Delhi: Government of India.

National Health Profile (2007). New Delhi: Central Bureau of Health Intelligence, Government of India.

— (2008). New Delhi: Central Bureau of Health Intelligence, Government of India.

National Institute of Health and Family Welfare (2002). *Report of Evaluation of Implementation Status of National Cancer Control Programme in India*. New Delhi: Department of Planning and Evaluation, NIHFW.

Taylor, W.D. (2010). *The Burden of Non-Communicable Diseases in India*. Hamilton, ON: The Cameron Institute.

WHO-SEARO. (2008). Health Situation in the South-East Asia Region 2001–2007. New Delhi: WHO Regional Office for South-East Asia.

CHAPTER 18

Counteracting the Inertia to Balance Gender Equation in Science

Vandana Saxena

Any discussion founded on reach and participation in science has consistently focused on issues of gender representation in this field. The following global map (see Figure 1) depicts the number of female researchers in science as a share of the worldwide total. The vast majority of data are presented in headcounts (HC), which are the total number of persons employed in Research and Development. This includes staff employed both full-time and part-time. The regional averages (based on available data only) for 2009 are: 45.2 per

Figure 1 *Gender gap in science*

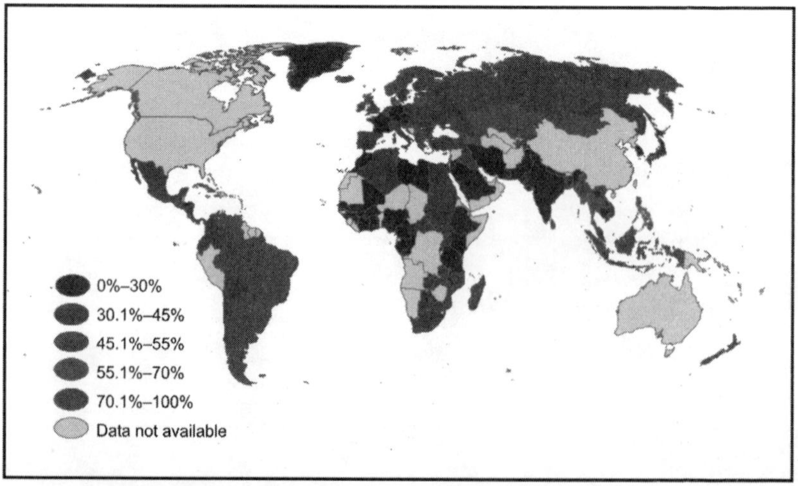

Source: UNESCO Institute for Statistics (July 2011).

Note: Data in this map are based on HC, except for Congo and India (based on FTE).

cent for Latin America and the Caribbean, 34.0 per cent for Europe, 34.5 per cent for Africa, 18.9 per cent for Asia, 39.2 per cent for Oceania; and unfortunately, there is no regional average available for North America due to a lack of data (UNESCO 2011).

These data endorse the much contested position of women in science at a global level and reinforces the significance of continuous thinking and persistent focused action in this field. This chapter attempts to study the Indian scenario regarding the presence of women in fields of science and technology. It analyses the reasons for the gap between male and female performance in these vital areas of academic enquiry.

INDIAN WOMEN IN SCIENCE

The case of India with specific reference to access, retention and progression of women in science, is a peculiar one. Neelam Kumar conducted a study addressing biographical, attitudinal and performance aspects related to scientific research in India. The study reflected the gendered nature of Indian Science. Unequal access and advancement emerged as principal forms of gender inequality within Indian scientific institutions (universally too women form just a tiny minority in top scientific jobs). The disproportionate number of women from urban area and their higher social class background indicates the role of cultural and socio-economic obstacle in the equal access to science education for Indian girls. Only the urban and very selective group of women is able to be in the career of science (Kumar 2009).

The history of women scientist in India is inherently the history of incongruities and diametric oppositions. These histories embody a quagmire of contractions – of privilege and penalty, of exaltation and damnation and of power and subservience. The success of women scientists sits rather uncomfortably within the larger context of science and society (Sur 2011). Barring her in as many ways as possible and as subtly as possible (making it sound like her own protection) was the easiest way, coupled with argument that women did not possess the strength or skills of intellect for establishment work anyways (Shankardass 2012).

The phenomenon of *leaking pipe* is omnipresent in the educational system of India, more typically vis-à-vis science education. Girls in the families are the first casualties. On a comparative scale, they either don't reach the school or are the first ones to drop out of the schools or denied access to science-related courses at senior secondary level. In a study conducted to comprehend the issues and challenges associated with teaching-learning of physics at senior secondary level in the government schools of Delhi, Saxena and Rautela (2010) found that the reasons of girls dropping out of the science stream at senior secondary level are manifold. First and foremost is the issue of non-availability of science stream in neighbourhood girls' schools. Next is the cost of studying science, which notionally includes attending additional coaching classes and buying reference books, and lastly the time required to strengthen the foundations of the subject, which is just not available to most of the girls studying in these schools as they are required to share household responsibilities with mother or other members of the family.

The girls are prepared to realize their social role much in advanced as compared to the boys. There is a clear distinction between the roles specified for both girls and boys since early childhood, which includes the toys they are provided to play with and various games that carry gender labels. Boys, in most contexts, get more attention as also more appreciation. Their work and activities are considered superior to those by girls; their inappropriate behaviours are ignored, more often.

Howard and Alamilla (2001) raise obvious yet pertinent questions that why certain behaviours are rewarded when performed by boys but punished when girls perform them. Or why the sorts of behaviours girls are encouraged to perform are often valued less than the sorts of behaviours boys are encouraged to perform. They further quote Barrie Thorne's book *Gender Play* (1993) that illustrates how girls and boys in school settings learn how to play together and apart. Children may initially learn from others how to separate into lines or into assigned seating, but Thorne observes that they continue to separate themselves through *border work.*

Gender boundaries are strengthened by contests between boys and girls, cross-gender rituals of chasing and invasions, mostly by boys of girls' public spaces. Boys invade girls' groups and activities more often than the reverse; girls complain more often to adults when boys invade. These inequalities reflect dominant cultural images – the processes and the values of the community. Gendering of the body in childhood is the foundation on which further gendering of the body occurs throughout the life course. The gendering of children's bodies makes gender differences feel and appear natural, which allows for such bodily differences to emerge throughout the life course. The hidden school curriculum of disciplining the body is gendered and contributes to the embodiment of gender in childhood, making gendered bodies appear and feel natural (Martin 1998).

Male prestige is linked to 'public' roles, such as chief or Brahmin, while female prestige is defined in relation to men, in such roles as wife, sister and mother; in other words, the female prestige structure is encompassed by the male structure (Barnard and Spencer 2009). While discussing the gendered culture in Japan, Hiroko Hara (2012) informs that the family system, known as '*ie*', traditionally set out specific roles for family head, successors, children and even the deceased. It was taken for granted that women, typically the wife of the oldest son or the daughters, should care for elderly parents. This social norm used to be deep rooted, as signified by 'most dutiful daughter-in-law awards' presented by the head of local governments every year until the 1980s in some regions.

The mismatch between cultural stereotypes of women and scientists makes many bright young girls summarily reject the option of selecting a career in science (Kumar 2009). This happens more regularly due to the dearth of female role models who can inspire girls and with whom girls can identify.

IS SCIENCE MASCULINE: BY NATURE OR BY PRACTICE OR BOTH?

Both science and culture are human activities. Early socialization patterns encourage girls to develop different adult priorities then boys. This necessitates a critical inspection of the epistemological basis of science along with the research and pedagogical practices associated with science. There are certain preconceived notions and stereotyping that is instrumental in discouraging young women from taking up a career in science. Even for women in professional scientific careers, some attitudes and values of the traditional male bastion retard progress. Even in the biological sciences, which have a higher proportion of women, they are limited at junior faculty positions, where their

Figure 2 *University enrolment in 2005–2006 (percentage): University Grants Commission*

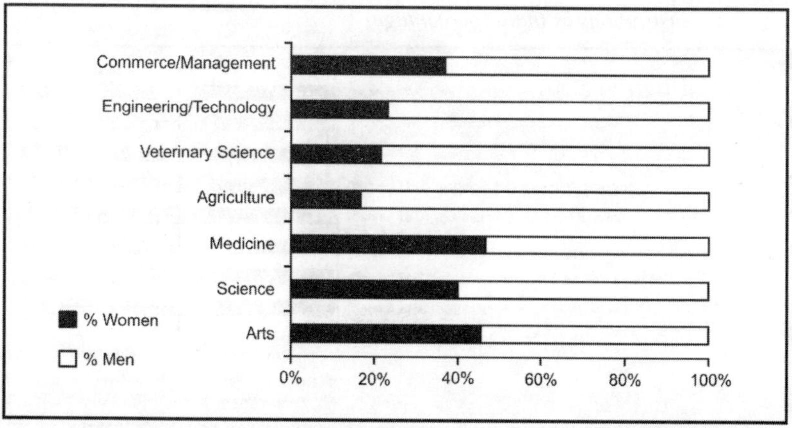

Source: Department of Science & Technology's National Task Force for Women in Science report.

proportion ranges from 18 to 33 per cent (Bal 2005). Figure 2 illustrates their presence in Indian context. The following two graphs represent the position of women in formal sector (Figures 3 and 4).

Historically with the emergence of era of enlightenment, *reason* was seen as the principal means of emancipation. The attribute of *reason* was more closely associated with men as opposed to the socially constructed feminine attribute of emotion. The key question, thus, would be how far is the nature of science bound up with the masculine ways of thinking and can science be truly universal and objective if it is so conceived? The type of thinking commonly

Figure 3 *Women scientists in government scientific institutions in India (%age)*

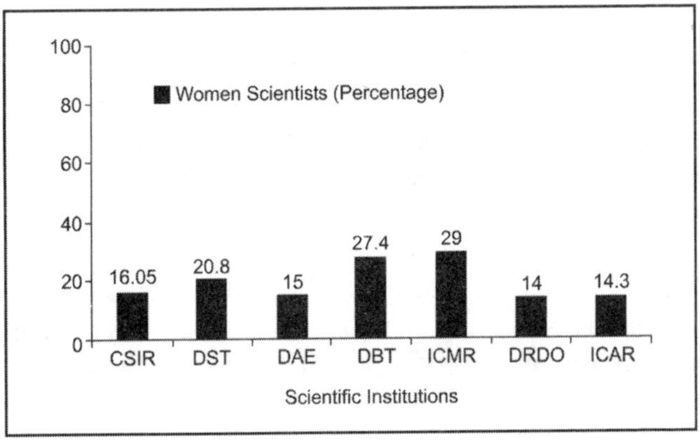

Source: Department of Science & Technology's National Task Force for Women in Science report.

Figure 4 *Women scientists at junior and senior ranks in government scientific institutions in India (percentage)*

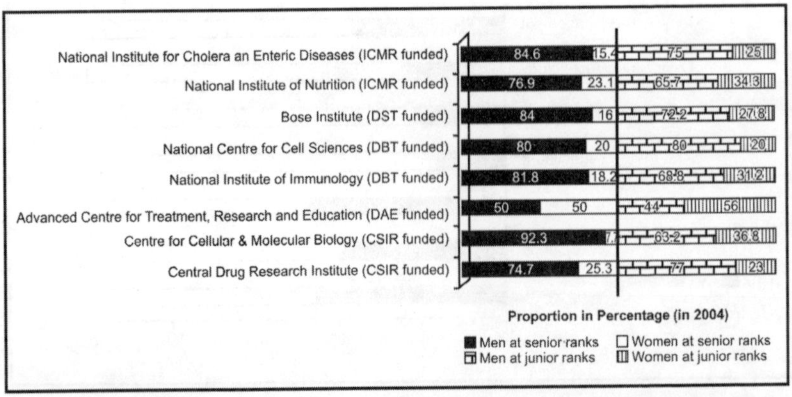

Source: Department of Biotechnology's Biotech News, Volume IV, No. 5, October 2009.

labelled scientific embodies an intrinsically masculine worldview. Science does pose itself as an authority, and patriarchs would be least interested in sharing authority with women. Patriarchy within the scientific community is manifested through male control of elite positions and various exclusionary devices. The scientific method incorporates masculine features such as the objectification of nature. Scientific knowledge is masculine in its neglect of women's experience and its adoption of paradigms built on assumptions of competition and hierarchy (Bowling and Martin 1985).

When faced with a claim that something is true, scientists respond by asking what evidence supports it. But scientific evidence can be biased in how the data are interpreted, in the recording or reporting of the data, or even in the choice of what data to consider in the first place. Scientist's nationality, sex, ethnic origin, age, political convictions and so on may incline them to look for or emphasize one or another kind of evidence or interpretation. For example, for many years the study of primates – by male scientists – focused on the competitive social behaviour of males. When the female scientists entered the field, the importance of female primates community-building behaviour was recognized.

The discourse in Western science is labelled as hegemonic and biased towards certain groups of people, particularly women. The 'value-neutral' and 'objective' tag on science is characteristically under scrutiny by scholars working in the field of feminist science studies. Feminists also challenge the prevalent reductionist approach, which seeks to understand things primarily in terms of their parts. A female-gendered approach, by contrast, would give equal emphasis to context or the larger system in which a thing operates. For example, we tend to reduce sex to chromosomes suppressing the role of development in how the genetic information variably unfolds. We talk about genes, rather than the contexts in which genes are or are not expressed. A reductionist approach is limited, though we often regard it as an essential part of a scientific posture.

To reinforce some of the basic skills in science such as observation, measurement, classification, hypothesizing, inferring, predicting, relationships, experimenting and data analysis and representation, the examples and situations used in school science classrooms are predominantly from the world of boys or adult males. Whereas a lot about simple machines can be taught through various kitchen-based activities they seldom appear during the classroom discussion. Lot of washing and cleaning practices followed as part of housekeeping can be examples for many basic chemical reactions, but are rarely brought to the classroom. Though there is a great deal of affection for 'mum', she is definitely accorded an inferior role. And within the home there is a clear sense that men have a right to be waited on by the mother (Arun et al.

2011). In the context of intergroup relations, discrimination has a pejorative meaning. It not only implies more than simply distinguishing among social objects, but also refers to inappropriate and potentially unfair treatment to individuals due to group membership (Dovidio et al. 2010).

The classrooms communicate rather emphatically that none of the features of the expected profile of an adult woman have any presence in science-related discussions; that the science requires the highest level of focused commitment and perseverance, which would not be possible for women given their requirements as a care taker in the family; and paradoxically women are constantly appreciated for same virtues of commitment and perseverance as a home maker. The masculine and feminine stereotypes are reinforced through classroom interactions and establish science as a male preserve.

There is complex mechanism of denial, suspicion and restriction, which quite systematically keep the women outside or on the margins of male-oriented world of science. Science and technology, together, have developed a wide range of machines and appliances to ease the physical effort. The household tasks are now less complicated and time efficient. Most men, however, are yet to rediscover their role as equal partners in household chores. They call themselves tech-savvy, enjoy buying latest appliances and are most happy learning to operate any gadget but those meant for household task. In rural India where scarcity of electricity is still a reality, most of the technology is developed to support male-oriented task.

It is generally acknowledged, except by those with an extreme *scientific* turn of mind, that though science might tell us how the world is, and how it might be materially altered, it does not speak of the ethical judgements we might make in intervening in the world; of how, so to speak, it ought to be (Donnelly 2001). The scientific knowledge is normally presented as pure and uncontaminated by social processes. Just beneath the surface of a scientific text are a myriad of alternative perspectives and interpretations. It is these currents of different worldviews and epistemological positions that we argue need to be identified, uncovered and rewritten (Phillips and Hausbeck 2000). Science and patriarchy then must be seen in the context of wider social relations. An individual action can be more effective if it fits into a well-planned overall strategy. If there are fundamental structural reasons for women's exclusion from science, then it is apparent that it is necessary to change those structures, hence the very nature of science, before women can enter into a more egalitarian science. It is valuable to have developed a long-term strategy, which incorporates a structural analysis of the major forces operating to construct both science and patriarchy in particular ways (Bowling and Martin 1985).

We stake our lives every day on what we take ourselves to know. It would be unsettling to revise this stance and retreat to the view that at best we have justification to believe. But if we had to give up even this moderate view and to conclude, say, that what we believe is not even justified, we would face a crisis (Audi 2011). A variety of researches and popular surveys have established the paucity of women in scientific pursuits. In this current climate of reform, we need to actively challenge and change the prevalent image of science as a masculine preserve, while concurrently revising the concept of femininity and masculinity. Girls' experiences in the science classroom must change in order to enhance both their participation rates and achievement levels (Scantlebury 1998). Generally, gender-inclusive practices within the classroom either address the interests and strength of girls or provide opportunities for activities that girls tend not to engage in outside the school. An encouraging or even allowing single-sex group to operate within the classroom seems to be a strategy which should encourage girls to participate more in manipulating materials and experimenting (McGinnis and Tippins 2002).

The socio-cultural proscribes lead to partition on the basis of sex within the classroom; girls and boys adhere to their prescribed roles and limits. Stereotypically, the boys, too, are under immense pressure to pursue science with an underlying assumption of facilitating their access to a socially and financially prestigious setting. Many boys resist their entry to these pigeonholes and strive to carve a niche for themselves. This opportunity is seldom presented to them. Under such situations, the probability of developing an enriched, gender neutral understanding of science and its processes is particularly low.

It is time to make a conscious effort and recognize the need to rethink the pedagogical frameworks to promote gender-inclusive practices. The myth has to be broken for both the girls and the boys. Both will have to grow with a belief that, conceptually, gender is not a polarized position rather a continuum that reflects in different compositions across each individual; that science is a gender neutral activity and that both girls and boys are equally capable of doing science. The practitioners in science are now required to acknowledge the marginalizing nature of science and issue a public apology with a commitment to redesign an inclusive epistemological basis of science.

REFERENCES

Arun R., Beattie, I.R. and Ford, K. (Eds) (2011). *The Structure of Schooling: Readings in the Sociology of Education*. 2nd ed. Thousand Oaks, CA: Pine Forge Press.

Audi, R. (2011). *Epistemology: A Contemporary Introduction to the Theory of Knowledge*. London, UK: Routledge.

Bal, V. (2005). Women Scientists in India: Nowhere Near the Glass Ceiling. *Current Science 88*(6), pp. 872–878.

Barnard, A. and Spencer, J. (Eds) (2009). *The Routledge Encyclopaedia of Social and Cultural Anthropology*. London/New York: Routledge.

Bowling, J. and Martin, B. (1985). Science: A Masculine Disorder? *Science and Public Policy 12*(6), pp. 308–316.

Donnelly, J. (2001). Instrumentality, Hermeneutics and the Place of Science in the School Curriculum. In F. Bevilacqua, E. Giannetto and M.R. Mathews (Eds), *Science Education and Culture: The Contribution of History and Philosophy of Science*. Netherlands: Kluwer Academic Publishers, pp. 109–127.

Dovidio, J.F., Hewstone, M., Glick, P. and Esses, V.M. (Eds) (2010). *The SAGE Handbook of Prejudice, Stereotyping and Discrimination*. New Delhi: Sage.

Hara, Hiroko (2012). Modernity, Technology and Progress of Women in Japan: Problems and Prospects. In D. Jain and D. Elson (Eds), *Harvesting Feminist Knowledge for Public Policy Rebuilding Progress*. New Delhi: Sage, p. 224.

Howard, J.A. and Alamilla, H.M. (2001). Gender and Identity. In Diana Vannoy (Ed.), *Gender Mosaics: Social Perspective*. Los Angeles, CA: Roxbury Publishing Co., pp. 54–64.

http://www.indousstf.org/upload/women%20in% 20science%20report% 20(1).pdf

http://www.project2061.org/publications/sfaa/online/chap1.htm

http://www.uis.unesco.org/sciencetechnology/documents/fs14-women-science-2011-en.pdf

Kumar, N. (Ed.) (2009). *Women and Science in India: A Reader*. New Delhi: OUP.

Martin, K.A. (1998). Becoming a Gendered Body. *American Sociological Review 3*(4), pp. 494–511.

McGinnis, J.R. and Tippins, D.J. (2002). Gender. In J. Wallace and W. Louden (Eds), *Dilemmas of Science Teaching Perspectives on Problems of Practice*. London: Routledge Falmer, pp. 59–72.

Phillips, J. and Hausbeck, K. (2000). Just Beneath the Surface: Rereading Geology, Rescripting the Knowledge/Power Nexus. *Women's Studies Quarterly 28*(1), pp. 181–202.

Saxena, V. and Rautela, S. (2010). *Pedagogical Challenges in Learning Physics at Senior Secondary Level: Student's Perspective*. Unpublished M.Ed. Dissertation, University of Delhi, India.

Scantlebury, K. (1998). An Untold Story: Gender, Constructivism and Science Education. In W.W. Cobern (Ed.), *Socio-Cultural Perspectives on Science Education: An International Dialogue*. Dordrecht, Netherlands: Kluwer Academic Publishers, pp. 99–120.

Shankardass, R.D. (2012). *Of Women 'Inside': Prison Voices from India*. New Delhi: Taylor & Francis.

Sur, A. (2011). *Dispersed Radiance: Caste, Gender and Modern Science in India*. New Delhi: Navayana.

Thorne, B. (1993). *Gender Play: Girls and Boys in School*. Buckingham: Open University Press.

Index